Library Promotion Handbook

Library Promotion Handbook

By Marian S. Edsall

A Neal–Schuman Professional Book

ORYX PRESS
1980

The rare Arabian Oryx, a desert antelope dating from Biblical times, is believed to be the prototype of the mythical unicorn. Nearing extinction two decades ago, the World Wildlife Fund found three of the animals in 1962, and sent them to the Phoenix Zoo as the nucleus of a breeding herd in captivity. Today the Oryx population is nearing 200 and herds have been returned to breeding grounds in Israel and Jordan.

Published by The Oryx Press
2214 North Central at Encanto
Phoenix, AZ 85004

Published simultaneously in Canada

Printed and Bound in the United States of America

Distributed outside North America by
Mansell Publishing
3 Bloomsbury Place
London WC1A 2QA, England
ISBN 0-7201-0832-2

Library of Congress Cataloging in Publication Data

Main Entry under title:

Edsall, Marian S
   Library promotion handbook.

   Bibliography: p.
   1. Public relations—Libraries—Handbooks, manuals, etc. I. Title.
Z716.3.E3   021.7   79-26984
ISBN 0-912700-15-7

Contents

Foreword

There is a wealth of information available on the subject of public relations, although it is not widely understood nor clearly defined. One definition, adopted by the Public Relations Society of America, states "Public relations is the function that maintains an organization's relationship with society in a way that effectively achieves the organization's goals." Another theory is that "Public relations is the planned pursuit of public understanding and acceptance of an agency's purposes, goals, objectives, programs, and services."

Despite a rather general misconception, there is a great deal more to public relations than publicity, promotion, and communication; the latter are important tools, not the function itself. This handbook is designed to aid library directors, public information officers, and library staff members in using those tools, and in that sense, the scope is self-limited. It is intended only as a ready reference, a how-to guide, not as a treatise on the total spectrum of public relations, for public relations is what an institution does as well as what it communicates.

One word of warning: there is a great deal of repetition in the following material, a restatement of principles ad nauseum until they become, I hope, a part of your subconscious modus operandi. Repetition is also the heart of good promotion, for once is not enough! A rule of thumb for a radio announcement or an advertisement says "Mention the name three times," and so you must repeat your message. Repeat your message. Repeat your message.

It is customary in a foreword to extend thanks to all who have helped in the preparation of a book. In this case it is impossible, for thanks are due to each and every one of the hundreds of librarians all over the country who have shared ideas, reports, suggestions, and advice, of which this is a distillation.

Marian S. Edsall
February, 1980

Library Promotion Handbook

The Library "Image" and Imagery— Or Is All This Necessary?

"I didn't know the library had that . . ."

This is one of the most common and disheartening comments that a librarian hears.

It is topped, for outright despair, only by the all-too-frequent announcement, "The library budget has been cut by 20 percent."

The two are related.

The lack of effective communication about what the library is, what it has, and what it can do for an individual has resulted in public misunderstanding, disinterest, or bare tolerance on the part of many.

The cliché-ridden library "image" is one that is (a) deplored, (b) ignored, (c) laughed off, or (d) believed overcome. Unfortunately, that image is very much alive and well.

". . . the lack of effective communication about the library has resulted in public misunderstanding, disinterest . . ."

Not long ago an advertising agency "donated" $300 to the book fund of a small library in return for permission to film a candy bar commercial in the building. A dowdily-dressed, stringy-haired actress played the part of the librarian, the TV crew put up the good old "quiet" signs, and the stern-faced "librarian" proceeded to admonish a youngster for crunching a candy bar! Shortly after this was filmed and aired, an agency for a cereal company approached an eastern library system office for advice on where to find a small, old-fashioned library for a similar setup. (This one was nipped in the bud when the Public Information Office of the American Library Association was alerted.)

Outmoded signs must be updated, as in this poster example.

Whatever you may think of the Madison Avenue approach to advertising, the fact remains that the practitioners zero in on prevalent attitudes and play on them to give instant credibility and association to their message. In short, a majority of the viewers of that candy bar commercial do—consciously or unconsciously—carry a mental image of the library as plastered with "Silence!" signs and visualize a librarian with a frown and her hair in a bun. When was the last time you saw a "Silence" sign in a library? (The desirable degree and place of quiet in a library room or building is a matter of legitimate debate and concern, but stern admonitions for a tomb-like atmosphere went out with the nineteenth century.)

Old stereotypes and outmoded reputations are difficult to erase. As the columnist Sydney Harris wrote, "Once the stereotype hardens, it is almost impossible to break. . . . Our need for clinging to stereotypes of the past is part of the infantilism that remains in all of us." But he went on to point out that our world is dynamic and constantly changing. Libraries, too, are changing, but we are not getting the message across effectively.

In many communities the library is regarded simply as a community status symbol. The results of a Gallup Poll commissioned by the New Jersey State Library showed that 87 percent of those interviewed believed that libraries were essential to a community; however, only 27 percent said that it would make much difference to them personally if a public library was not available for their use. Further evidence that the library is more often regarded as a monument than as a service agency is the fact that it is easier to pass a bond issue for a new building than to get an increase in the library budget.

". . . the inherited reservoir of good will is dwindling . . ."

In this changing world, the inherited reservoir of good will and credibility is dwindling. It must be refilled through better public information and communication if libraries are to be more than "status symbols."

Despite the fact that more and more librarians rank public relations and communications near the top of their list of concerns, despite the fact that study after study recommends more significant efforts in this area on every level, too many library administrators and professional nabobs continue to downgrade such activity as beneath the library's dignity and outside the scope of its responsibilities. For them, public relations is equated with slogans, imagery, and publicity gimmicks. This widespread misunderstanding is often reflected in the professional literature, as witnessed by these excerpts from an editorial in *Library Journal*, January 15, 1974:

> Library publicity and public relations folk have long treated existing library services as if they were for sale . . . it can safely be said that library publicity . . . as represented in radio and TV public service spots and space advertising . . . has the same look, sound, and tone of all the slick stuff . . . this commercial pap

when applied to an institution like the public library may be effective to a degree, if we want to pack 'em in, but beyond its lack of dignity, it overlooks the basic justification for all public services—that people need them.

Although it is obvious that people need libraries, three out of four nonusers are not aware that the library has what they need. Adopting and adapting tested, successful promotional methods to attract the attention of these people long enough to get the message across can hardly be termed "commercial pap." What of that phrase—"if we want to pack 'em in?" Is that bad? Or is the writer afraid that the great unwashed will somehow sully the nice, quiet library atmosphere? And the clincher—"lack of dignity." How much dignity is needed to let a blue collar worker know that the library has the information on how to make home repairs? How much dignity is needed in the message to school dropouts that the library can help to fill the gaps in their education? How much dignity is required to alert a child that the library has a book on stars or buried treasure? Standing on its dignity is part of the library's problem. Too many people will never enter a library because of this "dignified" image.

> When we persist in telling the people with groovy music and full color that the library is roughly akin to Macy's and Gimbels . . . the people will simply accept our description of libraries, and write them off as another social frill of little importance and less substance.

The trouble with the preceding statement is that, groovy music or not, too many people and too many legislators are willing to continue to write off libraries as a frill, or as a less-than-essential public service, simply because they are unaware of the breadth of the available materials and services. We haven't been able to get their attention. We haven't been able to get the majority inside the door. And too often we do not talk their language!

> But a library . . . is a serious, substantive, essential institution whose mission is to provide information and the means of education that an enlightened public needs.

Would that we had an enlightened public. Would that we could enlighten the public with discreet low-keyed pronouncements. The library's problem is not how to reach an enlightened public, but how to enlighten that public. Unfortunately, we are in competition for attention—competition that is better financed, better planned, more astutely used, and more in tune with the times.

A library is a necessary public service, publicly supported because individuals couldn't possibly afford to amass the incredible amount of data needed to insure that every citizen can find what he needs there or to pay individually what that would cost. . . . When we sharpen up that message, broadcast it, and provide the information service to back it up, perhaps we'll gain the public support we need and we won't have to hire hucksters to create a phony pitch to draw crowds. We won't have to sell the library.

Is it hucksterism with a phony pitch to lure teenagers into the library with groovy music to an array of materials from auto mechanics to Zen meditation? They just might discover that they can find the answer to some of their questions and problems. It *is* hucksterism with a phony pitch if we bleat about something we don't deliver or promote a service we can't provide (even the gaudiest hucksters are now forced to abide by "truth-in-advertising"), but what's wrong with twentieth

century methods to promote what we do have? To sell the library, in short.

Traditionally we have been able to reach a proverbial 20 percent epitomized by the middle-class housewife in Dayton, Ohio, and the white-haired scholar, but what of the others who we presume need us—the Black, the senior citizen, the small businessperson, the farmer, etc.?

If it takes jingles and brass bands to let them know we have something they need, we had better opt for jingles and brass bands on occasion, because otherwise we must be content to settle for that "enlightened" 20 percent—and 20 percent of the necessary financing.

Public funds are spent for the purchase of library materials and for staff services, but too many still believe that very little or no funds should be spent to let that same public know what is available, in a form that will gain attention. To spend money for a public service and keep it a secret that can be unearthed only by the most determined bibliophile or devoted patron with unusually good eyesight would appear to be immoral and unethical. It is akin to a "public be damned" attitude.

A good public relations program must be implemented in many ways, and publicity and promotion are but two of the means by which such a program is carried out, although they are the most

visible and tangible. They are, indeed, basic and essential.

Libraries are struggling to go on-line, to become automated, to computerize some activities—in short, to use twentieth century means to deliver twentieth century services. The average library patron is not interested in the how or why of the technology that will deliver more and faster service, but simply needs to be informed that it is available, in terms that are meaningful. The patron couldn't care less about OCLC, data banks, or PLESSEY circulation terminals. On the other hand, communication with legislators, city council members, businesspeople, and trustees is needed to inform them of the need and potential of such technology so that support and financing will be forthcoming. This is public information, and it must go out in many forms.

Obviously, no amount of publicity, of soft or hard sell, could or should cover up the deficiencies of poor resources and poor service. We know that library service is not as good as it could be, is not as good as it should be in many places, and often is not as good as we like to say it is. Then why promote it? Because, in order to reach the potential and to satisfy an ever-expanding need, a person must understand what the library offers, what it is, and what it can be; that can come about only through better communication.

Effective public communication depends on some specific skills and knowledge, just as do cataloging and reference work. There are some practical suggestions and techniques for communicating effectively with the public in the following pages, which include some instructions on "jingles and brass bands. . . ."

Getting Started: How to Plan a Public Information Program

If the purpose of promotion and communication is to "inform, influence, and persuade," then tough questions have to be answered before an effective public information program can be designed.

What are you communicating?

Why?

To whom?

How?

And *whose job* is it?

Finding answers to these questions is a lot more difficult than making up a schedule of library events, ordering posters or bookmarks, or preparing booklists and news releases. However, these means used to "inform, influence, and persuade," have little value without the answers: in writing.

It is not enough to assume that the why and wherefore are understood; too often they are not. It may take more time and soul-searching than you think you can spare to determine the answers, but it must be done.

The Big Think: What Are You Communicating?

As the library's communicator, you must know and be able to interpret the library's goals, objectives, and priorities, as determined by the governing body and the library administration. If these have not been clearly formulated, someone must push the responsible parties into writing out

and adopting them. This is a sticky maneuver; the question "What are we doing and why?" is one that most groups hate to face. There may not be consensus, either, since many schisms exist between and among professional librarians and lay persons. Is the library's main function to be a "caretaker of a cultural monument or a facilitator of ideas?" as Richard J. Wolfert, North Dakota State Librarian, phrased it. Is the emphasis to be on clerical and custodial functions or on service activities? Is the library to serve all the people, or just the enlightened who seek it out?

All libraries have much in common, but each is also an entity with characteristics and goals that reflect, to some extent, the community and the past and present leadership. Without a clear understanding of this, communication and promotion will be based on little more than generalities, which may or may not apply.

Above all, keep in mind that, unless you are in a decision-making role, you must accept the established policies and objectives and communicate them as best you can. It is to be hoped that you are in a position to influence, suggest, and effect constructive policy changes, but your major task is to inform, to overcome ignorance and misunderstanding—to "tell it like it is."

Why Are You Communicating?

Whether your library is dynamic and progressive, evolving and changing, or content with status quo and "holding the line," the growing public demand for accountability means that you must communicate—explain and defend, if necessary—what the library is and why, if it is to continue to exist and receive the support to which it lays claim.

Accountability means that you must be able to answer the taxpayer who asks, "I never use the library so why should I pay for it?" This is bad enough, but it is worse when s/he asks, "I know I pay for this, but what's in it for me?"

The communication process must also be continuous and repetitious; it is not a once-a-month or once-a-year activity. Many governing boards and library administrators have not faced these facts, nor do they understand the implications; public information and promotion usually receive a very low priority in the budgetary and organizational scheme or are considered frills, which are summarily axed in the face of a financial crunch. Paradoxically, this is the time when they are most needed!

Thus, the next step in planning a program may be dictated by the need for convincing boards and others of the importance of what you propose and for gaining their support. You need a lot more than lip service, and so prepare to go forth and do battle if you must. Start by requesting time at staff meetings, board meetings, or in individual conferences to discuss the function of public information and the importance of a planned program. In short, you may have to start to "inform, influence, and persuade" right at home.

Then get something in writing. If a policy statement that defines the purpose and procedures for a public information and public relations program has not been adopted as a matter of record (and too few have), prepare and submit one. The very process of discussion and consideration will be both educational and helpful, and the final draft will serve as a tangible expression of intent, a guide for planning, and justification for future budget requests. Any such policy must be tailored to local situations, but the following statement can serve as a model to be adapted and revised as needed.

Public Relations and Public Information: A Policy Statement

In recognition of the ____ Library's responsibility to maintain continuing communication with present and potential users of the ____ Library's services and resources, so as to assure effective and maximum usage by all citizens, the Board of Trustees of the ____ Library adopts the following resolution as a matter of policy.

The objectives of the ____ Library's public relations program are:
- To promote community awareness of library service.
- To stimulate public interest in and usage of the ____ Library.
- To develop public understanding and support of the ____ Library and its role in the community.

The following means may be used to accomplish the foregoing objectives:

1. An annual plan of specific goals and activities shall be developed, sufficient funds shall be allocated to carry out the program, and the program shall be evaluated periodically.

2. Training sessions, workshops, and other aids shall be made available to library staff members to assure courteous, efficient, and friendly contact with library patrons and the general public.

3. Personal and informational group contacts shall be maintained with government officials, opinion leaders, service clubs, civic associations, and other community organizations by library staff and Board members.

4. Local media shall be utilized to keep the public aware of and informed about the ____ Library's resources and services.

5. Newsletters, brochures, and other promotional materials shall be produced and distributed through effective methods of reaching the public.

6. The ____ Library may sponsor programs, classes, exhibits, and other library-centered activities and shall cooperate with other groups in organizing these to fulfill the community's needs for educational, cultural, informational, or recreational opportunities.

7. The Library Director or a designated qualified staff member shall have the responsibility for coordinating the ____ Library's public relations and public information activities.

It is not enough, however, to secure passage of a policy statement and file it away. Communication with the board and library administration must be constant; your own accountability is at stake. Plan time, in the future, to:

a) Attend staff and board meetings, in your role as library communicator.

b) Send brief, interesting memos to staff and board members, or otherwise keep them informed of the public information activities or programs planned or undertaken. Distribute samples of all printed materials prepared.

c) Prepare an annual summary of activities, with a fair evaluation of the results.

d) Present short-term and long-range plans to the board periodically, with objectives, justifications, costs. Occasionally submit one creative, individual proposal to gain attention, support, and approval.

To Whom Are You Talking?

If your mission is to "inform, influence, and persuade," to whom will you talk? The general public? There really isn't any such animal. There are taxpayers, homemakers, Blacks, businesspeople, senior citizens, young adults, lawyers, people over 50, people under 10, readers, nonreaders, TV viewers, consumers, mechanics, high school graduates, nurses, clerks. . . . But all are part of the public which needs to be informed and influenced, whether directly served or not.

For most purposes, the public can be broken down into two general audiences for the library's message—users and nonusers. The users are regular patrons, irregular patrons, and those with expired library cards. The nonusers include a very large group that will never enter the library, even if you give away $100 bills. A smaller group of nonusers (potential users) may be tempted if one or more obstacles were removed, such as inconvenient hours; inaccessible location; lack of sufficient resources to meet the needs; forbidding regulations, procedures, personnel, and layout; and lack

of information about what is available or how to secure it. Removal of most of these obstacles is an administrative function, but a good communication and promotion program can help to hasten the day, and will, at the very least, aid in breaking down the barrier of ignorance of the service and materials.

". . . messages go out to different audiences in different forms . . ."

The messages you want to convey should be designed to:

a) Encourage usage of the library

b) Increase support of the library

c) Increase understanding of the role and function of the library

In cases (a) and (b), you want people to *do* something, e.g., come into the building, ask questions, read more, give time or money, speak up for funding or vote; for (c) you may only be seeking recognition of the value of library service so that it can continue to be provided.

Those messages go out to different audiences, both users and nonusers, and in different forms. To be effective, target audiences must be identified and the communication method must be chosen carefully. There is, of course, considerable spillover in some forms; for example, a news release about an exhibit of Eskimo sculpture in the library will inform those patrons who wish to see it, but may also reach a nonuser and increase or reinforce an understanding and/or approval of the library as a valuable cultural center.

No library has sufficient funds and staff to conduct as comprehensive a public information program as it would like or feels is needed. It is essential, therefore, to establish priority messages and priority target audiences and to design a program accordingly.

It is customary, at this point, to recommend a "market" or community survey. These can be useful in realigning or redesigning the library's goals, functions, and procedures in terms of a community's needs and makeup, but they seldom reveal much that an astute or even novice publicist does not know or suspect. Questionnaires and surveys can be a good form of publicity in themselves—evidence to people that the library cares about what they think—but they are expensive, a very technical process if done properly, and the validity or usefulness of most of them is open to question. As a matter of fact, have you ever seen published reports of a home-grown survey that did not "prove" that the library was well-regarded, doing a good job, and reasonably well-used? On the other hand, professionally conducted surveys tend to damn with faint praise, and most reveal an abysmal lack of information about library services at all levels of society.

There is a certain irony in the fact that the public is aware of this lack, and this was evidenced at the time that citizen input and opinions were sought throughout a midwestern state as a preliminary to formulating resolutions for consideration at the White House Conference on Library and Information Services. "More effective publicity regarding library services" received the second highest number of votes from those attending regional meetings. Despite this clear-cut expression, the professionals' concerns for technology, networking, and even for designating the Library of Congress as the National Library and for preferential library postal rates, overrode the public concern, and the matter received a low priority in the final tally. In the Gallup Poll conducted in that same state, the most frequently made suggestion in answer to a question about how the public library could be of more service to the community was that "libraries advertise what they offer." There have been similar public reactions in other states and regions.

". . . know your community . . ."

A local survey may reveal what people do not know about the library (e.g., availability of films, large print books, interlibrary loan, etc.) but the percentages are not likely to vary much from those of state or national surveys. The fact that only 1 percent of the people polled knew that the library has microfilms is not sufficient information to aid in designing an effective public information program, because it raises more questions than it answers. A general opinion or attitude poll is no panacea for library promotional ills nor of much aid in correcting them. Limited, specific "before and after" surveys, on the other hand, are an important but often overlooked means of evaluating the effectiveness of particular promotional activities, and these should be plugged in during the planning process.

The dictim, know your community, is a valid one, however. Much can be gleaned from census reports and other local and national government materials without going to the trouble and expense of a survey. The interests and characteristics of various segments of the public—market segments—can be interpolated from data collected by others and used in designing promotional programs and publicity for target groups. For example, information about the income levels, age levels, and destination preferences of travelers, data available from the annual yearbook of the travel market, could be of assistance in planning travel and film programs for specific audiences and in determining the best channels for publicity. It would, at the very least, be preferable to a hit-or-miss method of booking such programs on the basis of what is most readily available, and trusting that the one-line newspaper listing or the monthly library events calendar would reach all those who might be interested.

Statistics may give some clues, but a publicist must put an ear to the ground before taking pen in hand—a fairly demanding exercise! Comments and reactions from staff, library patrons, and the man-on-the-street are ways of knowing your community. Wide reading is necessary to spot trends in interests and social changes so as to keep the promotional program in tune with all segments of the population. A good publicist must also know, or know about, the local opinion leaders and the important organizations and groups in the community.

The directives to know your community and to research your audience are far more easily said than done, particularly when time and money are limited. Inasmuch as no truly scientific or simple methods have been devised to do so, and few operative methods are available to the average library, much depends on such intangibles as common sense, intuition, imagination, and empathy.

How Will You Communicate? The Strategy-Action Plan

Programing public information and library promotion is the act of translating objectives, as determined by the administration, into communication actions and techniques. There is considerable confusion between general objectives and communication program goals, and the lack of distinction between the two results in few measurable effects and little impact.

Writing the program is essentially a one-person job, albeit the hardest one is likely to undertake. It should be drawn up in specific terms after consultation with and input from the administration and staff. It is essentially the details of when, how, and why certain things will be done to carry out established or agreed-upon objectives and policies.

Planning the program is carried out in three steps:

1. Establishing goals and priorities

2. Determining procedures and actions

3. Scheduling

Your goals, whether short-term or long-range, should be as specific as possible, and the means of measuring or evaluating the success or failure of the methods used must be built-in from the beginning, not attempted after the fact. You have to know where you are going, but you also must know if you have gotten there!

". . . set your goals . . ."

If a general objective is stated as "to make the public more aware of the library," for example, the job is to translate this into reasonable action procedures or tactics on some sort of a priority basis, and within a time frame.

When the means of achieving that objective is stated in terms of a measurable goal, you can get a handle on it. For example, you might decide that the goal should be "to keep newspaper readers better informed about activities at the library." You can establish a schedule for this, plan a series of releases about library programs and services, and be able to build in some measurement of the impact, not only in terms of inches of newsprint, but in feedback from staff, patrons, and others.

If the idea of using the newspaper for publicity seems pretty obvious and routine, scarcely worth the effort of writing it out as a specific goal, consider this. You have—or should have—made a value judgment that the local newspaper is the most effective media outlet with which you can work. Is it? Researching and writing good, usable press releases and making and keeping the necessary newspaper contacts is time-consuming. How much of the available time should and can be given to this? Should it receive more or less emphasis than preparing a newsletter or a radio program? Is it as important, more important, or less so, than the production of brochures, bookmarks, or other printed materials? If you are not sure of the answers to these questions, go back to square A, and reconsider the priority of this goal.

". . . are specific goals established?"

Although the establishment of specific goals and priorities is absolutely essential to the development of any meaningful program, it is "more honored in the breach than the observance." There is evidence of increasing interest on the part of librarians in learning how to use the tools of promotion—how to write a news release, plan a library program or exhibit, etc.—but very little evidence that this knowledge is put to use with a purposeful and measurable end result firmly in mind. It's a bit like taking a short course in how to handle a hammer, nails, and a saw, and then proceeding to use them without a blueprint or pattern. You can knock a lot of boards together expertly, and the results will be tangible, but not necessarily practical or useful. You could even build a good dog house without a blueprint, but it would certainly be wiser first to determine (a) if you have a dog, (b) if or why you need a house for the dog, (c) whether the dog can be taught to use it when built, and (d) the actual size of the dog for whom it is intended. Now you can draw a diagram, buy a specific amount of material, and use your tools well. You certainly shouldn't build one because everyone else in the neighborhood is doing it, or because you have heard that dogs need houses.

In an effort to determine how libraries actually set goals, plan, budget, and evaluate their public information and promotional programs, I recently canvassed 15 representative libraries around the country, both large and small, which have active and highly visible programs. Many of the answers to a key question, "Are specific objectives established?" were vague or ambiguous.

"It is our intent to set specific objectives."

"We make such efforts, but they are sporadic. . . . A plan would help."

"We try to reach all areas of the community."

"We send different items to special interest groups."

The respondents all had excellent tools and skills, but their effectiveness would be difficult to evaluate.

On the other hand, an excellent (and unusual) example of specific, measurable goals was reported by the Denver Public Library. "Specific goals for 1979 are: raise reference questions asked 15%, raise circulation 10%, raise registration 10%, increase the number of business borrower's cards to 1,500 by December, 1979." The goals/objectives/timetable for the Public Information Office of that library was 32 pages long one year! Few libraries do such detailed planning, but all can profit from the exercise of developing a strategy-action plan.

Let's take a not-entirely-hypothetical but fairly typical situation at the far end of the scale from the Denver Public Library to illustrate possible program planning strategies and principles.

Assume that the library is in a small community (under 10,000 population), employs a staff of 2½, and is the member of a regional system. There is a small and relatively inactive Friends group. Staffing and budget constraints, plus the library director's lack of interest, ability, or initiative has limited promotional efforts to terse announcements, or a short list of new books in the weekly newspaper and the posting of a notice of the hours in a few areas around the community. The librarian complains that the local businesspeople do not come into the library and have very little interest in it, despite the recent acquisition of a good basic

business collection. She also reports to her board that attendance at the children's film program has fallen off so badly that it has temporarily been postponed, adding, "maybe there will be more interest later." Despite an influx of new residents in recent years, circulation figures have shown no increase in the past three years. In addition, the system-provided large print book collection is used little, although there are a large number of elderly, retired persons in the town. Thus, a number of problems have been identified in the mind of the librarian, but not, to date, included as a board agenda item.

The first step would be a discussion with the library board, outlining the problems, exploring possible remedies, and seeking agreement on promotional priorities. After full discussion, the goals might be listed:

---

1. Encourage better use of the library by local businesspeople. (Rationale: the library has sufficient resources and has access to the comprehensive business collection of the large resource library, all of which could be useful to local merchants; businesspeople are important leaders in influencing community opinions, and their political and financial support of the library is essential to its growth.)

2. Improve attendance at the children's film programs. (Rationale: good films are available through the system; such programs have proved stimulating to children in other libraries in the area, and attendance at them has increased the circulation of children's books and other materials.)

3. Increase the number of new card-holders, particularly among the relative newcomers in the community. (Rationale: circulation has not kept pace with the population growth; the percentage of active users is below that of comparable libraries in the system area; the collection is up-to-date and there is access to a wealth of material through interlibrary loan.)

4. Increase the usage of large print books. (Rationale: there is an unknown but substantial number of sight-impaired persons, including youngsters, in the community; the large print collection is adequate and supplemented regularly by deposit from the system.)

There are a number of factors, both pro and con, to be weighed as a program is planned. On the plus side, there is a trained public information consultant on the system staff whose assistance has not been used up to this time. Printing of flyers, brochures, and other materials can be done free of charge by the system staff. Grants from the system for special projects are available, and a well-devised promotional program might qualify. A pool of potential volunteers exists in the Friends group from which assistance for specific activities might be secured. An abundance of statistical information about the town exists as the result of various studies that have been carried out by nearby county, state, and university agencies.

Some of the roadblocks to implementing a goal-oriented promotional program can be foreseen and are fairly common.

There is no budget for promotional activities. (Possible remedy: internal budget adjustment by the board; a small grant sought from the system.)

The staff is small, and has no time for other than custodial and service activities. (Possible remedies: shift of responsibilities and work schedule to free the director for initiation and supervision of a promotional program; active assistance by members of the board; cooperation sought from members of the Friends group and specific assignments worked out for them.)

Readership of the local weekly newspaper is very limited and coverage of library news is poor. (Possible remedies: explore use of widely-circulated free shoppers and other publicity outlets; prepare more extensive news releases for the local newspaper with aid of volunteer writer or Friend; make better use of system-provided news releases.)

Although the listed goals are all commendable, and no doubt attainable in time, it is apparent that it would be most unrealistic to make an effort to cover them all in one year. The choice of priorities, by both the board and the librarian, might then be:

1. Increased contact with businesspeople

2. Some measurable increase in the number of cardholders

With this decision made, a program of ways and means can be developed and a tentative schedule written out. The system consultant can be called in for advice, and these possible action plans explored:

An informal survey of the needs and interests of the local businesspeople to be conducted by the Friends; appropriate news release about the survey issued.

Cooperation and advice sought from several representative merchants in planning proposed activities.

One or more in-house library programs planned and scheduled at times deemed most convenient according to survey results; a speaker from the resource library asked to discuss available business resources and the function of the interlibrary loan service; an outside speaker selected for an in-house talk on a topic of interest to local merchants, as expressed in the survey; a specially assembled collection of business-related materials from both the local and resource library collections displayed; flyers concerning program and exhibit posted in community; invitations to the meeting, hand-delivered by Friends and/or trustees.

A booklist of business materials prepared with system aid, and supplemented at intervals with listings of recent additions.

A timetable developed for implementing various phases of the project.

". . . a ripple effect results . . ."

Evaluation of the short-range effect of this effort would consist of a count of the number of attendees at the program; a count or estimate of the number of cards issued, reference inquiries, or visits made by businesspeople; reactions or comments reported by staff and trustees. Concentration of efforts on this identified segment of the community would also have a ripple effect, which is less easily measured, but which will contribute, in time, to a shift of opinion of the library from one of a passive institution to one of an active service agency.

Although these activities would undoubtedly absorb most if not all of the time and energy available, a start might also be made toward the secondary goal of an overall increase in the number of card-holders. Part of the difficulty in attracting the patronage of new residents may be lack of effective publicity about the library. Many are commuters to the city and do not subscribe to the weekly paper, the only media outlet heretofore used. Those who have not been inside the library tend to dismiss it as small, with a limited collection, and are unaware both of the recently updated collection and the resources available through the interlibrary loan service and rapid delivery provided by the system.

It could be assumed, simply on the basis of the socioeconomic grouping of many of those recently attracted to the area, that a fair number of the newcomers are potential library patrons, and that more information and increased publicity would provide considerable stimulus to usage.

At the same time, the library board would be wise to study the need for a change in the schedule of the hours to make it more convenient for these potential new users, and to consider providing a centrally located book-drop in the Main Street area, to help overcome the obstacle of a building location outside the main traffic stream. These two actions in themselves would generate good publicity.

Several avenues could be followed, as time or opportunity allowed, to reach this targeted group.

The two free shoppers distributed to all residents in the area could serve as media outlets; a library feature story might be run in the one which carries such material, and a paid advertisement or flyer inserted in the other.

The county edition of the metropolitan paper is read by a majority of residents; news and feature material about the local library might occasionally warrant space in the proper section.

Newcomers to the community could be reached through distribution of a simple, informational flyer by the bank when new accounts are opened, by real estate agents, and by the school during the registration period. Other agencies might be asked to include such a sheet in a routine mailing.

A short canned talk might be prepared, and members of the Friends, library board, and staff encouraged to present this at the meetings of various local social and service groups to which they belong.

On the theory that present users can be the best pipeline to others, a goal of a specific number of new registrants might be set and pursued in-

house by conducting a contest to induce patrons to bring in one or more persons, and the number of new card-holders could be reported by a thermometer device or other visual.

These various activities all require a measure of skill and initiative, and it may seem to be an ambitious program for a small library, but it is well within the range of the ability of those who could assist if asked. The system can also provide technical aid. By establishing goals, procedures, and

". . . measurable results can be anticipated . . ."

a schedule, some measurable results can be anticipated which will help to encourage and motivate those involved.

This hypothetical exercise illustrates how some basic promotional planning principles can be applied. It also serves as an example of how isolating and tackling a few promotional problems—or even one—in depth, rather than dealing with many superficially, can make it possible to use limited time and money productively.

In other situations the planning procedure would be more involved and detailed, but the steps would be the same: setting attainable goals based on objectives and priorities determined in consultation; analyzing target groups; selecting techniques to reach them; preparing a schedule of time, personnel, and budget; evaluating the results. The process may seem formidable and unnecessarily elaborate, but the failure to go through it is one reason for the inadequacy and ineffectiveness of most library public information programs, on whatever scale.

". . . evaluation is essential . . ."

Evaluation of various activities is generally given too little attention, in part because of confusion about the meaning of the term and in part because much is not readily measured in concrete terms. Although often presented as such, evaluation is *not* a report of what was done. It is a report of whether or not what was done accomplished a specific, understood purpose that was identified in advance. Measurement is carried out in various ways, according to the activity. It can be based on records or statistics that are kept: for example, the effectiveness of a particular piece or type of publicity can be evaluated by devising a simple form for staff members to use in recording related telephone calls or in-person inquiries, including a sample question to be asked about how the person heard about it. Casual comments made to the staff or letters received are measures of sorts. Formal discussions at staff meetings, including both impressions and reported reactions, can be helpful in some situations. Such measurement is not very scientific but is better than none at all. Structured before-and-after surveys may be highly desirable or necessary in some cases.

The three progressive levels of results that are expected from publicity and promotion are:

1. Increase in knowledge

2. Change of opinion

3. Actual behavior change

In evaluating the results of any phase of the program, avoid the pitfall of measuring success or failure solely at the third level. Only a novice expects to make a large-scale behavior change (which in this case might be converting nonusers to library users) and becomes discouraged by what is perceived as failure. The objective of seeking approval of the library by the nonusing public is equally important, and despite the difficulty of measuring such an intangible, research has shown that the more a person knows about an agency (level 1), the more favorably he is likely to regard it. This is an acceptable rationale for much that cannot be measured and documented.

Whose Job?

It would be ideal if every library had a trained publicist on the staff, full- or part-time. Progress toward this ideal has been slow, but the increasing awareness on the part of both library directors and trustees of the importance of this function and the need for qualified assistance are good portents for the future.

Diffusing the responsibility for carrying out the library's public information and promotion program among various staff members and department heads is an all-too-common practice at present. This is primarily because of the failure to distinguish between the implementation of a service (an in-house library program, for example, or an outreach activity) and the process or technique of publicizing or promoting it. It's unrealistic to expect the children's librarian or department heads to carry out their primary duties and activities and assume that they know how to promote them effectively as well. Most activities should be joint efforts that require consultation and cooperation. But ultimately one person must ride herd and channel and carry out the actual communication process. In some cases the library director must assume this role, and be both the chief and the Indian. In other situations a staff member may be assigned the responsibility, or, where possible, a person specifically hired on a part- or full-time basis. The latter need not be a trained librarian, since most library school training has little relevance to this function. Journalism experience and/or public contact work with another agency is far more important. A properly qualified person will quickly learn all that is necessary about library operation and philosophy—in less time in fact than it will take a trained librarian to acquire the skills of a publicist. As a less costly alternative, some libraries contract with an outside professional on an annual basis or for specific projects to receive the benefit of professional expertise, contacts, and equipment, and to profit from an outsider's viewpoint.

". . . other aids . . ."

The best immediate hope for hard-pressed small- and medium-sized libraries lies in the consultation and assistance that may be available from the staff of the library system or network of which they are members. Such aid will be more or less useful in accordance with the degree of understanding and responsibility assumed by the member library for setting goals and priorities within the context of the local situation. Experienced volunteers, Friends, or trustees have been invaluable in providing aid in carrying out one or more aspects of a promotional program in some libraries.

What's in a name? If "that which we call a rose, by any other name would smell as sweet," perhaps the title assigned to the person is relatively unimportant as long as the function and duties are clearly understood. "Public relations officer" is clearly misleading, since public relations in its entirety is everyone's job and a prime management responsibility. "Public information specialist" is no doubt preferable, but "public affairs officer," "communications specialist," "community relations officer," and "community service director" are some of the terms used. A job description should be drawn up which clearly states the basic function, relationship, and duties. No one model would be suitable for all types and sizes of libraries, but this statement could serve as a starting point:

> Basic functions: the public information officer shall have the responsibility for informing the public about the services and activities of the ___ Library by all acceptable communication techniques; shall coordinate the promotional activities within and for the library; shall report directly to the Library Director; and shall supervise assigned clerical, graphic art, or other assisting personnel.

The specific duties can then be spelled out in as much or as little detail as is deemed necessary and in the form used for job descriptions of other staff members.

This is the list of duties drawn up by the Greenville County Library in South Carolina, for example:

> The purpose of the Community Relations Department of the Greenville County Library is to inform every segment of the community of the services and facilities provided by the library and to encourage the fullest possible utilization of those services and facilities. Relating the library to the community includes:
>
> 1. Directing, editing and participating in the production and distribution of news releases, articles and various publications including house organs.
>
> 2. Meeting with civic, industrial and business groups and the general public to deliver and discuss topics relating to the library.
>
> 3. Planning and coordinating special promotions and publicity programs (National Library Week, Arts Festival, Textile Hall, John Cotton Dana Scrapbook, Billboards, Transit Advertising).
>
> 4. Arranging conferences and special events and escorting and briefing interested groups and public officials through the library.
>
> 5. Supervising the writing, editing and publications of booklets, catalogs and sustaining publications.
>
> 6. Representing the library at various public meetings and conferences.
>
> 7. Participating in outside literary groups, book discussions, educational committees, etc. as a spokesman for the library. (Thursday Club, Literary Hour at Woman's Club, Westminster Discussion Groups, Books Sandwiched-In, Y.W.C.A.)
>
> 8. Setting up press conferences as needed.
>
> 9. Consulting with and advising director and agency personnel as to the best use of the various media for public relations effectiveness.
>
> 10. Working with personnel on exhibits displayed in library.
>
> 11. Acting in a liaison capacity with the Friends of the Library organization.

The State of the Art

The following questions were included in the questionnaire sent to a limited number of libraries around the country. The libraries are not representative of public libraries as a whole; they were contacted simply because there was evidence of aggressive and on-going promotion programs. The following selected answers illustrate the disparity in the state of the art.

Who plans the library's publicity and promotional activities and what other staff members are involved?

"As Public Relations and Programming Coordinator, I have primary responsibility for all planning. Initial planning is always done with the department head, and from then on we work in concert as much as possible. Large events involving the whole library are planned initially with the whole professional staff on hand."
(small Wisconsin library)

"These activities are planned by the Director and the Assistant to the Director."
(small New York Library)

"The head librarian."
(small Wisconsin library, medium-sized Nebraska library)

"The Administrative Assistant is responsible for public relations. She prepares news releases, public service announcements, brochures, annual reports, and other public information. She coordinates bulletin boards and displays. However, it is the philosophy of this administration to involve each department head . . . the staff there generally uses their ideas and art work."
(small Alabama library)

"The PR/Programming Coordinator with the Library Director. There is a Board member who chairs the PR Committee."
(medium-sized New York library)

"This is presently a joint thing shared about equally by the Library Director, the Head of Children's Services and the Head of Adult Services. This does not always work out well. However, we are hiring a half-time professional public relations officer to coordinate things."
(medium-sized Illinois library)

"Many people are involved."
(large Indiana library)

"The library's information writer, graphic artists, deputy director plus all public services staff members."
(large Minnesota library)

"The Assistant Director of Community Services plans the adult programs and the promotional activities . . . does publicity for all programs."
(medium-sized South Carolina library)

"The Head of Public Relations plans publicity in conjunction with the staff members most closely involved with the activity."
(large Pennsylvania library)

"The Community Services Officer does all the planning."
(large Iowa library)

Is an overall plan for activities and projects planned annually? Is an annual schedule or calendar written out on a weekly, monthly or semiannual basis?

Eight of the fifteen replies indicated that an overall plan was prepared, more or less formally. The Greenville County Library (South Carolina) forwarded this detailed list:

1. To conduct 50 tours of the library.

2. To conduct 40 programs for the general public.

3. To update and republish 1000 copies of the Directory of Greenville County Clubs and Organizations.

4. To prepare and distribute 6000 copies of eight monthly Calendars of Events, one nine month Calendar and one summer Calendar of Events.

5. To prepare and distribute 7200 copies of 12 different book lists.

6. To prepare and distribute 12,000 copies of six different movie brochures.

7. To prepare and distribute 4000 copies of four film brochures.

8. To prepare and distribute 5000 copies of five bibliographies for government publications.

9. To prepare and distribute four book-mobile schedules, 12,000 copies.

10. To answer suggestion box inquiries monthly.

11. To publish 50 issues of *Ad-Libs*.

12. To publish four issues of *Leaves*.

13. To publish 30 additional brochures on various subjects, approximately 30,000 copies.

14. To prepare and distribute 1000 copies of 25 different bookmarks.

15. To prepare and distribute 20,000 copies of ten different flyers.

16. To publish 1000 certificates for summer reading program.

17. To provide 72 regular exhibits and 2 special exhibits.

18. To maintain monthly door count for main library.

19. To attend as library representative 40 meetings, such as PR-16, RSVP, Thursday Club, Community Council Public Information Task Force, Friends of the Library.

20. To complete a procedural manual for the community relations department.

21. To maintain schedule for public meeting rooms on a daily basis.

22. To provide news releases to five local papers on a weekly basis.

23. To provide spot announcements to 16 radio stations on a weekly basis.

24. To work with local TV station for PSA's throughout the year.

25. To print 5000 movie tickets for Children's Room.

26. To print 5000 *Help for You* brochures in conjunction with Community Planning Council.

27. To answer unlimited number of phone calls regarding library services and facilities.

28. To promote library services through participation in community wide events such as Arts Festival, Up-Country Jubilee, PEP, etc.

29. To promote special library events such as National Library Week, Symmes Reception, receptions for Friends of Library speakers, etc.

30. To send LA IV to one local or state workshop or convention for professional development.

31. To attend one or two regional or national conventions in order to actively participate in membership committee of SELA, and public relations committee of ALA.

Sample Annual Schedule

The Hennepin County Library (Minnesota) summarized one annual program:

1. Prepare budget request for Public Information Section including addition of a part-time Library Assistant—April 10, 1978.

2. Plan and implement a library card registration campaign that will include radio public service announcements, a TV public service announcement, printed materials and posters—October 18, 1978.

3. Produce children's and young adult audiovisual shows on how to use the materials catalog—June 30, 1978.

4. Annually update HCL's general slide show; to annually produce a general brochure and guide to HCL rules.

5. Have 1978 annual report ready for distribution one week before the library board's annual meeting.

Are specific objectives established?

"We make an attempt to hit one new segment of the public each year, in addition to our ongoing activities. There is not a lot of pre-planning in this—it usually comes about through a suggestion from a user, or as part of a promotion or activity being presented by another community group."

"Yes, for example, we had a legislative luncheon to acquaint area legislators with the needs of the library before they went to the capitol to vote on the budget."

"We try to reach all areas of the community. . . ."

"Yes, in 1978 we will emphasize library card registration. . . ."

"The staff meets annually to determine which goals have priority."

Are the promotional methods (publicity, special events or contacts, exhibits, etc.) determined in advance according to specific described objectives?

"Yes, in a flexible way. Highly important events are tightly planned. However, over the long haul, some flexibility is left to take advantage of opportunities that may present themselves to bring in contingency plans if a course of action appears not to be delivering the desired effect."

"Not usually. . . ."

"Yes, according to very specific financial limitations."

Is any attempt made to evaluate the results of particular activities in terms of the objectives?

"This is our weakest area. Evaluations are done informally . . . we operate largely on 'feelings.' . . ."

"To the extent that results are measurable—i.e., attendance at programs, number of persons receiving special interest newsletters, etc. In addition, the Library has surveyed 20% of the householders in the community annually. . . ."

"Yes, a narrative commenting on the success is written. Recommendations are made for future reference."

"Yes, I frequently use questionnaires. . . ."

"Very loosely! If an event was a success, its success was 'self-generated'; if a 'bust', there was 'not enough publicity.' . . ."

"Results directly attributable to the promotional activities: increase in program attendance—16%; increase in circulation—2.2%; increase in library card registration—2.6%."

"Yes, evaluation is always done to determine the best methods of publicizing and the overall effectiveness. . . . Members of community organizations assist the staff in evaluating library programs. . . ."

"When the objective is specific and may be quantified, yes. If the objective is not quantifiable, usually there is a wrap-up discussion with staff to set the ground work for future objectives."

Is there a line item in your budget for publicity and promotion?

The answers to this question ranged, predictably, from: "No line item," "Not readily identifiable," to percentages of the total budget (from 3/10ths of 1 percent to 1.6 percent). Dollar amount figures that were reported included salaries of designated personnel in some cases, and figures budgeted for supplies and activities only in others.

Only one valid conclusion could be drawn from these varied reports: the degree of understanding of the principles of planning and the sophistication demonstrated in establishing and evaluating goals does not depend on the size or budget of the library, large or small. It would appear to depend entirely on the knowledge, insight, and/or experience of the persons involved, whether library director or designated public information officer. The foregoing questions can serve as a quick review of the planning situation in any library.

A communications "audit" may be worthwhile for larger libraries, which have had a planned public information program over a period of time. An outside consultant can be called upon, or it can be conducted on a self-evaluation basis. A very useful guide for in-house review, one of the few available, has been developed by the American Society for Hospital Public Relations, entitled "Hospital Public Relations Management Development Program." The review process is described in hospital-related terms, but with the simple substitution of library identifications and situations, most of the steps can be followed easily and systematically. Each statement or objective in the guide (under such sections as "Philosophy and Objectives," "Organization," "Programming") is followed by columns headed "yes," "in process," "planned," "no," or "not applicable." The result is an overall review or assessment of the current status, which pinpoints deficiencies.

Communicating One-to-One: The Library User as a "Customer"

Libraries are for Customers

Librarians serve people, not books.

Right? Of course. That seems too obvious to state. And people are individuals. Thus the consideration afforded an individual in the one-to-one communication process between librarian and patron must be the foundation upon which all other library promotion is built. If the foundation is shaky, the best-conceived promotional program will be left in midair, with neither validity nor substance.

The person entering the library from need or habit—or perhaps lured in by a new awareness of materials and services—who is met with indifference or disdain will react with dismay, disappointment, frustration, or anger. This will lead to disinterest, or even hostility, toward the library, the very attitudes that most need to be overcome.

Unfortunately, indifference or insensitivity to patrons' needs is, if not endemic, at least still extant in too many libraries, both large and small. When the so-called affability factor is lacking, it is of little use to try to create an environment that will encourage the first visit to a library, let alone repeat visits.

Almost everyone has a horror story. (In all fairness, we must admit that almost everyone can and will repeat a horror story about treatment received in some other agency, business, or institution. Rudeness or indifference is not confined to librarians, but that's no excuse!)

Just recently I had occasion to seek some information about an unusual geological formation off the coast of Belize, in Central America. I went the usual route of consulting the card catalog and the indices with which I am most familiar but found nothing. Time was running short, so I "bothered" the reference librarian on duty with a request for assistance to hasten the search. And bother it obviously was, although she was not particularly busy; she waved airily toward a shelf, and said, "Well, I don't know . . . did you try that index over there?" She promptly turned around to something else on her desk. It was a classic example of the waving-arm-over-there syndrome.

There's a sequel to this episode. It happens that I am a trustee of the system to which this large library belongs, and so I told the story to one of the administrators, without naming the staff member. (I didn't know her name, because there are no

The message comes through loud and clear when it is printed in big letters on the front of a desk that is too often something of a barrier between patron and librarian. Laurel F. Goodgion, Children's Librarian, New Britain Public Library (CT) demonstrates that the sign means what it says.

name tags used in this library, despite the fact that this is one of the simple things that helps to overcome the impersonal atmosphere of a good-sized library.) My excuse for repeating the story was to make a discreet suggestion that some training was obviously needed in staff-patron relationships, especially in view of the fact that money for a substantially expanded public information and promotional program had just been approved. Ah yes, a book containing the information I needed was given to me a few days later, with an apology—a perquisite of trusteeship, I'm afraid—but at least a recognition at the administrative level of the importance of one-to-one communication.

On the other hand, many library administrators not only recognize the importance of customer consideration, but personally convey this concern to staff, as illustrated by this story told by Dr. Martha Jane Zachert, as reported in *Oklahoma Librarian,* October, 1976:

> When she first went to work as a beginning library page, the director took her aside and told her she was the most important employee in the library. Martha Jane thought he was kidding until he started explaining to her that she was the most visible of all employees:
> . . . you're on your feet among the shelves, next to the people who are searching for material. If they ask you a question and you turn them off with a curt "I don't know" or "go ask the lady in the blue dress," then our patrons will think of our library as cold and uninterested in their problems. However, if the supportive staff is easy to approach, if the person answering the phone has a pleasant voice, if that employee knows what she is doing and does it well, the patrons will feel at home in the library and confident of the library's ability.

The responsibility for maintaining the affability factor lies with each individual, but only those who, by nature or training, can and are willing to relate well to patrons should be in the front line of service to the public.

Human nature being what it is, good humor, composure, and a smile are difficult to maintain, however motivated you may be, when your feet hurt, you've heard the same question 19 times in an hour, and the other person is unpleasant. And even the best of intentions can seem to go astray,

as Katherine E. Moore, Balsam Lake, Wisconsin librarian, relates:

> I was busy helping a patron with a reference question when someone else asked me a question about a book title.
> I started to respond, "I've Only Got Two Hands. . . ."
> With an icy stare, she asked her question again. Again I stated, "I've Only Got Two Hands and I'm Busy. . . ."
> With that she lost all composure and said, "Yes, I know you're busy, but all I want to know is the title of a book!"
> "That's what I'm trying to tell you," I answered. "The book is *I've Only Got Two Hands and I'm Busy Wringing Them,* by Jane Goodsell."

The customer relations training practices employed by businesses are applicable to libraries, and many of the reminders and aids so used can be adapted. The following version of a creed, the origins of which are variously attributed, is a reminder worth distributing and posting:

> A library user is the most important person in our business. A user is not dependent on us. We are dependent on him/her.
>
> A user is not an interruption of our work. S/he is the purpose of it.
>
> A patron does <u>us</u> a favor when s/he comes in. We aren't doing a favor by helping him/her.
>
> A user is our business—not an outsider.
>
> A patron is not just a statistic on the monthly report. S/he is a human being with feelings, like our own.
>
> A patron is a person who comes to us with his/her needs and wants. It is our job to fill them as best we can.
>
> A library patron deserves the most courteous attention we can give him/her. S/he is the lifeblood of this library. S/he pays our salary. Without him/her we would have to close our doors. Don't ever forget it.

Librarians serve people, not books, and doing this pleasantly and in a spirit of helpfulness is the first step in successful library promotion. Indeed, you may not always be able to aid a patron satisfactorily, but the intent will come through and the user will have a better image of the library, whatever other inadequacies may exist. This is doubly important because the library is, in effect, a monopoly, and unlike most other community agencies or businesses, the patron cannot go elsewhere for the service. It's a take-it-or-leave-it situation.

Looking at Ourselves

Attitude changes are difficult to effect, but they can often be initiated when problems are acknowledged. For example, an information survey taken in the library may reveal some negative reactions and opinions on the part of library users that may surprise—even disturb—staff members, and provide incentive for behavioral change. It could take the following form:

How Do We Rate with You?

Please cross out two headlines to each of these questions, leaving only those that approximately express what you yourself would say.

1. How were you treated by the staff?

2. Were you greeted pleasantly?

3. Were your questions answered satisfactorily?

4. Have we made you feel "at home" in *your* library?

5. Did you get all the help you needed?

Since none of the headlines provided above adequately expresses my feelings, I shall make one myself:

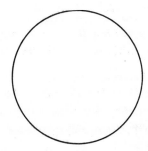

And because this isn't the way I feel either, I shall give vent to my feelings in the following lines:

_____

_____

_____

_____

Name (if you wish): _____

The following exercises, based on questionnaires used in a Baltimore, Maryland staff training session, can be done in a group to aid individuals in becoming more aware of personal attitudes and how they can effect work in a library.

Values Clarification

(The intent of this exercise is to stimulate individual thought in the process of answering questions. Caution should be taken in making generalizations from the response, since the questions are open to individual interpretation. After completion of the exercise, the spread of anonymous yes and no answers can be tallied, and each question can be used for discussion of the significance and meaning of the attitudes implied.)

Answer yes or no to each question:

1. Should librarians answer homework questions? __Yes __No

2. Should librarians answer homework questions asked by the student's parent? __Yes __No

3. Should you make a judgment as to the importance of questions asked? __Yes __No

4. Should loitering be allowed in the library? __Yes __No

5. Do you think you will be only too happy to retire when the time comes? __Yes __No

6. Could you invite someone you don't like to your home? __Yes __No

7. Do you think marijuana should be legalized? __Yes __No

8. Are you willing to admit it when you are wrong? __Yes __No

9. Have you lived in this community all your life? __Yes __No

10. Would you really rather live somewhere else? __Yes __No

11. Do you think most people cheat on something? __Yes __No

12. Do you find it difficult to listen to people sometimes? __Yes __No

13. Were you attracted to library work primarily by a love of books and reading? __Yes __No

14. Do you think you are racially prejudiced? __Yes __No

15. Do you dislike dealing with people with handicaps? __Yes __No

16. Do you think familiarity breeds contempt? __Yes __No

17. Do you know many patrons by name? __Yes __No

18. Are you reluctant to give your name to patrons who ask for it? __Yes __No

19. Do you fear for your personal safety while in the library? __Yes __No

20. Do you have a close friend of another race? __Yes __No

21. Do you have friends of various ages? __Yes __No

22. Do you think sex education in the schools should include techniques for contraception? __Yes __No

23. Do you think that a homosexual should be allowed to teach in the public schools? __Yes __No

24. Would you prefer to have all library employees address each other by their first names? __Yes __No

25. Would you be in favor of a "halfway house" for drug addicts in your neighborhood? __Yes __No

26. Do you think that young people today are spoiled and lazy? __Yes __No

27. Do you think your library is giving the best service it can? __Yes __No

Characteristics of a Public Service Librarian

(The intent of this exercise in setting priorities for traits of librarians is to stimulate thought about the skills, interests, and personal characteristics that make effective a library staff member who is approached by or approaches the public in the library.)

Mark each trait either (1) very important; (2) important; or (3) not as important:

1. Knows the collection well __1 __2 __3

2. Reads professional literature __1 __2 __3

3. Has a genuine liking for people __1 __2 __3

4. Is a good listener __1 __2 __3

5. Can communicate effectively __1 __2 __3

6. Can relate to people of various ages, races, and cultural backgrounds __1 __2 __3

7. Is involved in the community __1 __2 __3

8. Has a sense of humor __1 __2 __3

9. Has cultural interests __1 __2 __3

10. Reads widely __1 __2 __3

11. Has hobbies and interests outside the profession __1 __2 __3

12. Has experience in library work __1 __2 __3

13. Is open to new ideas __1 __2 __3

14. Is well organized __1 __2 __3

15. Is intelligent __1 __2 __3

16. Has a good memory __1 __2 __3

17. Has good reference skills __1 __2 __3

18. Maintains professional attitude in dealing with the public __1 __2 __3

Self-Analysis Quiz

(This is for individual use only, to encourage self-examination.)

1. Do you consider yourself very sociable? Moderately sociable? Antisocial?

2. Do you genuinely like people?

3. How many people have you invited into your home in the last three months?

4. How many homes have you been invited to in the last three months?

5. How many times have you gone out with friends in the last three months? At whose invitation—yours or theirs?

6. Do children make friends with you quickly? Slowly? Not at all?

7. Do people with physical or mental handicaps upset you or arouse fear?

8. Are you at ease with strangers in a social situation? In the library?

9. What is your general attitude toward society? Are you objective? Optimistic? Pessimistic? Indifferent? Resigned?

10. Do people seem to like you? What could you do to make them like you more?

11. Do you feel superior socially or professionally to most people you meet? On a par with them? Below them?

12. Do you adhere rigidly to your moral or ethical standards?

13. Do you practice flexibility by deciding right or wrong on the merits of each situation?

Positive Communication

There is more to positive communication than simply dishing out information. Communication is a two-way street. You not only provide information; you must also be sure that information is heard and understood by the people whom you want to reach.

There are many studies on the subject of interpersonal relationships and communication which are well worth reading, but there are also some very simple dos and don'ts with immediate practical application to everyday situations in the library that will help to enhance the affability factor.

Do use name-tags to identify library staff members. This helps to break down the gap between a patron and a nameless face behind the desk. The badge or card can also carry a "May I Help?" phrase to reinforce the intent, if not always the practice, of that message. In a very large or highly departmentalized library or library system, this identification is also an aid to staff members who may not know or recognize all other co-workers. Be sure that the name is printed in letters large enough to be read from a normal approach distance; it defeats the purpose if a patron must squint, lean close, or stare hard to make out the letters.

Don't use jargon in assisting patrons. Many do not know the meaning of the terms "interlibrary loan," "computerized catalog," or "vertical file," and it increases a feeling of inadequacy or embarrassment when a librarian makes such references. The expression, "charging" or "transaction card," for example, are inexcusable and subject to misinterpretation. The "circulation desk" is the more familiar "check-out counter"; and what's a periodical if it is not a magazine, newspaper, or journal?

Do make friends for the library on a person-to-person basis:

1. With a smile, not a blank look

2. With a genuine response to the patron's needs, not indifference

3. With attentive listening, not impatience

4. With enthusiasm, not boredom

5. With recognition of the other person's individuality and importance, not irritation

6. With obvious pride in the library and its services, not smugness

"All very elementary, my dear Watson," but often overlooked or forgotten in the day-to-day hassle.

Don't use buck-passing phrases. Have you ever heard these, or used them?

"I don't know. It's a rule of the library. . . ."

"I'm not allowed to do that. . . ."

"That's not in this department."

"You'll have to see the library director about that."

"Don't blame me, I didn't have anything to do with that."

"Don't ask me—I only work here."

Do use the telephone properly as a communication aid. Few things are as annoying as a long delay in answering the phone, being put on "hold" and left dangling for an indeterminate period, or encountering a curtness that implies you are interrupting a very busy person—just a few of commonplace situations that turn the telephone into a weapon rather than a tool. Training staff to use tactful phrases and proper responses is an administrative responsibility, as is allocating the time and place for efficient use to prevent disruption of service to patrons in the building. It is extremely difficult to erase the impression received by those who have a bad experience in calling the library; prevention is the best cure. You might want to explore the situation at your library by calling from the other end and playing patron. In an experiment in Baltimore County, for example, one participant reported, unhappily, "We heard employees dismiss our questions, provide meaningless referrals, give incorrect answers, and leave the phone unattended as long as twenty minutes at a time." If such an experiment smacks of spying to the staff, turn it into an announced effort to reward recognition to those who handle it best.

Do initiate individual contact. Some patrons may shrink from a too-friendly approach or obvious concern, but many more are reluctant or embarrassed to approach a librarian for assistance, especially if that person appears occupied or authoritative, and often will leave without communicating his/her needs. One experiment in a conscious and organized effort to overcome that problem was reported by Dr. Richard Madaus, in *Arkansas Libraries,* Vol. 33, No. 2, 1976:

> When we first started talking about investigating the concept of organization toward aggressive reference service, some people said we were crazy—it couldn't be done. . . . And many observers noted that there would be no way to measure its success even if we could try it. Well, we probably are crazy—we did it . . . and it has almost doubled our circulation while tripling the number of people in the building. . . . We do feel that aggressive reference, i.e., putting patron service as the first priority of the library, does indeed flesh the skeleton of library theory we all learned in library school, and all too often put aside due to lack of budget, staff, and available time.

He described the restructuring of the library service and priorities undertaken to develop the program. This report was designed for a university library, but the first three aggressive reference rules would apply to a public library:

> 1. At the reference desk, a librarian may not be seated more than 10-15 minutes. After 10 minutes without a reference question, the librarian should start roaming the floors asking patrons if they need assistance. (Usually they never make it past the card catalog—someone *always* needs help there.) As a rule, we have found more questions being answered from the floor than from the desk. In fact, many hours the librarian never even gets to sit down at all.

> 2. No one walks past the reference desk without being acknowledged. (A smile, "Hello," "May I help you?" etc.)

> 3. Patrons are never merely directed to material—they are taken to it.

He concluded,

> We feel that aggressive reference is nothing more than basically sound minimum library service. It does require a shift in priorities and responsibilities, but we feel that in the age of information science, the traditional library must examine its objectives and evaluate performance in terms of those objectives.

In other libraries, this contact initiation has been termed "floor walking."

The "Problem" Patron—Or the Library with "Problems"

It is a wondrous, wild, and wooly assortment of people who come into the library. Some are problems because of their demands, misconceptions, or their personality traits. (Or maybe just because they got a parking ticket while trying to return an overdue book.)

A fair share of those regarded as problem patrons are made so because of problems in library operation and because the attitude prevails that using the library is a privilege, not a right. A good, objective look at the rationale for existing library rules and regulations is necessary when there seems to be an excessive number of problem patrons.

Eileen Cooke, Washington, D.C. Representative of the American Library Association told this story in *Drexel Library Quarterly,* Vol. 1, No. 1:

> The public is inclined to question anything from the classification of a book to the information requested on the borrower's application form. We must adjust ourselves to serving an endless variety of personalities in an endless array of moods. I remember one difficult patron whose library card had expired and who complained bitterly, not only about being required to fill out a form, but about the quantity and content of the questions asked on the form. 'What do you want, my life history?' I merely listened, and sometimes merely listening is important. As he continued to grumble, I said, 'The information requested on the form is actually of no use to us, but we do need your grandmother's maiden name.' This bit of levity clicked with the patron and solved a difficult situation. Timing and a light touch can be very important in our relations with the public. In this case, a borrower known for his irascibility became a more pleasant patron because a staff member bothered to add a touch of sympathetic humor.

She might well have added to this report the question of whether that lengthy form was really needed!

Requiring a local reference on an application for a library card is another example of a time-worn practice that needs to be examined. Is the reference ever checked? Does one need to know someone before he has a right to use the library? A news story told of the experience of John Dean, a well-known figure in the Watergate scandals. He applied for a card at a California library, but did not fill in the lines for references. When an adamant staffer told him he must list a reference, he was quoted as saying, "I don't have a friend. If I ever get one, I'll come back."

It takes a great deal of tact to explain or justify library regulations to a patron. If they are not readily self-evident and capable of being explained in three sentences of two-syllable words they may be questionable, and lead to problem patrons. A Sunday comic strip feature illustrated this in full color. Two youngsters were in the library, one saying "I'm looking for a book on how to build a dog house." He is shown with the book, entitled *How to Build a Dog House,* "Just what I want!" At the librarians' desk he says, "I'd like to take this book out," and she replies, "You can't take the book out." The last frame pictures the two children carrying tools, boards, and nails into the library.

". . . take a look at your rules and regulations . . ."

Regulations are designed, presumably, to ensure fair service to the greatest number, but they tend to be self-perpetuating or promulgated for the convenience of the library, not the user. What factors determine library hours, for example? Tradition and custom? Convenience of staff? Civil service regulations? *Or user needs?* How often is there a full complement of staff in a quiet library on a weekday and a frantic handful serving a full house on an evening or week-end?

Developing and justifying the rules and policies that govern all such matters, including disposition of material discards, lost cards, acceptance of gifts, and handling unacceptable or disturbed patron behavior are administrative responsibilities, but the staffer on the front line of public contact must be able to understand and explain these matters, so as to forestall patrons from becoming problems. Heresy or not, it may be necessary to grant a reasonable request of a borrower, to bend a rule if it causes no undue harm to others, in the name of goodwill and service.

Not long ago I was all but bowled over by the social worker in a nursing home as she rushed out the door. She explained breathlessly, "I've had a call from the public librarian about a resident's overdue book [the resident is in a wheelchair], and I've been told to get it back *right now.* She's just impossible. And she's so unpleasant to the kids, too, except those she happens to like."

PRISCILLA'S POP   **by Al Vermeer**

Reprinted by permission of Newspaper Enterprise Association

Which brings us to the much cussed and discussed matter of fines and overdues. Collecting fines for late return of materials is probably the single most annoying practice of libraries in the eyes of the public, and one of the greatest deterrents to better library use by many. It epitomizes the bad image of the library as a closed-fisted institution, zealously intent on guarding its wares. The number of cartoons on the subject of library fines that appear regularly in all kinds of periodicals is mute testimony to the widespread disdain and dislike of the practice.

What are the usual justifications given for charging fines?

"To get the books back on time." If so, the amount should be set high; a few pennies per day is scarcely a deterrent to late returns. A large fine may be a deterrent to the eventual return of the books; it doesn't work in reducing book losses according to many studies. Most libraries that have eliminated fines find that the number of overdues *remains at the same level*.

The need for getting materials back "on time," whatever arbitrary period that may encompass, is also based on the presumption that another patron wants or needs that particular book on or before the due date. This is nonsense for many items.

"To serve as punishment for those who do not abide by the rules." Librarians scarcely need to be cast any further into the role of disciplinarians. Public scofflaws will not be deterred by a nominal fine. Borrowers should return books on time for the right reason—the needs of others—rather than from the fear of penalty. And the patron who is happy to pay a fine because s/he thinks it benefits the library has actually denied his/her responsibility to others and is guilty of strange reasoning.

"To serve as a source of income." The less said about that the better. The amount of fine money collected is generally small; if you need "petty cash," *budget* petty cash! Or solicit contributions. Or have a book or bake sale. In many cases the money collected goes into a municipal or school general fund rather than to the library, or the amount collected is applied against the library budget to reduce the number of tax dollars spent. Here again the principle is wrong, because it has

". . . amnesty—bad PR!"

become a "user fee"; if that were valid, a charge should be levied on every book loaned. But even more to the point, it costs more to collect fines than the amount produced.

An overdue book notice, in the form of a postcard, can use a little humor.

A postcard overdue book notice need not be threatening.

Consider these facts: "Good" patrons get less attention and/or must wait while clerks collect fines and argue with delinquents. There is an opportunity for favoritism in levying fines, a tacit admission that there is something wrong about the whole idea. (How do *you* treat your trustees?) Whether or not children are the worst offenders, the fault may not be theirs. A usually responsible or conscientious patron may be the victim of an unusual or extenuating circumstance, even of a clerk's error, and scarcely deserves punishment or a penalty. The eagerness to check out more books is effectively stifled when a user is made to pay a fine for an overdue book.

The deplorable privilege-not-a-right attitude is exemplified by the circulation librarian of a state college who wrote, "Those repelled or alienated from the library by a firm but fair [overdue] policy will most likely be undesirables and misfits which the library would not want as patrons anyway." (Ergo: levying fines will make it easier to sort out the right kind from the wrong kind of users?)

Some very strange and convoluted reasoning is evidenced on the part of those librarians who make rules about fines and then devise self-defeating methods to reward or forgive those who break them. "Amnesty days" are a good example of this reverse logic. They encourage miscreants to expect and await expiation of their sins on an occasional or regular basis, and they penalize the nonoffenders. But, even worse, the widespread publicity is focused on one of the least desirable and disliked aspects of library service. After a lengthy discussion in *School Library Journal,* April, 1977 on publicizing a "Free Week" in a high school in Council Bluffs, Iowa, the author concluded,

> Essentially a library 'Free Week' will evolve into a concerted *public relations effort* that can be conducted *on a regular basis* [italics added; ed] to make patrons more aware of the library and the services it provides. The small amount of money that is lost will be more than compensated for by the immediate and visible increase in circulation and library patrons.

This is a good example of total misunderstanding of the effects of such publicity on the public.

Incredible as it may seem, there are other outrageous gimmicks that have been used to get back overdue materials: a Wisconsin library of-fered ten cents for each overdue item that was returned during a specified week; in New Jersey and Ohio, libraries have inserted coupons in local grocery ads for return of overdue books without fine; a university library publicized the fact that it would "forgive" one dollar of any fine due, reporting this as an effort to create good will for the library; a Canadian library offered a McDonalds' coupon good for an order of French fries for every overdue item returned, adding the parenthetical note, "16mm films excepted." A Virginia library offered to forgive fines if the patron could write the name of the town through which Sinclair Lewis' *Main Street* ran; a South Carolina library offered coupon "rebates" on fines during National Library Week, with 50 percent off during that period, or, "the coupons could be held for future use during the next twelve months at a 30% level"—perhaps the worst example of all!

Occasionally a library does retrieve a fair number of overdue books, but the price in terms of prejudicial publicity is much too high.

A paragraph from a library staff newsletter sums up the utter illogic of it all: "As the elderly patron walked up to the desk he explained, 'I feel just awful. I have been coming to the library since 1912 and this is the first time I have had to pay a fine.' " Then the editor had the gall to add, "Too bad he missed the fine-free week."

Abolishing or modifying the barrier of fines does not solve the problem of overdue materials, but there are more constructive methods to encourage prompt return that are used successfully by many libraries. One of the simplest and most obvious is placing return book drops in convenient locations around the community. Printed materials in the form of posted notices, bookmarks, and news releases are all used to explain the problems caused to the library and other patrons by negligence or oversight.

Putting people on the spot by posting or publicizing names of those with overdues is a dubious practice, although it has had some fair success in schools, perhaps as a result of peer pressure. But avoid, at all costs, any chance of a news report singling out individuals, such as the one that appeared in a weekly Wisconsin paper under the headline, "Caught in the Act." The article described the librarian's appearance before the City Council with a plea for more money. She explained some of the problems, and then was quoted as saying, "The mayor has an overdue right now. That's why she looked down when I was talking about them." The article didn't say, but the chances of getting more money would appear pretty slim after that remark.

Overdue notices do not make friends, but they are a necessary evil. Sugar them a bit with a friendly phrase, an unusual format, or a cartoon. They also can do double duty by carrying a timely bit of information about a program or something new at the library, as a way of saying "we aren't angry with you." Use such phrases as "We hope you enjoyed the material you borrowed several weeks ago, and that you'll find time in the next few days to stop in at the library to return it. See you soon!" Or, "We find ourselves in the uncomfortable position of again having to ask, won't you please return the material you borrowed from us as soon as possible?" Both were used by the East Syracuse Free Library. Your notice would be sure to be read if you wrote it out on a white paneled card resembling a formal invitation in this form:

You are cordially invited

to call at One Hundred Main Street

beween nine and six o'clock

any day this week

to return your library books

R.S.V.P.

You might even get some leverage and some laughs by offering membership in the Procrastinators' Club of America (yes, there *is* such a thing) or set up your own club, with cards, bylaws, etc.

Congratulations for being late.

You now qualify for membership in the Procrastinators' Club of America.

(over)

APPLICATION FOR MEMBERSHIP

I hereby certify that I am an active procrastinator who qualifies for membership in the Procrastinators' Club of America, Inc.

NAME _____

ADDRESS _____

CITY _____ STATE _____ ZIP _____

(Signature) _____

ENCLOSE $10.00 INITIATION FEE

Membership entitles you to an official membership card . . . a "License to Procrastinate" . . . participation in all events and affairs . . . a recent calendar and many surprises.

Procrastinators' Club of America, 1405 Locust St., Phila., Pa. 19102

The membership card for the Procrastinator's Club of America could be a model for your own Overdue-Book-of-the-Month Club.

Lost or stolen books are quite another problem, and when overdues slide into the lost category, a very different approach is obviously called for; stringent measures to recover the books or recoup the cost would meet with general public understanding and acceptance. However, again, the problem is often aggravated by the library's negative actions in combatting it, such as little or no duplication of most-needed or most-wanted titles, "hiding" theft-prone items, and unduly restricting circulation.

These suggestions for coping with the problem are excerpts from an article by Theodore C. Hines, "Theft, Mutilation, and the Loss-to-Use Ratio," in *Library Security Newsletter,* Vol. 1, No. 3:

The [first] . . . step is to remove the obstacles to *honest* use of your library, and these questions will serve as guidelines to what might be done:

Can your users take out a reasonable amount of materials at one time?

Is the loan period long enough? Can materials be renewed by phone? Are charge-out procedures rapid and efficient, not requiring users to fill out long forms? Is desk scheduling so arranged as to avoid users having to wait to check out materials at peak periods? Is the circulation desk convenient to the exit?

Are there enough multiple copies of high-demand items such as auto repair manuals, books on karate, civil service and other examination materials, shorthand and typing manuals? Do these items have as long a charge period as others? Are you making as much use of paperbacks as possible, especially in areas where loss/use ratios tend to be high? Do you circulate copies of at least some reference books and encyclopedias? Does your selection policy reflect user needs?

If a title requested is not available, will you really try to get it for your users promptly, by interlibrary loan or purchase—or by calling another library to which your user can go and borrow the book (lest s/he be driven there to "borrow" in a more unofficial manner)? Do you advertise these services constantly?

Is your periodicals subscription list adequate and are your back files what they should be?

Are [photocopying] facilities readily available, cheap, and easy to use? [Ed: Why not offer free photocopying of one to three pages of high-cost, high-loss references, such as repair manuals?]

Have you considered microform subscriptions for back files as a cheaper and better substitute for hardbound collections, back issue ordering, and binding? If so, are reader-printers easily available and cheap to use?

Do you charge fines, especially for children? Do you realize the motivation this generates, first for non-return because the child may think he hasn't enough to pay the fine, and then, because he owes fines, for engaging in informal "use" of materials rather than checking them out? Do you visit the sins of siblings upon siblings, so that if your sister owes a book or fines, you can't get books—legally, at any rate?

Does staff behave as if late or lost books are a type of crime rather than something that can happen to anyone and that is much more likely to happen to honest, frequent, and good library users than to others? Is their attitude about mistakes, lost books, fines, adequate and friendly?

Have you buried your microforms in a separate room or section so they are hard to use? Do you have enough readers and reader-printers? Are all materials, but especially non-print and microforms, fully cataloged and easy to find?

Are there typewriters for use in the library? Are the seats the kind you could stand to sit and work in for a reasonable time? Can a user talk if he wants to without feeling he is disturbing other users or antagonizing the staff?

If you have teachers, scoutmasters, church groups in your neighborhood who persistently give the same assignment simultaneously to a hundred children, have you gone and talked to them about trying to work something out positively, to give the children what they need without·the unpleasant experience of scrambling for too few materials before their peers get them? Have you ever tried to work out preparing packets of material in advance?

A lot of time and effort is spent on retrieving lost library materials. Is as much spent on retrieving "lost" patrons? For example, the Clinton Public Library in Iowa checks expired registration cards against the current phone directory; if the person is listed, a letter is sent saying that s/he has been missed, and asking whether the library service has been at fault. Some reasons for renewing the lapsed cards are listed, with reminder of the variety of services available.

In the beginning and in the end, it is the one-to-one contact and consideration that counts; without the affability factor hard at work, no amount of publicity, bright-colored posters or special events will successfully promote library use.

Using the Media for Publicity

Publicity Is What You Make of It

Publicity in the media is one of the most important facets of a library promotional program; it is the factual or advocated information put out in the form of news.

Although the dictionary definition of news gives emphasis to timeliness, rest assured that media representatives, too, are aware that the expression "That's news to me!" refers as much to facts well-known to some (i.e., that the library has more than books) as to the news concerning an event that happened today (new appointments to the board of trustees) or is anticipated soon (a film program scheduled next week). The media will use both your topical news items and your advocacy interpretations or information features when you know how to present them.

No news is bad news for any library that wants better usage, better funding, and better public support, but the news must be actively disseminated. Media people rarely come to the library to publicize its program—and many never come in at all. (On the other hand, they may turn up unbidden at the first hint of controversy.)

In all likelihood, you will never get all the media exposure you think you are entitled to as a worthwhile community resource and institution. And you won't get any simply on the premise that you deserve it. The competition for free space and time in the media is tough. To enter the lists successfully you must be armed with an understanding of the rules and strategies of the game.

Game Plan

You need a game plan and schedule. You must know what you want to say, why, when, and to whom. Sound familiar? You faced those same questions when you were formulating your total promotional program; if you did that, you know the direction your publicity activities should take and the relative priority you must give them. Whether you have three newspapers, five radio stations, four television stations, and dozens of house organs and newsletters as media outlets, or a single weekly newspaper and area radio station, your aim is the same—to get across an effective message at the right time, in the right place, and in the right way. You will never have complete free choice as to which medium you will use for what purpose unless, of course, you buy time or space. Among the factors outside your control are the local newspaper or station policies or prejudices and the media prerogative to determine whether, when, or how much of a release will be used. You must plan and schedule realistically within these limitations.

A tentative calendar, listing and dating the routine and major media publicity you plan, particularly feature material, is an indispensable aid. All available outlets should be noted so that you can determine which will be most effective in terms of audience, timing, message format, and necessary lead time preparation. Determine how the various units fit into the total picture or message you hope to project. Publicity for its own sake or without a planned purpose is pointless.

Library service has a long and rich history, but society is now asking the question "What are you doing for us and why?" Your publicity must be designed to provide some answers and justifications. It is no longer enough to take the easy way out with only occasional appealing shots of tiny tots with picture books or rapt children at a story hour. Not only does this tend to reinforce an unwarranted opinion that the library is mainly for kids, but it begs the question. One significant message that must be conveyed by more than cute photos is that the library has an important role in helping to combat the appalling level of semiliteracy in our communities today; the important and necessary story is the *how* and *why*. Only planned publicity can accomplish that. Too many librarians still believe that any publicity or mention, however haphazard, is good; this is the old "I-don't-care-what-you-say-about-me-just-so-you-spell-my-name-correctly" theory. It may not hurt, but it doesn't do much good either.

There is a great deal of questionable advice given to novice publicists regarding the rules for releases, but there is one fundamental rule that applies to all. Contact your media people personally, and find out about their preferences, needs, and interests. Learn the names of the persons with whom you will be dealing and send your material through the proper channels. This does not guarantee that more of your publicity will be used, but it will improve the chances about 50 percent.

Ideally, your path should be cleared by the library director and trustees who have the basic responsibility for establishing good relations and peer liaison with media managements. The contact at this level will help immensely to assure the coverage you want. If there have been no previous efforts made in this direction, set up appointments and have your director or an eloquent trustee accompany you to briefing interviews. A frank and friendly approach will pay real dividends. Should you take an editor or station manager to lunch? Why not, if you have a good reason and something of value to impart to him/her? Their time is limited and important, but you may also be able to give them background information and news that will be helpful to them now and in the future. Don't be afraid to ask for advice; it will help everyone to do a better job. (You might also lobby for the appointment of a media representative to the board of trustees!)

Maintaining Good Media Relations

Be accurate at all times. Never release material that you have not checked and rechecked, right down to the certainty of the spelling of names. One good brouhaha with the media may wipe out a lot of past efforts to prove your reliability.

Be available. Make sure that the media people know how to reach you at all times. When a reporter needs background information, verification, or details of a late-breaking story, s/he wants it now, not tomorrow or next week.

Be consistent. When you have established a routine for sending out publicity, stick to it, so that the media can depend on you to fill available or reserved time or space.

Be discriminating. Know what is news and of interest to the public; avoid an overabundance of releases and trivial content. A form of Gresham's Law applies; if you send out too many unimportant releases, they will drive down the value of important ones.

Be fair. Send out the same or a similar release so that it arrives at the proper time for use by each medium, but give each one an occasional "exclusive" on an impartial basis.

Keep background information handy, whether it is general facts about the library or material dealing with specific issues. Part of the job of dealing with the media is educational. Uninformed reporters or new ones assigned to cover the library are one of the hazards of maintaining good relations. You will have to fill them in constantly, and be willing to repeat what may seem obvious to you.

Ask for due credit. Media people may use the library for personal reasons, but many depend primarily on their newspaper morgues or reference collections for the information they need in their daily work. Remind them of your reference service and encourage them to use it. Ironically, those who are aware of this and take full advantage seldom, if ever, publicly credit the library as the source. Following a call for assistance, you can tactfully suggest that the newspaper, radio, or television station use the phrase, "according to information supplied by the Cityville Public Library . . ." when appropriate in their stories. Remind them that the library is dependent upon public support to maintain the service and that their acknowledgment of help from the library is invaluable.

Say thank you. Express appreciation in a letter or in person when the library has received good coverage. Monitor the media as best you can, and enlist the support of staff and others so that you will be fully aware of what is being said, when, and where.

Don't argue. How do you correct misinformation and counter criticism? Very, very carefully. The media always has the last word, so react accordingly. Use good judgment in determining how serious the matter is, and nine times out of ten it will be best to ignore it. If you feel that something must be done, you can write a letter or make a phone call to the person responsible; keep your tone polite and factual, not unduly defensive, and you will, at the very least, educate him/her. Writing to or phoning a reporter's superior puts the employee on the spot and may malign your future relations. If criticism is printed or aired as an editorial opinion, that is an editor's right; about all you can do is to present your side, either in a memo or personal discussion. As a last resort, you can issue a formal statement to counter serious charges.

Controversy makes good copy in the eyes of the media, and although you may regard such publicity as unfortunate, it does give the library additional exposure and an opportunity to present valid information and explanations. An unwarranted or prejudiced attack on the part of a few may also rally unexpected support for the library, if you keep cool. This is also the time when the good press relations you have established will pay off.

the censors are coming!
the censors are coming!
the censors are coming!

Keep your ears tuned for the sound of distant thunder. If there are rumblings of trouble ahead over such issues as censorship, book selection, personnel changes or budgetary requests, take action in advance and head off the storm as best you can with the timely release of interpretative information. Be honest, never repress facts, and admit mistakes if necessary. You will get a fair hearing for the most part. In times of crisis and close scrutiny by the media, keep staff and trustees

informed of the situation and of the action that is being taken. Request that all questions or interviews be referred to a designated library spokesperson, whether that is you, the library director, or the board president.

A few simple techniques will aid in dealing with an aggressive or hostile press. Discuss the issue from the point of view of the public, not of the public library; explain why the action taken (or not taken) is in the best interest of the public as a whole. Watch your language, and do not make any statement that you do not want quoted. State your reasons or recommendations directly and clearly in the beginning, and follow up with supporting facts or figures. Your first words may be all that remains in a reporter's printed story or in a film clip that was cut to fit the available space or time.

Be wary of attempts to put words in your mouth. If a question contains the proverbial "when did you stop beating your wife?" twist, do not repeat the phrase or deny the charge. The question as posed will not appear in the report, but the answer might—"I never beat my wife"—and the headline could read "Librarian denies beating wife." It's a tricky maneuver that often works in the heat of exchange, so take time to answer, ignore the offensive phrase, and word the answer carefully. Use the expression, "No comment!" at your own peril; instead, give an honest reason for not replying.

The Press Conference

You may have occasion to consider calling a press conference by asking media representatives to come to you at a stated time and place. There must be a good reason or the turnout will be sparse; if you have any doubt about the matter, don't hold the conference. Among the situations that might warrant this would be the appointment of a new library director, the opening of a new facility, inauguration of a new and important service, or announcement of a special event of community-wide interest.

Prepare a special press kit, which would include one or more news releases, additional background information or angles that would flesh out the story, a fact sheet about the library, biographical data about any persons involved, and, if possible, one or more good 8 x 10 glossy pictures with full captions.

Alert the press well in advance—a week or more—and include enough information so that persons making assignments can determine whether to cover it or not. Use judgment and imagination to pique editorial interest, with emphasis on why this would be of interest to readers, listeners, or viewers.

Equipment You Will Need

It is assumed that you have the basic "equipment"—an ability to use words properly, spell correctly, express ideas clearly in language that is easily understood, plus a little creative imagination. You have assumed or been assigned the job of publicist because of these attributes, and it is the distinction between you and other representatives of the library. (Some library directors, for example, are skilled in many aspects of public relations, but are unable to write a simple direct sentence; his/her academic prose or technical jargon never will or should appear in print in the community media.)

A typewriter is, of course, absolutely essential. Handwritten releases went out with the buggy whip, and are picked up by the media just about as often.

A good camera, plus the ability to operate it well, will give you a distinct edge in securing media coverage, and you will find many more uses for it than simply supplying photos for releases. Unless photography is your hobby or you are willing to learn the basics of journalistic photography, you will not match the skill of a newspaper photographer or a television cameraman. On the other hand, they are not always available or do not turn up when needed, and your pictures will help to tell your story. Admittedly, the throwaway rate of unsolicited photos is high, but it can be worth a try on occasion. Consult the editor in advance, if possible, or try submitting a sheet of contact prints for consideration. Never send the same photo to competing media; mark those you submit "for exclusive use of _____." A good quality 35-mm single lens reflex camera is necessary to do an adequate job; an "instant image" camera is much too limited to serve your purposes.

A small tape recorder will free you from note-taking during interviews and meetings, or supplement your notes, and will assist you in verifying

statements made by others. It is also a handy way to record those great ideas that come when you are driving or otherwise unable to write down fleeting thoughts or memos to yourself.

Your personal reference collection may need to contain only a good dictionary, thesaurus, and style manual, because you have the unique advantage of easy access (surely!) to all of the library's reference resources. A duplicate copy of something you use very often may be in order, and some specialized publications and periodicals (see bibliography) may be helpful to have close at hand.

Working with Newspapers

Local newspapers provide the best way for the library to reach the greatest number of people on a regular basis, and you should, therefore, assign a high priority to securing coverage. Despite the rather widespread editorial notion that libraries do not make good copy, that is not true. Libraries get extensive coverage on occasion, although it is not always the type of publicity desired. Screaming headlines and inches of space may be devoted to a "seven day wonder" such as an attack on a particular book title held by the library, a budget slash proposed by a disenchanted council member, or a dispute over a library policy or request.

Reporters also like to poke fun at what they regard as a staid institution. An amusing example of this was reported from England, where news of the Mansfield Library in Nottinghamshire County appeared under the headings, "Thirst after Knowledge" and "Thirst for Books," brought about by the fact that an application had been made by the library for a license to sell liquor. Journalists envisaged topless librarians serving booze with books and holding drunken orgies. The facts in the matter were considerably less sensational, as reported by Anita Wright in *New Library World,* January 1978:

> This library, as is the case with many other central libraries built in the last few years, has included in the building a lecture theater, a group of meeting rooms, and a coffee bar, so it seemed a natural extension to be able to serve alcoholic refreshments to those people attending a function.
> The magistrates took half a day to hear the application as the local publicans, the pro-

prietor of the wine cellar, and the Temperance Society had all sent objectors. . . .

The license has now been granted and the seven day wonder is over. But take note: a first class library service is not newsworthy but the thought of boozy bookworms and rowdy reading stirs the imagination, and our news coverage in the press and on television will probably never be repeated.

It is very unlikely that you will make news by applying for a liquor license for the library, but you can make good copy with more routine information about library services and activities. It is up to you to learn how to look at it from the editor's viewpoint, and thereby garner a fair share of space. Generally, only about 40 percent of a newspaper is alloted to news (60 percent to "paid space") and many editors receive ten times as much material as they can use. Your release must be timely, interesting, and brief to warrant some of that 40 percent.

"Getting to Know You . . . Getting to Know All About You"

Again, your first step is to get acquainted with the editors with whom you will be dealing, and learn their requirements, preferences, and deadlines. Some papers, for example, will devote considerable space to feature and human interest stories, to a regular column, or to library-supplied feature material; others want only so-called "hard" news (announcements of activities, staff or board appointments, etc.), except, perhaps, for National Library Week or Children's Book Week. Learn the name of the city editor, and the departments of the paper other than the city desk, so that you can route material to the appropriate section, such as the entertainment page, the woman's page, the sports section, etc. Find out if the editors want a written story ready for the printer, or if all submitted material is routinely rewritten. Is a simple fact sheet sufficient? Is the editor or a reporter amenable to phone calls, and if so, what is the best time?

For example, here is the kind of information that was gleaned from talks with representatives of two competing newspapers in a medium-sized midwestern city. One did not want finished copy, just the basic information; the other accepted complete releases. One would not use any submitted photos but would assign a photographer if warranted; the other would consider supplied photos. Any news that appeared in the Sunday edition of the morning paper would not be used in the other newspaper at any time because of a 70 percent overlapping readership for that issue. Telephone calls were acceptable to one, discouraged by the other, which preferred mailed releases.

Incidentally, a good way to secure this kind of information or to refresh your own knowledge is to arrange a "workshop" at the library for publicity chairpersons of various agencies and organizations to which representatives of all the media are invited to discuss their specific requirements.

Many publications issue publicity tip sheets, detailing their needs and rules. It would be advisable to request these from newspapers outside your own community, in the event that you have news worthy of consideration by big city papers that are read in your area.

Despite the fact that reporters and editors are prone to say that they never use publicity handouts, surveys have shown that such stories are printed, and that library-generated releases are the major source of any news that does appear.

It is the editor's privilege to decide whether a story will be used, what pictures if any will be run, how long the article will be, and on what page it will appear. Only a rank amateur would be foolish enough to say, "This should go on the front page," demand that a photographer be sent, or request to see a story before it is printed.

". . . news, information, or advertising?"

The question of whether material is advertising or legitimate publicity is a sticky one which can surface unexpectedly, particularly in a small community with a single weekly paper. Editorial distinctions vary widely in this regard, often seeming to be based as much on personal idiosyncrasies or the financial state of the paper as upon journalistic principles. In a recent case, the publisher of a rural weekly was outraged to discover that the bookmobile schedule he was running as a public service was also being printed as a paid advertisement in a free advertising giveaway shopper. Right or wrong, he was not mollified when the library director explained that the shopper was circulated entirely outside his area, and was the only inexpensive way to reach those people.

Information about events intended solely as fund-raisers are another case in point. An editor who gives the library very good free publicity concerning a book sale, for example, may be unhappy to learn that money has been spent elsewhere for printing or advertising in other ways. Placing an ad in a small publication can be money well spent on occasion; at any rate, if any question is likely to arise about a specific situation, it would be well to discuss it in advance rather than risk displeasure. (However, buying a lot of display ad space won't guarantee that your news will be published!)

House Organs and Other News Outlets

In addition to free shopper giveaways, other channels for your news releases should not be overlooked. There are employee publications of companies and manufacturers in your area, newsletters or magazines put out by various clubs and organizations, neighborhood newspapers, and church bulletins. Many of these are probably sent to you or can be located through the library's various directories or organization lists. These publications reach selected groups with specific interests. Look them all over carefully; then make a phone call or write a note to the editors inquiring about their interest in receiving selected information or news about the library. Include a sample of the kind of notice or release you have in mind, if possible. The type of information should be tailored to the special interests of the reader, for example, a release for the newsletter of the local kennel club might list some new films, magazines, or books the library has acquired on the subject of dogs. A quick personal canvass will save time and postage, and will open up some valuable publicity outlets.

ABC's of Story Angles and Possibilities

Where can you find a good library news story? All around you!

One of the essential attributes of a good publicist is the ability to look at the library as an outsider. Familiarity breeds not contempt, but oversight. You must be able to see what is or could be of interest to others and write about it—or alert a reporter—with enthusiasm and imagination. Keep abreast of both national and local interests, know what is in the news and what is being talked about so that your feature and background stories or ideas are timely and current. *People and names* make news (patrons, staff, trustees), *events* make news (both before and after the fact), *human interest* incidents make news, *services, activities and materials* make news (both new and old), *changes* (in schedule, regulations, staff) make news; the possibilities are limited only by your ability to recognize the fact or angle that is news from an editor's viewpoint and that is of potential interest to readers.

Here are some of the topics, from A–Z, that make news regularly or occasionally, plus selected actual samples from releases or as written up by a reporter at the library's suggestion. This list may help you to see areas that you have overlooked in the past or suggest new angles to be covered. The topics are also possibilities for your library newsletter. (The names and places have been changed in the actual examples cited "to protect the innocent.")

ANNUAL REPORT highlights make good copy. Prepare your own release or point out interesting items in a marked copy sent to the newspaper. Here are typical clips:

> If you were an average patron of the Cityville Public Library last year you read about seven books, one magazine, and listened to about half a record, according to the annual report received from the librarian. Using the census count for the city, the library investment was $6.29 per person. . . .
>
> *   *   *   *
>
> The Cityville Public Library, which circulates a book every 28.5 seconds, had its largest collection of books and its largest budget in the past fiscal year. . . .

ANNIVERSARIES take many forms; these can be round-numbered anniversary dates for the opening of the library; years served by the librarian, staff members, or trustees; or the beginning of various services.

CITYVILLE CITY-COUNTY LIBRARY
NOTES 75th ANNIVERSARY

The Cityville City-County Library has a long history of dedicated service to this community and the rural area it serves. It is the culmination of the dreams and hopes of a small group of Cityville women who were the first to act to provide a library after Cityville became a city. From a humble reading room in the old Andrews store, containing books and papers partly for the rivermen who were waiting for drives to come down, the present library emerged. . . .

* * * *

New Year's Day, 1912, ushered in a new era of library service to the people of Cityville. The city celebrated that day with an open house at the library. The afternoon's informal reception was followed by an evening of speeches and entertainment. History will repeat itself as the library staff will hold an open house. . . .

AIDS, ACTIVITIES, AND ASSISTANCE available to special groups, organizations, and people can take the form of simple announcements:

LIBRARY OFFERS ENGLISH
LANGUAGE AIDS TO VIETNAMESE

Sponsors and teachers of Vietnamese refugee families are finding a lack of adequate materials available to assist in English language instruction. To help alleviate this situation, the Cityville Library now has Vietnamese dictionaries, plus American language instruction texts with accompanying cassette tapes available. . . .

* * * *

VIDEOTAPE COURSE AT LIBRARY

Cityville Library has gained permission to videotape a university-sponsored course so that library users can view the course at their own convenience, for pleasure or for university credit. . . .

* * * *

CITYVILLE LIBRARY INITIATES
"JOB BANK" TO AID UNEMPLOYED

The Department of Employment Service and the Cityville Library announce the installation of a "job bank" viewer for public use in the library. This service provides, free of charge, a daily listing of current local and statewide job openings. Persons wishing to use this free service may ask any staff member for assistance. . . .

You must constantly look for new angles to call attention to the variety of resources of the library. One way to repeat the obvious is in a feature vignette such as this:

LOCAL LIBRARY MEANS MANY THINGS

A summer visitor at a local resort needed to listen to a specific kind of music to provide inspiration for a ballet. The library provided phonograph, earphones, a quiet room, and the needed records, much to the surprise of both the visitor and the resort owner. . . .

ACKNOWLEDGEMENTS AND TESTIMONIALS from users are invaluable aids to publicity. Use them as often as good examples present themselves (see the following page):

Mr. and Mrs. John Smith, novices at home building, constructed their beautiful home from the ground up using information from library books. With the help of the staff at the Cityville Library, the Smiths learned about carpentry, bricklaying . . . .

* * * *

Brown said he learned much of his magic from books and then developed his own routines. He advises those wanting to get started in magic to read library books and then contact magicians in town. . . .

* * * *

NEW FAIR ENTRANT "FAIRLY"
DELIGHTED

Betty Smith couldn't believe it; the first time she exhibited at a county fair, she won four ribbons. Mrs. Smith said her most helpful resource finding recipes and helpful hints is the Cityville Public Library . . . .

* * * *

MADE $30,000 STOCK PROFIT WITH
$500 IN BANK

A conversation about Ralph Nader led John Smith, armed with a telephone and $500 in the bank, to buy and sell $200,000 worth of stock, make a $30,000 profit and never spend a penny. . . . "To tell the truth, when I began I knew absolutely nothing about it," he admitted. He went to the Cityville Public Library, looked up magazines that dealt with stocks, read the stock exchange rules, and researched the market for one week. . . .

BUDGET REQUESTS and BUILDING PROGRAMS are hard news items that regularly warrant space.

BOARD MEETINGS are covered infrequently for two reasons; reporters rarely attend meetings, and a release concerning action that has been taken is seldom sent out. Routine business is not newsworthy, of course, but a brief summary of significant agenda items or sidelights with human interest may get into print, and are certainly worth the time to prepare. Compare the space given to school board meetings, for example, with that of library board meetings. Almost any board meeting would yield a note such as this:

Crime pays for the Library Board—when it's someone else's crime. The Board learned Tuesday that the Library recently received a $65 contribution from an anonymous source. Library Director M. Dewey explained that the donation was engineered by a local shopkeeper. . . . (Ed. note: the merchant dropped a shoplifting charge in exchange for a donation to the library by the miscreant.)

* * * *

Mr. Dewey informed the Library Board that the County Administrative Officer has set a ceiling on the Library's budget request for 1978-79 that was $300,000 under the current budget. He noted that only the Board of Education and the Library had been given ceilings below the current operating budget, and that only the Library had been singled out for the omission of staff increment funds. . . .

BOOKMOBILE publicity can be generated by releases concerning the schedule, new materials, or activities; in addition, it is an excellent source of human interest material.

BOOK LISTS and BOOK REVIEWS are too often the only form of newspaper publicity that is prepared by the library. Undoubtedly there are a few avid readers of book lists, but a little creativity in compiling them would undoubtedly increase the readership. A list of titles, whether new or old, is much more meaningful when it is focused on a subject area, pertains to a topic in the news, or is related to community events or interests. Lists of current titles can also be prepared occasionally for special sections of the newspaper such as the sports section, the business page, etc. Editors in small communities might also be interested in short reviews of books by library patrons, complete with a photo of the reviewer.

BOOK SELECTION, the how and why of the process, is not front-page material, but it is background information that may merit a feature article, particularly if there is a timely news peg involved. A release on this subject builds understanding that helps to ward off or counter censorship attacks. Here is an example of such an article:

HOW LIBRARIANS SELECT BOOKS

Selecting the books that appear on the shelves of the Cityville Public Library is a never-ending massive task. Accountability to the Public Library Board and the public for the entire collection rests with Library Director M. Dewey, who says, "We are given the budget and work within it. The Board feels I know what types of books are wanted by our patrons and leaves the job to me."

Suggestions from county library patrons and staff members are also taken into consideration, Dewey said. . . .

In choosing books, the library follows the Library Bill of Rights which provides for books to be obtained both pro and con on various issues. . . .

"Persons frequently wish to donate items they find in their homes," Dewey said. "We are happy to accept these with the understanding that once they are left with us we may do what we wish with them." The items must be checked to determine if they are worthwhile. Dewey also believes a sound knowledge of the community, its characteristics and needs is essential to the sound acquisition of materials. . . .

CHANGES in hours, regulations, and rules are "musts" for news releases.

CONVENTIONS, COURSES, OR CONFERENCES attended by staff members are newsworthy items.

CARD-HOLDERS in terms of numbers or milestones in registration can be the basis for a story, tied in with an explanation of where and how to apply for a card and illustrated, perhaps, by an anecdote of how a library card was used to provide identification for cashing a check or securing a driver's license (every library has one such story). If you are reregistering patrons, give the Mayor card number 1 for publicity's sake. Who holds card number 13? Number 10,000? Who has the oldest card?

CALENDAR DATES and seasonal events provide a good excuse for a "background" story with information about special days, weeks, or months:

They call it "Ground Hog Day" in the United States, but in other parts of the world February 2 is known as Candlemas or the Feast of the Purification of the Blessed Virgin, when candles are blessed in the churches, symbolic of the reference to the "light to lighten the Gentiles."

The custom of observing the weather on this day to forecast for the next six weeks was brought to America from Great Britain and Germany, according to sources in the Cityville Public Library. . . .

* * * *

It may be February 6 to you, but among the Chinese people, it is New Year's Day, by the old Chinese calendar.

The year, according to that calendar, has 354 days and 12 lunar months, about half of them with 30 days and the other half with 29, reported Dewey, director of the Cityville Public Library, who dug out the facts from materials on the library's shelves. . . .

COMPARISONS with other libraries, taken from local surveys or studies or from professional journal reports, can be used in a release that points up local inadequacy and unmet needs or can be used as an occasion for plaudits to the community for support. Lead off with a direct quote from the library director or a trustee.

COMPUTERS are a fact of life in the library world, but the public has little knowledge or understanding of this. You could build a story this way:

Suppose you are a librarian and a local magazine editor needs a review of an obscure off-Broadway play that is not listed in the play indexes? Or a television newsroom cannot find a photograph of a key person who is involved in a major breaking story? Or a trivia club member wants to know how much the original Mickey Mouse watch cost?

Do what Cityville Public Library's information staff did in each of these situations— use computerized information retrieval.

Anyone living in the Cityville Library service area qualifies for library-assisted computer searches. . . .

COOPERATIVE publicity is a two-for-one return, and items about the cooperation between the library and other agencies helps to emphasize the fact that the library is in the mainstream of community service and in partnership with others. Play up all joint activities or services; consult your counterpart in the other agency, and initiate the releases if you want top billing.

STUDENT FINANCIAL AID FORMS
AVAILABLE AT PUBLIC LIBRARY

The Cityville Public Library is cooperating with the Department of Health, Education, and Welfare by providing applications for assistance to eligible needy persons who are attending or planning to attend institutions of post-secondary education. . . .

* * * *

LIBRARY, SCHOOL SPONSOR
TRIP TO CHILDREN'S THEATER

The Cityville Public Library in conjunction with the Elementary School is sponsoring a trip to the Children's Theater on August 8th. . . .

* * * *

LIBRARY, SCIENCE UNIT SIGN PACT

The Cityville Public Library and the Cityville Science Museum announced today that they have signed an agreement to provide improved science services to the public at no cost to taxpayers. . . .

DISPLAYS and exhibits are traditional and routine reasons for news releases, but do beware of letting these constitute an undue proportion of your "news." In addition to the usual where, when, and what, include other details of interest, particularly about the people involved. It may not all be used, but then again it might! Here's a good example from a library system news release:

VISITING ARTIST STRESSES
COMMUNICATION

"A tall young man came in this summer," said Library Director M. Dewey, "and asked if his papa came to America, could his paintings be hung in the library. Well, he was so charming and so obviously adored his father that we would have agreed even if the paintings looked like grass," she joked.

The tall young man was 19-year-old John Smithsson, on a summer visit from Sweden. His "papa" did come to America— and his paintings, far from looking like grass, will be on display through November in the Cityville Public Library. . . .

* * * *

A display of paintings and framed needlework by Mrs. Betty Smith will be on exhibit in the Cityville Public Library during May.

Mrs. Smith, of 233 Main Street, Cityville, a housewife and an amateur painter, retired in 1970 after 15 years of working as a registered nurse. In addition to raising her family, she found time to pursue her interests in painting, needlecraft, toymaking and short story writing.

Mrs. Smith's art career has included a semester of art at State College, instruction from the Famous Artist Correspondence Course and lessons from several local artists. She hopes to limit her interest to painting in the future and to advance to the professional level.

Admission to the exhibit is free, and the Cityville Library is open from 9 A.M. to 6 P.M. every day except Sunday. For a complete listing of art displays and other library activites, pick up a free copy of the monthly schedule at the Library.

EQUIPMENT acquired, through donation or purchase, is important news, and would rate a photograph. Here are some recent sample headlines:

MICROFICHE AT LIBRARY
HAS BOOKS LIKE SARDINES

LIBRARY ADDS TAPE PLAYER
TO AUDIO-VISUAL EQUIPMENT

'BILLY GOAT GRUFF' JOINS
CITYVILLE LIBRARY
(Stuffed animal added
to children's room)

LIBRARY BOOK DROP INSTALLED
IN SHOPPING MALL

An unusual or appealing photo will help to gain space for a release about a new system or piece of equipment that may otherwise seem highly technical and difficult to explain.

It's not easy to publicize a card catalog, but when the Baltimore County Public Library (MD) converted the old system to a new microfilm catalog, this appealing photo called attention to the new operation, claiming "everyone is curious."

FILM collection additions and film showings should be announced regularly, but it is advisable to flesh out the bald listings with mini-reviews in the release:

GREAT MYSTERIES ON TAP
AT LIBRARY

A mysterious epidemic that drains the body of blood plagues a quiet village in the film "Mrs. Ainsworth," to be shown at 7:30 July 19 at the Cityville Library.

Glynis Johns stars as the glamorous Mrs. Ainsworth, who has charmed everyone in the community, except for two men who are wary of her nocturnal appearances. . . .

You may also be able to get still photos from the film company or producer to use in publicizing the new acquisitions or programs. Another valuable service that might be acceptable to your editor would be the compilation of summaries from various sources of reviews of the movies playing locally. This is a worthwhile exercise even if the newspaper does not wish to print them; publicize the fact that you have these capsule comments on tape for library patrons who want to read them or telephone for information. Remind newspaper readers that films are available for group and club use with a release about the number loaned out in a specified period of time, name the various agencies that used them, and mention some of the more popular titles.

FAMILY activities and features about the "best read" families are good subject angles.

FRIENDS of the library are a source of release material; if they have their own publicity chairperson, offer to assist with and coordinate the material that is sent out so that there is no overlap or delay.

GIFTS, GRANTS, and bequests to the library are news; enumeration of small gifts will be acceptable to some community newspapers, and unusual or large gifts or bequests will often warrant space in metropolitan newspapers.

CITYVILLE LIBRARY RECEIVES
MONEY GIFT FROM LOCAL DONORS

Cityville Library will be able to offer its patrons a greater variety of written and visual materials, the result of recent donations made by a group of local industries and individuals. The donors included. . . .

M. Dewey, Librarian, reports that a portion of the money will be used to purchase an 8mm movie projector, which patrons and Cityville organizations may use to view the wide variety of films which Cityville Library offers. . . .

Memorial Day could be used as an excuse for releasing a list of recent gifts; you can declare your own "Recognition Day," if only for the sake of publicity. Gifts of special collections or additions to specialized areas by clubs or organizations can take the form of joint releases. The publication of a brochure on the subject of memorials can be a news peg:

GIFTS STRENGTHEN LIBRARY
COLLECTION

A new brochure explaining how gifts, memorials, and bequests can help strengthen its collection of books and other materials has been prepared by the Cityville Library.

"Over the years the library has received gifts ranging from single volumes to donations of whole collections," M. Dewey, Library Director, said. Donations are also made to purchase other library materials, such as fine art reproductions. All gifts and bequests to the Library are tax deductible, according to John Jones, City Attorney.

"Two recent donors," M. Dewey said, "have urged us to provide the public with more information so we have prepared a brochure, 'Gifts for the Library.'"

One of the donors, Mrs. B. Smith, recently gave . . . .

GROWTH of circulation or the collection can be dramatized in many ways:

LIBRARY BREAKS CIRCULATION
RECORD

Whose circulation was better than yours on Wednesday, July 11?

The Cityville Public Library's!

On that day an all-time record of 2,156 books found homes in the arms of avid north shore readers. . . .

TWO NEW RECORDS ESTABLISHED

June 16 was a red-letter day for the Cityville Library for at 10:13 A.M., exactly, the one-millionth item to be circulated during the year was taken out by a patron. The patron who brought the library over the one million mark for the year was John Smith. . . .

The second record to be broken was circulation for the entire library system which, at closing time, had reached 6,906,306, an 8.1 percent increase over the previous year. . . .

* * * *

LIBRARY WITH NUMBER 200,000 DOUBLES COLLECTION IN LESS THAN FIVE YEARS

The two-hundred-thousandth volume was added to the Cityville Library collection Thursday, April 9.

The book, "Books that Changed America" by Robert B. Downs, was assigned the 200,000th accession number, an indication of the dramatically rapid growth of the Library, M. Dewey, Director, pointed out. . . .

LIBRARY IN LINE FOR HISTORIC MARKING

The Cityville Library has been nominated for marking as a registered landmark. M. Dewey, librarian, said there seems to be little question that the library was the first established under the Public Library Law of 1872. . . .

HISTORICAL items or materials found, received, or held in the collection can be the subject of a release. Here's an unusual report:

OLD CITYVILLE 16mm FILM DISCOVERED BY CITY LIBRARY

Libraries have traditionally been the breeding ground of scholarly surprises, which vary anywhere from discovery of an unknown manuscript between the mildewed pages of an old book, to locating an unknown documentary film.

Last week Cityville Public Library became the site of one of these discoveries. A documentary film taken of Cityville in 1939 has been offered for sale to the library by a North Carolina man who says he owns the only copy of the film in existence. . . .

GROUP use of the library, such as special visits, materials supplied for meetings, and group meetings held in the library are worth routine reporting.

HONORS awarded to staff, trustees, or to the library itself should be duly noted:

CITYVILLE LIBRARY RECEIVES RECOGNITION

Cityville Library received recognition in the July-August publication of. . . .

HOBBY materials and HOW-TO information are of perennial interest; feature releases can be developed for appropriate times or in relation to community activities and interests.

INTERLIBRARY LOAN is a matter that is little understood by the public, but an increasingly important and necessary facet of library service. This is best publicized by the example on the following page:

TOP INTERLIBRARY LOAN
BORROWER

The Cityville Library announces that John Smith is the "Interlibrary Loan Borrower" of the year. Mr. Smith's interlibrary loan requests have come from his interest in the computer field. He is using this library service to get the latest technical material available on the computer and computer languages.

During the past year other residents made a total of 1745 interlibrary loan requests for materials to further their education or satisfy their curiosity. . . .

The germ of a story was found in the report of a staff newsletter:

The application for a library card contained this note from a branch librarian: "Please rush this application; patron is leaving for Europe for one year and would like a card before leaving."

This was a good chance to point out the fact that the library's services are very wide-ranging, but that interlibrary loan did not reach clear across the ocean—yet!

JUVENILE literature news can be reported in ways that are both timely and topical. Announcements of national book awards can be made, with listing of titles held by the library; trends in children's books and interests can be discussed in the form of an interview with the children's librarian; the acquisition of works by local children's book authors or illustrators is local "news"; current TV series or movies based on children's books can be reason for an article. Reporters and photographers are prone to feature children in story and picture to the exclusion of other areas of service; try to balance this by suggesting other angles with reasons why they will be of interest to many.

KITS of special library materials are often available from the library, but the public's knowledge of this is taken for granted. Don't. Write it up.

LEGISLATION at both the state and national level can affect the local library, although this is seldom mentioned in the community press. Keep up with the action (or lack of it) for releases describing how new laws or project funding directly affects the home town library, particularly in terms of dollars and cents and/or as direct quotes from legislators and the library director.

LOCAL LORE and little-known facts about the community or region, uncovered in new books, research studies, or in donated materials could be the basis for a feature.

LIBRARY IS MINE OF STATE LORE

Area residents will observe Wonderful Wisconsin Week, September 17-23, with the aid of Cityville Public Library.

Residents are encouraged to utilize the special display of books about Wisconsin available at the Cityville Library to learn details of the following facts:

—Ten flags have flown over Wisconsin, and the Wisconsin flag has flown over four other states. No other state can match that record. . . .

MUSIC MATERIALS—musical scores, song books, and recordings—are worth a mention; use National Music Month as the "peg."

MAPS are a little-known part of the library's collection; publicize them on the occasion of new acquisitions or an unusual use by a patron for travel or research.

NEW MAP COLLECTION ADDED
TO CITYVILLE LIBRARY

A collection of interesting, unique, and useful maps has recently been added to the Cityville Library's reference department.

The collection includes maps of the county, state, metropolitan areas, an historical map series, lake maps, and even treasure maps. A listing of the Library's entire collection of maps, as well as atlases, pamphlets, and books that contain maps, are indexed and kept on file at the reference desk. . . .

NAMES make news, so watch for opportunities to capitalize on this (see photo captions that follow).

Eighty-two-year old John Brown, one of the library's oldest patrons, and little three-year-old Betty Smith, visited the Cityville Library and got together for a picture. Brown comes to the library every single Saturday regardless of the elements and he reads four books a week. Betty brings her mother to the library once a week and the little girl picks out the books that she wants her mother to read to her. . . .

*   *   *   *

Spring is in the air and the birds are beginning to return. In preparation for the season, John Smith, of 213 Main Street, has been constructing birdhouses during the winter months. Plans for the "caboose" birdhouse shown can be found in the pamphlet "102 Birdhouses, Feeders" which is available at the Cityville Public Library. The library has many more books and pamphlets containing plans for a variety of different types of bird shelters and feeders.

NETWORKS are an important development in terms of local library service, but the concept is difficult to publicize. It is best reported by example (how the county or regional system actions or services affect local residents). All libraries belonging to a library network or system should make a habit of adding the phrase, "the Cityville Public Library, member of the South County Library System . . ." as part of the identification in all news releases.

OUTREACH SERVICES are subjects for releases when there is an occasion for an announcement of new services, expansion or change of program, request for aid in reaching new contacts, or report of the number served or the hours spent by volunteers.

SERVICE TO HOMEBOUND
NOW OFFERED

The Cityville Public Library is seeking to unite people with a few hours to spare with people who are confined to their homes because of illness, age, or disability.

"Service to the Homebound," a program established by the library in 1975, wants additional volunteers and clients. . . .

PROGRAMS and library events are routinely announced in news releases; the problem here is that for many libraries it is the beginning and the end of publicity efforts. Try for a lot more coverage!

PAPERBACKS are pretty standard now in libraries, and the fact is probably old hat to you, but it is news to a lot of others. You can call attention to the collection by discussing new titles, or with a fact piece on the pros and cons of cost vs durability.

POLICIES AND OBJECTIVES are often abstractions, but should be woven into news releases when possible. Major decisions or recommendations by the board after study are often timely, as in the following:

LONG-RANGE PLAN DEVELOPED
FOR LIBRARY

A long range plan for library service, 1978-1983, has been developed by the Cityville Library.

The long range plan recommends. . . .

And here's how the matter of confidentiality of library records and requests was handled in a newspaper article.

It's a big word—confidentiality. It's an important subject. What does it mean at the library?

It means that anyone can ask for an answer to any question and no one else need ever know. It means anyone can check out library materials on any subject and the library staff won't tell. . . .

Suppose you want to change jobs. There's a world of information at the library to help you, but you might not want your present employer to know you're looking. Suppose you have a valuable painting or coin collection at home. You want help finding more information about it but you don't want the whole town to know you have it. . . .

Weeding the collection is a procedure that can arouse controversy and rumors. A straightforward explanation will answer questions and head off criticism, such as this example from a small town newspaper.

SPRING CLEANING SENDS
DUST FLYING AT LIBRARY

Spring is here, and they're weeding at the Cityville Library.

However, Andrew Carnegie's gift to Cityville has not become overgrown with plant life. Rather, the term refers to the process that is removing many old dust collectors from the crowded shelves to make room for newer, more commonly read books.

Operating under the premise that quality counts over quantity at a modern library, Mrs. Dewey began last week in the fiction section at the head of the alphabet. Three days later, she was still at work on the D's. . . .

Weeding is not as ruthless as some friends of literature might fear at first. Each book in the library receives individual scrutiny . . . and Mrs. Dewey considers the book's physical condition and use in recent years. The selection process is guided by a number of bibliographic tools. . . .

One rule of thumb says that a book goes out if it has not circulated. . . .

PROGRESS REPORTS on building plans, remodeling, or expansion activities can be made before, during, and after the fact.

NEW LIBRARY A REALITY
WITH COUNTY BOARD VOTE

The new Cityville Library passed its third and final hurdle Tuesday night when the County Board in a special session voted to meet the county's share of the $550,000 facility. . . .

PUBLICATIONS issued by the library can be announced in brief releases about new book lists, a calendar of events, brochures, etc., that are ready for distribution:

> As the first 1,400 copies of the second edition of the Cityville Library book catalog were readied for mailing to the rural area this week, Director Dewey expressed pleasure with the unique program he termed "a pioneering effort—on a very low budget. . . ."

QUESTIONS posed to the library staff by patrons is a good feature subject to call attention to the reference service:

> ### LIBRARY REFERENCE DESK HAS THE ANSWERS
>
> What are the words to "Froggie Went A Courtin'"? Who was the first streaker? How do you trap turtles? What's the cost of an ad in the Wall Street Journal? How do you fix a Rambler transmission and what's no-fault divorce?
>
> Maybe you don't know. But you can find out, and someone already has.
>
> All these questions and many more were put to the staff at Cityville Library during the past six months as library reference questions.
>
> Telephone or ask in person; they'll find the answer to most any question if they can. . . .
>
> *   *   *   *

> ### LIBRARY SERVES BY ANSWERING QUESTIONS
>
> A multitude of questions is asked and answered at the Cityville Library. According to Mrs. Dewey, Librarian, the question heard most often is "Can you recommend a good book to read?"
>
> "This is probably a dumb question" prefaces many questions, but any question that needs an answer cannot possibly be a dumb question. The library is proud to be the "answer place," and even if it takes several days, if the answer is in print somewhere, the chances are good that it will be forthcoming.
>
> A sampling of the kind of questions and requests the Cityville Library has found answers for in the past months include. . . .

If a well-known person or agency seeks assistance, capitalize on it. Have you had a call for information from Walter Cronkite's secretary? From *Time* magazine? From the Governor's office? From an official of a foreign country?

QUIZZES often intrigue readers, and your newspaper might carry one on occasion. This appeared in a Wisconsin newspaper:

> How well do you know your library? Answer the following questions about the Cityville Public Library, and you will have your library IQ. Give yourself 5 points for every correct answer unless otherwise noted. The highest possible score is 100.
>
> If your score is 85 or better you are an exceptional citizen, aware of your city's needs and resources. If your score is 70 to 80 you can consider yourself to have an average knowledge of your community's information resources. If your score is below 70, your library card needs exercise.

QUESTIONS

1. What is the annual budget of the City-ville Public Library?
   a. More than the Swimming Pool.
   b. Less than the Swimming Pool.
   c. The same as the Swimming Pool.
2. How are the funds provided for the support of the Library?
3. Who is the president of the Library Board?
4. Who are the members of the Library Board? (Three correct names—5 points, two correct—3 points, one correct—1 point.)
5. Name one special service the Library offers in addition to lending books.
6. Approximately how many books does the Library have in its collection? (within 1000)
7. How many adults are on the Library staff?
8. Who does the art work at the Library?
9. What is the fee for a library card?
10. What is the fee for a lost library card?
11. Does the Library offer telephone reference service?
12. How many libraries are there in South County?
13. What is the fine for overdue books?
14. How many books does the Library lend in one year? (within 3000)
15. Who takes out more books in a year—children or adults?
16. What does a red line under a title mean?
17. To how many periodicals does the Library subscribe? (within 10)
18. How many hours each week is the Library open?
19. What animal lives in the children's section of the Library?
20. How many times have you used your library card in the last 6 months? Twelve times—5 points, eight times—3 points, less than 8—0, no library card—subtract 10 points.

The answers to these questions will be displayed at the Circulation Desk of the Cityville Public Library. Be sure to check your LIQ soon.

READERS who use the library for any number of (legitimate) reasons can be the source of human interest stories, from getting started on a hobby or business to romances in the stacks. Canvass the staff and desk clerks regularly for such information, and encourage them to make a note now and then to aid you in getting leads. Some papers will accept a regular "Reader of the Week" or "Reader of the Month" feature; careful selection will demonstrate the various interests and types of people served.

REPORTERS, columnists, and free-lance writers will help you generate good publicity if you suggest angles to them. Reminiscences, accounts of personal experiences, and a "new eye" approach to certain activities or services will often result. A reporter with a flair for humor could give you some invaluable coverage, as in this example:

Being an enterprising guy, I jumped at the offer when the people from the Cityville Library asked me to help "make a little dough."

Little did I realize the proposal entailed a training program on making and baking bread . . . part of the National Library Week festivities aimed at teaching adults how to make bread from scratch.

What the library people didn't know was they approached a culinary idiot; probably the only student who flunked the course twice in one day. . . .

SPEECHES made can be newsworthy if the topic is significant or controversial, whether the speech was given at the annual meeting of a national organization or to a local group. Don't expect the publicity officer of the club or organization to report it; make sure by doing it yourself. Write a brief four or five sentence summary for routine reporting; include a copy of the speech itself with the release if it is particularly significant.

LIBRARIAN ADDRESSES
KIWANIS CLUB

Mrs. Dewey, Head Librarian at the Cityville Library, told Cityville Kiwanians Monday night about the services offered by the Library.

Mrs. Dewey demonstrated talking books and magazines and told an interesting illustrated children's story. . . .

STAFF appointments, retirements, travel, special interests, educational courses taken or degrees earned are all news items.

LIBRARIAN BRINGS NEW
INTERESTS, DIFFERENT IDEAS

Shore fishing and antique collecting don't seem to be compatible hobbies, but they make sense to Cityville's new Librarian, Mrs. Dewey. They are two of the many interests of the university graduate who has a master's degree in library science. . . .

* * * *

LIBRARY EXHIBIT
TELLS PEN PAL STORY

A display of items from Japan has been placed in the lower level case of the Cityville Library by Mrs. Dewey. The colorful, well-arranged exhibit was prepared as part of her 64 hours work in a public library, required for her degree in library science. . . .

* * * *

STORY LADY CLOSES BOOK
ON LONG CAREER AT LIBRARY

Mrs. Dewey is retiring today.

The name may not ring a bell, but Mrs. Dewey's voice and face are familiar to innumerable Cityville area children and ex-children who knew her only as "the story lady."

SUGGESTION box contributions can be the focus for a story that offers a chance for explanations about library operations:

In the past several weeks, patrons of the Cityville Library were asked to contribute suggestions that they thought would help provide better service to them. The Library staff promised to reply to the suggestions and implement them if possible.

The following are some of the suggestions and the staff's responses:

Suggestion: Can you get another copy of "The Great Gatsby?" Every time I look for it, about once a week, I never get it.

Response: The Library has several copies of the book, but because the movie was just at an area theater, the book has become very popular. The next time you are in the Library, stop at the desk and reserve a copy. You'll be sure to get it that way. . . .

TRENDS in reading interest, particularly at the local level as indicated by title demands, can serve as a release subject:

The recent showing of the television program, "Roots," has substantially increased the interest in family geneology, and many more patrons are requesting aid and materials for tracing their ancestors, M. Dewey, Cityville Public Library Director, reported today.

"Whether casual interest or serious research, the library has books, pamphlets, and reference tools that will help," the Librarian said.

TRUSTEES should be "exposed" through interviews, reports of new appointments, participation in meetings of library associations, or other related activities. The example on the next page illustrates a less-than-usual aspect of library trusteeship:

Carpenters contacted were too busy, too expensive, or did not want the job, and so the senior member and Treasurer of the Library Board, Mr. Smith, took on the job of remodeling one of the rooms by himself. The job was made possible through additional county funds allocated to the Library.

UNUSUAL anything! Depicting the library as a "people" place is possible by keeping your eyes open for out-of-the-ordinary events:

TODDLER PROVES LIBRARY IS MUCH MORE THAN BOOKS

Betty Smith, age 1, has proved in her own way that the public library is more than books. She learned to walk in the library. For her accomplishment, the Library gave Betty a certificate of merit on Wednesday, May 23, which also, as it happened, was her first birthday.

For years children have been learning at Cityville Library, but a first was probably established when Betty learned how to walk while at the library.

It was just before the preschool story hour started. Betty's mother was sitting at a table in the children's room. . . .

The following items made the front page of a newspaper and the librarian reported that they attracted more notice than anything in years:

MECHANIC TURNS TRAPPER TO FIX CAR

The White Wagon had a persistent problem.

The White Wagon is a station wagon used by the Cityville Public Library to provide service to the villages in the county.

What looked like bits of insulation kept coming out of the heater. Finally, smoke came billowing out, and Mrs. Brown, Extension Librarian, headed toward the Pontiac garage.

When the itemized bill came back it read:
—Dissemble dash
—Check all wires under dash
—Clean out heater (mouse nest)
—Catch mouse

"The mouse was a field mouse, but we don't know whether he meant to look up a city cousin or just liked the mobile life," said Mrs. Brown.

*   *   *   *

WORKS FROM TOP DOWN AT LIBRARY

Most people start at the bottom and work up. John Smith started at the top and worked down.

Who's John Smith?

He's the curly headed, reddish haired young man some folks noticed clinging to the flag pole outside the Cityville Library.

Smith, an iron worker, dropped in at the Library and offered to paint the 70 foot pole, which hadn't had a paint job in many years, according to Library Director, M. Dewey.

*   *   *   *

WEBSTER'S NO ORDINARY CAT

The 14-pound cat named "Webster" is no ordinary cat. He has been a Library mascot, had his own news column in the Library periodical, receives mail in his name, had his biography published in "Cat Magazine," and has been tendered with affection by hundreds of children who visited the Children's Room at Cityville Library. . . .

* * * *

(Photo caption under a picture of two youngsters in baseball uniforms)

Rained out. John Smith and Bill Brown take refuge Friday afternoon in the Cityville Library after two inches of rain soaked the city ballfields. The boys play for the Hawks ball team in the league sponsored by the City Recreation Department.

VOLUNTEERS, their activities and assistance, are newsworthy. Photographs of them in action and receiving merit awards are two ways to get coverage.

VISITORS, from well-known personages to school classes, are possible news release subjects.

WINNERS of book awards—National Book Awards, Notable Book lists, the Newbery and Caldecott Awards, and various publishers prizes— can be listed and briefly reviewed in the local press.

XEROX® and other photocopying machines are available in most libraries now, and the fact bears repeating. Follow-up stories after acquisition can tell how it cuts down on book vandalism or loss, can offer free copying for certain materials, and can discuss copyright regulations pertaining to its use.

ZONING regulations and other government documents available from the library are often overlooked by the public, but can be a news release subject:

FEDERAL, STATE DOCUMENTS READILY AVAILABLE HERE

"Questions on everything from filling out federal income tax forms to constructing wells can be answered by using the 80,000 federal and state documents found at the Cityville Library," M. Dewey, Reference Librarian, points out.

Since 1908 the library has acted as a selective depository for federal documents. . . .

News Release Formats

There are only a few basic rules for the format of news release submissions. Naturally, you will type and double space the material, and use only one side of the paper. Leave wide margins and start typing about one-third of the way down the sheet. The space at the top is for the editor's notations. Type the Library name, address, your name, title, and telephone number in one corner at the top. Below this write the date. (If you will be issuing releases regularly, you may find it worthwhile to have some special paper printed for this purpose.)

Write *FOR IMMEDIATE RELEASE* to one side. If you wish the story held until a particular date write *FOR RELEASE:* Tuesday, October 15.

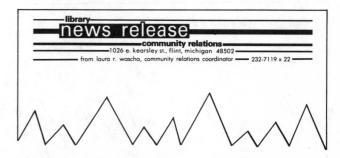

Sample News Release Format

Limit the length of your release to one or one-and-a-half pages, if possible. Write "—more—" at the bottom of the first page if the text is continued, and write "—add one—" at the top of the following sheet. (The "more" indicates that the story is not finished, and the "add one" means that it is an addition to the first sheet.) Do not break a paragraph between pages. Write "END" or "30" at the bottom of the release.

In many cases you will find that a simple fact sheet or information form is more practical to prepare than a formal news release. In this case, list the who, what, where, when and why in simple sentences, and the professionals will take it from there. For example:

(Who) The Cityville Public Library *(What)* will hold a series of programs entitled "Managing Your Money" *(Where)* in the Library Auditorium *(When)* on Wednesday evenings, beginning April 16 at 7:30 P.M. *(Why)* The programs are part of a series offered free to Cityville residents by the Library in response to patrons' requests noted in a recent survey of library users' interests. *(How)* The series is under the direction of Mr. Moneybanks, a well-known investment consultant and specialist on the staff of the County Extension Department.

If you are including photos with your release, add "with picture" on your release sheet under the date. Write the cut-lines (captions) for the photo on a separate sheet of paper, tape it to the back so that the typed copy portion extends below the bottom edge of the photo, and fold that part up and over the front of the picture. Here is a quick trick for a photo caption (but don't overdo it); pose your subject(s) in front of a blackboard and write the caption or a phrase in big letters on the board behind. Don't, repeat *don't,* try to arrange a photo of a dignitary signing a proclamation; this is an

empty cliché, and, in fact, many state and local officials are beginning to declare a moratorium on such rituals.

If you have not had much journalistic experience, it is still possible to learn how to write good news articles by reading the numerous texts on the subject and copying the style of the material in newspapers. Clip examples of various types of stories and use them as guides.

So Your Release Wasn't Used?

There are a number of reasons why your story never appeared in print. It is always a good possibility that there was simply no space that day or that your release was "killed" at the last minute when more important news came along. (However, it may be picked up later if it is not out-dated.) You can't control that, but there are other factors of timing which you can control. Get a release in at least 24 hours before it is to be published or observe the paper's stated deadlines. If you are reporting on an event, as opposed to announcing it, get the material in immediately afterward, not three days later. Daily papers usually have larger issues and therefore more space on particular days, often Thursday and Sunday; learn the best time for submitting feature material, which is more likely to be used on those days.

The editor will discard items which s/he considers trivial, of too limited reader interest, or that lack a local angle. In a metropolitan daily, for example, your release may be competing with as many as 500 or 600 others that were submitted that day; those are formidable odds.

Your release will hit the wastebasket immediately if it is handwritten, too lengthy (a thesis instead of a news release, with long sentences, unfamiliar words or professional jargon), contains misspellings, or has no date. It will be tossed out after a brief glance if it is incomplete and the essential who, what, and why are left out.

Don't irritate the editor by asking for clippings of your story; buy the paper and clip it yourself. Requesting the return of photos is a nuisance for busy people and should be avoided.

And finally, don't give up and stop sending in material after one or two unsuccessful attempts; even the most skilled publicist cannot bat 100 percent—or even 75 percent!

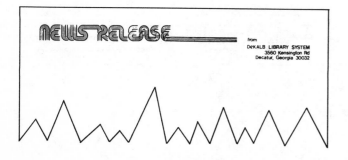

from
DeKALB LIBRARY SYSTEM
3560 Kensington Rd
Decatur, Georgia 30032

Sample News Release Format

Can You Make the "Big Time"?

Occasionally you may have a story that is of statewide or even national interest, in which case you should know how to contact the wire services. The item that will skip across the country on the wires is not necessarily one of great significance; it is, in fact, more likely to be of human interest or even may be trivia, but it could get your library's name in print from coast to coast. Some of these stories are picked up by the wire service representative from a local news account or from the local paper, but you can help, too. Get the name and phone number of the local or regional wire service people and keep it handy for quick reference when you spot a likely story; or even stage manage an event to capture interest and secure coverage. Here's an account of how Henry Theodore Wilkens, professor at Shippensburg State College, did just that, as reported in *Public Relations Journal,* September, 1973:

On another occasion, our students were going to walk books from the old library to the new library. Three colleges in the radius of 60 miles had walked books to their new libraries within a four months' period before our scheduled bookwalk, so my problem became one of interesting the saturated news media.

The solution started off slowly, but gained momentum as my willing participant warmed up to the project. My original plan was to dress someone in a cap and gown, put him on a white horse and let him ride off in the direction of the new library with a bunch of books under his arm. My star was a motorcycle fan, however, and he insisted on using the cycle instead of the horse. Since willing participants are not always easy to find, I accepted his suggestion. He showed up at the appointed time, cap, gown and doctoral degree in place, and started revving up the engine of the cycle. My rider had his quota of books and was ready to go, when at the last moment I suggested that he put a thin book in his mouth and then shove off. My lovable extrovert department head agreed, and off he went, roaring his way to immortality, books under one arm and one in his mouth.

Our cameras clicked . . . and TV also recorded the start of the bookwalk. We rushed the film to the UPI lab, they processed the film, and that print started off in the Sunday *New York Times* and bounced all around the country in newspapers for the next two weeks.

What was accomplished? Well, for one thing, people all over the country found out that our college had a brand new library. They also saw that our students were a fun-loving group, and willing to do a bit of work for the benefit of the school, when college students all over the country were being shown as raising hell, burning, destroying, and picketing. Destructive students were in the minority, but without a balance of activity in the news, America was getting a one-sided picture of what campus life was like. So the image of our student body was also enhanced.

Compile a list of state newspapers and send out selected releases that appear to have a possibility of regional or statewide interest. The following story is an example of an account of a local incident with statewide implications:

ERROR ON STATE FLOWER UNEARTHED AT LIBRARY

An innocent question directed to the Cityville Public Library uncovered a 24-year-old legislative error that put Wisconsin in the wrong official flower patch—and it all came about because of a needlepoint wall-hanging.

Back in 1908, school children throughout the state nominated the violet as one of the candidates for the state flower. . . . (When the bill was adopted in 1949, the violet was defined as "wood violet"—Viola papilionacea.) So it stood for 24 years until Mrs. Betty Smith decided to make a needlepoint wall hanging, depicting the official flowers and birds of the places the family had lived. To find out what they were, she called the Cityville reference librarian. In rounding up the information, they found that New Jersey and Wisconsin had the same state flower, which is not too unusual, except that Mrs. Smith noted Wisconsin's state flower could be translated from the Latin to "butterfly violet"—not wood violet. She double-checked it with the library and from there the hunt was on for the correct official Wisconsin state flower. . . .

LIBRARY NEWS

Library Notes By Jo Ellen Mulder

Balsam Lake—
Looking In At The Library

By Connie Hill

The Newspaper Column

A regular newspaper column can be an excellent vehicle for library publicity, but how well it is read will depend on the creativity and imagination of the writer. If the aim is to get across the idea of the library as an interesting, lively place and to motivate nonusers, it must be more than a list of new books. The "new books received" listing will be routinely skipped by all but a few devoted patrons who would undoubtedly make their way to the library in any case.

There are several advantages to a library column. You will have reserved space regularly, and you will be able to include information, anecdotes, and opinions that might not otherwise be considered news by the editor. Conversely, writing a regular column takes time, which must be specifically set aside for this purpose; deadlines must be met, and you run the risk of falling into a pat formula over a period of time which will not attract new readers or, indeed, hold old ones.

If you want to start a column or revamp the existing format, you will have to convince the editor that you can deliver the goods that will attract and hold readership. Prepare three or four sample columns. If the editor is still reluctant, citing space limitations or lack of potential interest, suggest that the column be given a fair trial for a few months and offer to evaluate the results with the editor. At the end of a trial period, you may be able to offer evidence of readership in the form of letters, increased registrations or circulation at the library,

and inquiries which you can directly attribute to material published in the column. A formal readership survey can be undertaken. A biweekly community newspaper did this and reported the following results:

> "LIBRARY CORNER" RATED
>
> How do Cityville Press readers use their "Library Corner"? Do they read it? How frequently? Do they enjoy "Library Corner"? "Library Corner," supplied by the local librarian, lists new books and films available from the library.
>
> Recently a poll was conducted; of the 500 surveys sent out, 250 were returned, considered an excellent response. In the urban area, with 58 replies of the 200 mailed, there was a 62 percent readership indicated. In the rural area, where 43 replies were returned out of 150 mailed, "Library Corner" has 58 percent readership, and 30 percent indicated they liked the column. "This is not considered really good readership, but enough to continue the column," a newspaper spokesman said. In the school area, 28 percent read the column, which is a very low readership.

There were some ominous undertones to this report (and some question of the validity, as well!). The decision to continue the column indicated more good nature than good judgment on the part of the editor. However, a few months after this poll was taken, a new librarian was appointed who changed the entire format and content of the column. In time a 30 percent increase in library circulation was reported, and numerous letters were received from readers. The newspaper editor was impressed, convinced of the value of the column, and subsequently increased the paper's coverage of other aspects of library news.

A library column generally appears under a standard caption and this may be, at least initially, a handicap to increased readership. The words "book" and "library" may hold promise of little immediate interest to many. One way to overcome this is to write a brief headline for the article to stimulate interest in the contents.

The biweekly column written by a librarian for a newspaper in a city of moderate size is captioned "Books Fortnightly," but good headlines attract attention:

> KIDS DRIVE YOU CRAZY ON
> AUTO TRIPS?
> HERE ARE GAMES TO
> ENTERTAIN THEM
>
> * * * *
>
> LIBRARY TO COME UP ROSES
>
> (Announcement of a rose show to be
> held at the library, with a list of
> books about roses.)

Another newspaper has carried regular book reviews in the form of a news article, with the writer's name and library identification by-line under these headlines:

> WOULD-BE TOURISTS WILL LIKE NEW
> LIBRARY BOOKS
>
> * * * *
>
> "THEY SHALL NOT PASS"
> A BOOK FOR PARENTS
>
> * * * *
>
> NEW LIBRARY BOOKS OFFER
> RELAXATION FOR HOLIDAYS

Then there is the library columnist who gets away with:

> SHERLOCK HOLMES NEVER SAID
> "ELEMENTARY, MY DEAR WATSON"
>
> * * * *
>
> CANDY IS DANDY, BUT LIQUOR IS
> QUICKER—POT IS NOT
>
> * * * *
>
> LAUDS FRISBEE . . . CHEAPEST SPORT
> SINCE HINDUSTANI HOPSCOTCH

If the format does not permit eye-catching headlines, you will have to try to get a reader's attention through the lead sentence or paragraph. Examples from library columns:

> NWPC/NAHW/NOW/NWAAC . . .
> No, the writer isn't misspelling nor the
> typesetter malfunctioning . . . the letters
> make sense, if you know how to decipher
> them.
>
> * * * *
>
> Income tax time again, fellow citi-
> zens! Unpleasant task as it is, your public
> library has some aids that may make it a
> bit easier and perhaps help save you
> some money in the bargain. There is, for
> example. . . .

The content and subjects treated in a library column can be as wide-ranging as your ability to relate the interests and concerns of the public to library materials and services—which is just about as wide open as you can get! You can editorialize, reminisce, do interviews, pontificate, be wry or humorous, discuss world affairs or the topic of conversation at the Main Street drug store. Check the ABC's of story angles for idea-starters. If time and all else fails, you can resort to a question-and-answer column. When a library system publicist proposed just such a question-and-answer column to eight county newspapers, seven of the eight accepted it for monthly publication, to her amazement.

What to Do with Press Clippings

A collection of press clippings mounted in a scrapbook can be impressive evidence to staff and trustees of your publicity efforts. Measuring the number of printed newspaper column inches is a favorite device for proving publicity effectiveness, but it actually is *not;* it is only a measure of potential reader exposure, which is quite another thing.

The collection will be an aid to your own evaluation, however, and will assist in planning the application of meaningful measurements in the future. You can also check coverage against your original plan and determine what areas or what kinds of information were not covered. Clippings filed in chronological order are valuable for reference, and can eventually become a part of the library's archives.

Some articles can be reprinted in your newsletter, brochures, or annual reports. A few may warrant multiple reproduction for mailing to legislators and others, a quick and easy way to communicate a special message.

Finally, send duplicates of your good clips to your system headquarters or state library agency. In Minnesota, for example, a four-page monthly publication, "Libraries in the News," contains reproductions of news clips from all over the state which keeps librarians informed of what others are doing, and is an excellent resource for publicity and promotion ideas.

More Ways to Get Newspaper Space

The news release and the library column are your two major newspaper publicity tools, but there are other ways to get in print. Here are some hints:

1. You may make a good friend of the editor by supplying "fillers," one- or two-line sentences or very brief paragraphs on subjects of timely or seasonal interest that can be dropped in to fill up a short column in the paper.

Odd things are left in books returned to the Cityville Library. Photographs, candy bars, bills, and a copy of a will have all been found recently. This week the book *How To Manage Your Money* was returned with a dollar bill inside!

*   *   *   *

Planning a vacation? You will enjoy it more by planning beforehand with the help of travel books and brochures from the Cityville Library.

*   *   *   *

Books on all aspects of football can be obtained from the Cityville Library.

*   *   *   *

Weight conscious persons will be interested in the excellent diet books at the Cityville Library.

*   *   *   *

Ideas for designing and building a patio are given in the recent book, *The Complete Book of Patio Gardening,* which has been added to the Cityville Library.

Over 300 new library cards were issued to residents of Cityville in June. This brings the total number of card-holders to 6,500.

*   *   *   *

The Cityville Library answered 535 questions over the telephone in October. One of the most interesting questions was "____."

*   *   *   *

The Cityville Library has a free 'answer' service. When you need to know the answer to a question, call 233-4343.

*   *   *   *

Your editor might be interested in a series of short feature fillers, under a heading, "Who Is It?" Example:

Born March 3, 1847 in Edinburgh, Scotland. Lived in Canada and Boston. Main interest was in helping the deaf. Most famous invention is a favorite of all teenagers. You can read about him in Thomas B. Costain's book *The Cord of Steel* at the Cityville Library. His name is Alexander Graham Bell!

2. Weekly or monthly calendars of community events have been compiled by libraries for local newspapers; if you prepare these, be sure you get a credit line, and, of course, include library hours and events. A Wisconsin library prepared a comprehensive and useful schedule for the newspaper during the summer months, with the heading, "Where to Take the Kids Next Week."

3. An occasional short list of new book titles with a one- or two-sentence annotation can be supplied to special sections of the newspaper, such as the entertainment page, business page, etc.

4. Your chances of getting a good photo spread in the paper may depend on your ability to interest the staff photographer in the possibilities, and by supplying a good reason, such as National Library Week, or a timely angle on special services. Photos that you submit, by an in-house photographer or a friendly camera bug, will rarely be used unless they are exceptionally good and of professional quality, but a sampling might be shown to the news photographer as suggestions.

5. The want ads are well-read sections of the paper, particularly in local weeklies and shopper guides. The cost is minimal, and in some cases editors donate the space or make a special rate. These can be fairly straightforward, or you can let your imagination go. Samples:

PERSONALS

Joe: Meet me at the library. I'll wait in the fiction section by the D's. Love, Betty.

*   *   *   *

MISCELLANEOUS

Will lend latest books on macrame, ceramics, knitting, other arts and crafts. Free. Apply in person, Cityville Library, Mon-Fri, 9-9.

*   *   *   *

BUSINESS SERVICES

Preparing a report or speech and need accurate statistics, or apt quotation? Our reference librarians can help. Phone Cityville Library, 233-4343.

*   *   *   *

HELP WANTED

113 patrons to sample new books at Cityville Library. Open Mon-Fri, 9-5.

*   *   *   *

FREE for loan to good home; brand-new copy of (book title); may be kept for 28 days. Pick up any time between 9 and 5, Mon-Fri, Cityville Library.

EMPLOYMENT SERVICES

Have hundreds of career books, civil service tests. Also latest information on scholarships, loans, study abroad. Call Cityville Library, 233-4343.

*   *   *   *

PLANTS, SEEDS, FLOWERS

Before you plant, check what the experts with nothing to sell have to say. Reference Department, Cityville Library, open 9-9, Mon-Fri.

*   *   *   *

---

6. Space for a display ad may be secured in various ways. Some newspapers have a fund for community-oriented ads which might be tapped by the library. The paper's advertising manager might assist in contacting local firms for underwriting an ad on a special occasion, or space might be purchased by the library itself or Friends of the library. This can be an institutional type ad or regular announcements of services and activities.

7. Occasionally a newspaper will publish a special section or supplement devoted to the library, most often on the pretext of National Library Week or the opening of a new building. Preparation of this amount of material takes a great deal of planning and work, but it offers an opportunity to reach a wide readership. There is a special bonus in the fact that additional copies, purchased at cost or made available by the newspaper as a public service, have a long life as a handout for

newcomers, for legislators and others. Usually such a section is compiled by the newspaper staff, with information and leads supplied by the library staff, but some libraries have done all the writing, editing, and makeup, and paid for the printing and insertion. The cost effectiveness of this is worth exploring, since the widespread distribution and the relatively inexpensive printing method may bring the unit cost down to 1¢ to 4¢ per household.

8. "Letters to the Editor" is a section of the newspaper with a high readership, and there are many reasons or excuses you can find for writing. You can express appreciation for good coverage:

Dear Editor:

Many thanks for your support and coverage of our recent open house at the Cityville Library. Over 7,000 people. . . .

*   *   *   *

(Call attention to the contributions of staff or trustees.)

Dear Editor:

We want to express our best wishes to the Cityville Library staff member who is leaving the community after four years of dedicated and responsive service to the information needs of all our patrons....

*   *   *   *

(Forward letters received for reprinting)

Mr. John Brown
President, Library Board

As our fiscal year draws to a close, we are reminded of the important part the Cityville Library plays in providing a source of knowledge and pleasure to our community. Please find enclosed with this letter our check for $300. . . .

You can comment on any question that has been raised, either in the news or in editorials, and correct or explain misunderstandings about library operations. Your comments can be timely by adding some interesting background facts about current news items, and by calling attention to the materials in the library on the subject, from famous persons to disasters. You can also encourage others to write and express their opinions.

The letters-to-the-editor column is a public forum. It can be, in effect, your editorial outlet if you take advantage of it. Keep letters short (200 words or so) and keep to the subject, whatever it may be. Use simple words and short sentences. If the first sentence refers to a news item or another letter that appeared in the paper, it will catch the eye of the editor quickly.

9. You may rate an editorial in the paper if you personally remind the editor of special weeks or contact him/her with background information for a thoughtful comment on a problem or new development at the library. Many newspapers receive "canned" editorial material from various sources (library associations, wire services, syndicates, etc.). Let the editor know that you will help in revising or amplifying the material to apply to the local situation.

10. Keep in touch with regular newspaper columnists and free-lancers in your community with memos about materials relevant to their special interests, and supply them with story angles from your "great ideas" file—all those bits that you have not had time to write up yourself. Keep an eye out for syndicated columnists who suggest that readers seek additional information at the library on the subject discussed, and follow up fast with a list of material available locally, whether the mention comes from Ann Landers or Sylvia Porter.

Sound Thinking—How to Get and Use Radio Time

There is at least one working radio in 98 percent of U.S. households, and the average number of sets per household is 5. There are radios in 99 percent of all cars, and they are turned on 62 percent of the time. Studies have indicated that more people get news from the radio than from television and newspapers combined.

There's a good sound publicity outlet awaiting libraries in every community, but it is sadly under-used, perhaps because librarians tend to be print-oriented. Radio has a very large and diverse audience, and many listeners may be people that can not be reached through newspaper publicity. An ominous note has been sounded as well; the shortage of newsprint and spiraling costs of publication are forcing many papers to reduce the number and size of pages, with a corresponding cut in space for public service news and features. Thus libraries may be forced to seek more radio and TV coverage to publicize services.

Radio has the additional advantage of being "instant communication" and the air time is free for public service announcements and programs, although, contrary to a widespread belief, there is no law that says a radio station must give a specific amount of time to public service. Stations must keep a log of broadcast time for the Federal Communication Commission and the amount of public service time logged is, at least theoretically, a factor in license renewal.

Use of radio time by libraries takes several forms. The simplest and easiest is a *public service announcement* (PSA) of 10-120 seconds in length; in effect, a nonprofit commercial. A recent national survey revealed that 60 percent of the radio stations contacted broadcast more than 100 PSA's a week, and 18 percent aired more than 200 spots a week. On the flip side of those facts, the reporting stations said that seven out of every ten PSA's submitted were rejected. This is not as discouraging as it sounds, however, for the count included material from national organizations and agencies which had little or no local tie-in. The rejected material was also characterized as "bland, dull, or boring." The library has the advantage of being a home-town agency, and there is no reason why copy should be dull or bland. Take heart. . . .

News items, similar in content to press releases, are materials sent in to be included in local newscasts. This includes both hard news and the human interest or humorous bits that newscasters like.

A *radio program* is a regular short feature, which can vary in length from 2–25 minutes, a longer daily, weekly, or monthly program of 15–30 minutes, a special presentation, or an occasional or scheduled segment of another program.

Getting Started

Your first job is simply to listen. Monitor each area station for at least a day or two so that you know the format of the programs and the potential audience. (This may be a bit of a hardship if you are not, for example, a hard rock fan, but the exercise will save you time and trouble in the future.) Note the times when PSAs, spot news items, or special programs are aired, and the type that the station uses, so that you can tailor your material or suggestions accordingly.

You must decide what kind of radio publicity you are capable of producing in terms of working time, ability, and resources, and the relative importance of this in your total promotion program. Once again you will have to make a prejudgment about the effectiveness of this form of publicity, but in the beginning you can establish some criteria or measurements for evaluating it after a period of time. (You should follow this same procedure if you are restructuring an existing program.) Don't jump in just because it seems like a good idea; air time may be free but your time is not, and a hasty or second-rate job will backfire.

Set aside a definite period of time, as part of the regular library promotion routine, to prepare the radio material. This can be as little as two or three hours a week or as much as eight hours or more, depending on the amount and type of programing you do. The important thing is to schedule a work period, and not consider the preparation of radio material as something to do when there is time.

Then, armed with some knowledge of the station programing and your proposals, the next step is to contact the station and talk to the people with whom you will deal, whether station manager, program director, or public service director. (It would be a good idea to renew this contact at intervals, even if you have established a working relationship, because personnel change, formats change, interests shift, and a good idea or proposal that was once rejected may now find a happy home.)

If your first reception is a little cool or skeptical, you may have to prove that you can deliver material that will interest the station's audience and enhance its image, as well as your own, in the public's eye. The station manager may not be familiar with the library, and so it will be up to you to be convincing, and show that you have something of widespread interest to say and will say it well. You might even go prepared to give the manager a library card and a special invitation to drop in at the library. A little familiarity may gain a higher priority in programing.

The Library's Radio Commercial

Public service announcements of 20–60 seconds are designed to call attention to the library, to remind the public that it is there, encourage use,

—————————————

". . . listen first, and learn . . ."

—————————————

and to purvey information about materials and services in as interesting and professional a manner as possible. These can be typed out for a station announcer to read, they can be recorded at the library if proper equipment is available, or they can be taped at the station.

Writing good spots is not difficult. Spot announcements come in three lengths: 20-seconds, 30-seconds, and 60-seconds. A spot doesn't permit the use of very many words. In fact, once you get going, you are going to have trouble keeping the number of words down. A 20-second spot is about 45-50 words, a 30-second spot is about 65 words, and you can only get 125–150 words in a one-minute segment. (A rule of thumb is two words per second.)

When you know the format that the station prefers and the audience reached, you can prepare the content accordingly. Once you have established a routine, be consistent and dependable. Get your material to the station well in advance of airing time and on a regular schedule if it is a daily or weekly series. Deliver your material in person, if possible. You will get better cooperation from the station if the station manager or continuity director knows that you can be depended upon for a certain amount of material.

You can write spots in simple, conversational form, just as if you were talking to someone— which is what the announcer or you will be doing. Count the number of words, time the spot, and

indicate the length accurately so that the station can log it properly. It is possible that the station will ask you or your stand-in voice to tape spot announcements in advance. This is helpful because it saves time and eliminates most of the stage fright that a live mike might bring on. A speaking voice that comes across well is the main requirement; you, someone on the staff, or a volunteer can do this at a convenient time at the station.

There is no limit to the subjects that can be used for spot announcements, in addition to the straightforward news releases about library programs and activities. A radio station seeks variety, and the library is in an enviable position to supply it.

What can you talk about? Here are a few suggestions to start.

1. The latest exhibit or display at the library.

2. The answer to a specific question that a patron asked recently.

3. Books or other library materials that tie in to a timely community interest or controversy. A simple format would read: "Did you see the article in the newspaper yesterday (or hear) about __? (Summarize content in a few words.) If you would like to know more about (subject), the library has this material available (books, magazine articles, etc.)."

4. A timely holiday or anniversay with an unusual fact about it and some pertinent reading material.

5. Mini-reviews of books have long been staple items for library PSAs. An Ohio librarian described the procedure at her library: "Several librarians troop to the station every three weeks or so and tape two-minute book reviews. These are heard five days a week at specific times in the afternoon, and again at 11 P.M. The response has been great. We also provide mimeographed sheets with the thumbnail reviews of the same books for library patrons."

The Alaska Library Association tapes 30 book reviews a month and sends them to stations with the tag, "This book tip was brought to you as a

public service by the Alaska Library Association."
In the July, 1977 issue of their newsletter, *Sourdough,* Betty Galbraith gave the following instructions and advice, reprinted here in part:

      1. These are tips to entice and draw the reader into the library, not formal reviews.

      2. Use a catchy first sentence to get the listener's attention fast.

      3. Tips should be 25 or 55 seconds; don't go over as the other 5 seconds are for the tag.

      4. Avoid unusual or hard to pronounce words—if you must use them, spell them phonetically.

      5. Punctuate for speaking. . . .

      6. Avoid "you will enjoy," "you are sure to like," etc.

      7. Vary the ending; we have used
● Look for it at your local library
● Check your local library
● Try your library first
● It's available through your local library.

      8. Rob from the blurb on the cover if it is good.

      9. Review books of general interest to the public, and only books that you consider very good, for example:

      Sit down, relax and enjoy a coffin break with Alfred Hitchcock. A freshly brewed pot of fear, and a most interesting group of people await you. They aren't exactly the beautiful people, but they'll go all out to give you the time of your life—as long as your life lasts, that is. So take a break from the tranquility of everyday life and pore through this deliciously diabolic collection of stories, brought together by Alfred Hitchcock's *Coffin Break.* Try your library first. This book tip was brought to you as public service by the Alaska Library Association.

Book-related capsules, prepared by the Grand Rapids (Michigan) Public Library, took this form:

Announcer: What was the loudest noise ever heard? William Vergara, in his book SCIENCE IN EVERYDAY THINGS, says: The loudest noise ever heard, at least in modern times, was the eruption in 1883 of the volcanic island of Krakatoa, in the Dutch East Indies. It was much louder than any atomic or hydrogen blast to date. After being dormant for two hundred years, the volcano erupted with such violence that it was audible in Australia, *two thousand miles away!* The violent explosions lasted for 36 hours and blew off half of the island. The final stupendous outburst on August 27, 1883 had enough sound energy to circle the earth completely, not once but seven times before it faded out! It left a record of its passing on all of the self-recording barometers in the world. Cinders and ash shot 20 miles into the atmosphere making it dark for one hundred miles around, even at noon! But even worse than the eruption were the tidal waves that followed. Hundreds of villages were wiped out by huge waves that rose one hundred feet in the air. The gigantic waves, rushing forward at speeds of up to seven hundred miles per hour finally dissipated themselves on the Australia and California coasts, thousands of miles away.

The one-minute "Accent on Books" spots aired in Washington state were in a conversational form:

Announcer: This is Sam Jones with "Accent on Books." Today we're discussing a book which was chosen for accenting by Becky Morrison because it is of particular interest to our senior citizens.

Becky Morrison: It is estimated that billions of dollars are bilked from America's senior citizens each year in the sale of disease cures, preburial contracts, land plots, and in various products and services. It is those people who have retired who have become the chief targets of these frauds and vicious rackets. Mr. Ducovny's book, which is now available at Cityville Library, discusses these schemes and guides the reader on how to spot them.

Announcer: Are these rackets explained? How will readers be able to identify a swindle or fraud?

Morrison: Well, a section of this book is a dictionary of the major areas in which these quacks operate, and advice is given by experts on how to recognize them.

Announcer: "The Billion Dollar Swindle: Frauds against the Elderly" is the title of this new volume, and it may be borrowed from the Cityville Library.

On-the-air book reviews present the possibility of a run on the titles mentioned, so be sure that multiple copies are available or you will run the risk of annoying patrons requesting them. It is also advisable to give the radio station the full listing of titles, authors, and call numbers, since the station will receive requests from listeners for further information.

The spots you submit, either script or taped, can also be very general in nature, as in the following examples. However, beware of ranging widely over a number of subjects in haphazard fashion. It is best to concentrate on one message over a period of time, varied in presentation, or to do a series in one category, so that there is some impact to the message through repetition.

When it comes to getting needed information or facts, there are two kinds of people in the world. One kind asks a friend or neighbor the question. The other kind calls the Cityville Public Library. The first group gets secondhand information; the others get the straight facts, from the authorities at the Cityville Public Library. Next time you need to know something, don't ask Joe; call 233-4343.

* * * *

Time is money, especially when you need information. What is *your* time worth? $2.00 an hour? $3? $5? $15? Don't fumble around trying to locate facts you need for your business or other activities; don't wander aimlessly along long bookshelves. When you need information, ask the reference librarian at Cityville Public Library for help. That's what the librarian is for! The librarian can probably locate what you need in three minutes. And that's only a few pennies worth of time for both of you. Save time *and* money and get what you need—fast—at the Cityville Public Library.

* * * *

There are a lot of famous addresses in history. There's Lincoln's Gettysburg Address, for example. And Napoleon's Farewell Speech to His Troops. And Washington's Second Inaugural Address. And then there's 25 E. Main St. What's that? Another important address: the address of the Cityville Public Library, where you can also find all those other famous addresses.

* * * *

Know any place in town where you can walk in and walk out with 10, 50, or 100 dollars worth of materials, use them for 28 days, and bring them back—WITHOUT ANY CHARGE? Well, there's *one* place in Cityville—the Cityville Public Library. Books, magazines, films, records, art prints—all *yours,* free for borrowing at the Cityville Public Library.

* * * *

People have different tastes. That's why they make chocolate and vanilla, as the saying goes. There's one place in town that caters to all tastes—the Cityville Public Library. Whether your preference is for Tolstoi, Toynbee, or Tolkien; whether you want to learn how to make a digital computer, a duck pond, or a dress; or whether you want to find out about the weather in Florida, the way to make wine, or the wattage of an electric light bulb, the Cityville Public Library will have something to suit your taste and to meet your need. The Library has a tasteful variety of *everything.* . . .

* * * *

Is there a new member about to be added to your family—a furred, feathered, or finny member? If you are about to acquire a new pet—whether a cat, dog, parakeet, or tropical fish—it's wise to be prepared ahead. And the best way is to find out all you can, by reading. Just about everything you may want to know about the care and feeding of pets can be found at the Cityville Library. Get a book before you get your pet, and welcome the new family member with confidence.

* * * *

"Laugh and the world laughs with you." Well, maybe yes, maybe no. But, no matter how grim you may feel at the moment, you can find something to make you chuckle, grin, or laugh out loud at the Cityville Library. If you have the "glooms," try a dose of humorous poetry, amusing essays, joke collections—even cartoon books. The Cityville Library can be a very funny place!

* * * *

Mind conditioning is as good as air conditioning to beat the heat in summer. If hot days get you down, cool it with a book on a cold subject. How about a trip to the Arctic? Or a story about polar bears? You can find a lot of refreshing subjects at the Cityville Library. It's a pretty "cool" place to visit.

* * * *

Are you willing to take a bet? The Cityville Library is offering a million to one odds to any taker who comes in the front door. And the bet? That you will learn something that you didn't know before you came in. The odds may be stacked against you, but it's a bet you will win when you lose. Come in to the Cityville Library and take a gamble on learning something new.

*   *   *   *

How many different ways can a story be brought to people? It can be told aloud. It can be printed, in a book, a magazine, or a pamphlet. It can be recorded or captured on film. If it's a good story, people will pay to read it, to hear it, or to hear and see it. *Or,* you can enjoy it free, thanks to the Cityville Public Library.

*   *   *   *

"Cold hands and warm hearts" is the motto now at the Cityville Library during the energy shortage. The thermostat has been lowered at the Cityville Library, too, to help conserve power, but the heat's on to supply you with heart-warming books, books hot off the press, even how-to-do-it books to occupy your cold hands. There's no shortage of information at the Cityville Library; it's a real "know" power plant.

*   *   *   *

Inflation has hit us all right where it hurts most, in the pocketbook. Prices zoom outta sight, and the cost of everything goes up. Everything? Well, not quite. The price of a library card hasn't changed at all—it's still *free*. There's a free one awaiting you at the Cityville Library now, just for the asking. And with that card you can get some of the information you need to combat the high cost of living. There's a wealth of material available to help you get your money's worth at the Cityville Library.

Inject some humor into your spots if you can, because this catches attention. Here are some tongue-in-cheek samples, which could be taped with various voices or read by a station announcer:

And now we have another in the series of true-life mini-success stories from the Cityville Public Library. . . .

Cyrus Cormick has a farm outside of Cityville. Every spring and fall he plows up over 120 acres of land. That's a lot of ruts to be in. To help keep out of a rut, Cyrus borrows dozens of books from the Cityville Public Library. Lately he has been reading up on how to drill for oil. He thinks now that he may try oil prospecting, because it would be a nice change from plowing the same fields. If he makes a strike, he says he will name the oil well after the Cityville Public Library.

*   *   *   *

Hilda Mae is a hairdresser at the Beau Monde Beauty Shop. She's pretty good. She's also hooked on making rugs, and she's pretty good at hooking rugs now, too. She learned how from a book she got at the Cityville Public Library. She read the book between appointments. Last week she gave five permanents and sold two rugs. She has returned the book, so you could borrow it now from the Cityville Public Library.

*   *   *   *

Hugo Hinterland is a game warden. He often has to hike or snowshoe great distances in the woods, and so he always carries a book or two from the Cityville Public Library in his rucksack. He was especially interested in books about the weather because he sure saw a lot of it. He learned so much from the books he read that pretty soon he could make a more accurate forecast than the local weather reporter. So he applied for a job with the Weather Bureau. And that's why you may soon get all the weather, courtesy of the Cityville Public Library.

*   *   *   *

Sam Bang is a cop. And he has to chase a lot of crazy birds on occasion. Sometimes, though, his patrol takes him out into the parks, and he became interested in a different kind of bird—the feathered ones. He stopped by the Cityville Public Library for some books about birds. Then the librarian suggested that he borrow some bird song records, too. Soon Sam was an expert at identifying a nuthatch at 700 paces. Recently, he was elected treasurer (bonded, of course) of the local bird watchers' society. "I owe it all to the Cityville Public Library," Sam says, modestly.

*   *   *   *

Horace Hackenbush lives in Cityville, but he's an outdoor nut. He likes to wander about in the woods. One day he found a tree that was loaded with ripe berries. He picked a lot and took some in to the Cityville Public Library to identify. Then he borrowed a book on how to use edible wild fruit and cooked up a big batch of the berries. He brought a jar into the Cityville Public Library recently. He calls it "Li-Berry Jam."

* * * *

Mary Bligh is a very good cook and her home is attractive, but she has never been called "the hostess with the mostest." In fact, people made excuses when she invited them to parties. Then Mary discovered that she could borrow films from the Cityville Public Library, such as (____) and (____). She decided to show these to her guests instead of her husband's home movies. She was an instant success, and now her parties are very well attended. She served (recipe) from the (cookbook title) that she got from the Cityville Public Library too. You can get the same recipe, and the films, too, from the Cityville Public Library and be a "hostess with the mostest."

A short spot series in the form of a weekly almanac can take this form:

For release: Week of January 17-24
Re: Benjamin Franklin's Birthday (January 17)

And now the Cityville Library brings you this week's mini-almanac.

Remember who said "Early to bed and early to rise makes a man healthy, wealthy and wise"? Benjamin Franklin. January 17 is Benjamin Franklin's birthday. This versatile man was a printer, author, philosopher, diplomat, scientist, and inventor.

He was also the originator of American lending libraries, and thus the "father" of the public libraries we know today. So, during Benjamin Franklin's birthday week, why not celebrate at your library—with a visit? Who knows—it may make you healthy, wealthy and wise!

This message is brought to you as a service of the Cityville Public Library and radio station _____.

For release: First week of February
Re: "Robinson Crusoe Day"

And now the Cityville Library brings you this week's mini-almanac.

Remember the story about Robinson Crusoe—the ship-wrecked sailor who spent 29 years on a deserted island?

That book, written by Daniel Defoe, is based on the true story of a sailor named Alexander Selkirk, who spent five years on an island in the Pacific Ocean, and who was finally found on February 1, 1708.

As a result, February 1 has been declared "Robinson Crusoe Day." It is a day to be adventurous, self-reliant, and self-sufficient. So why not visit the Cityville Library and discover the adventure of reading a rousing novel or listening to some stirring music? You might even check out *Robinson Crusoe!*

This message-of-the-week is brought to you by your Cityville Library and station _____.

For release: Second week of April
Re: Webster's Dictionary First Published (April 14)

And now the Cityville Library brings you this week's mini-almanac.

What's in a word? Perhaps you should consult a dictionary to find out. But that's not all a dictionary can do for you.

This week we celebrate Dictionary Day, because Webster's Dictionary was first published on April 14, 1828. It contained 70,000 words in two volumes.

What can you find in a dictionary besides words and definitions? There are pictures of flags of various nations, rules for spelling, information about abbreviations, explanations of signs and symbols and a pronouncing gazetteer. There are many different kinds of dictionaries available today, in addition to the standard *Webster's.*

Your library has good dictionaries and dozens of other reference books to help answer your questions. So come in and "have words" with the Cityville Library this week.

This message is brought to you as a service of the Cityville Public Library and radio station _____.

For release: Second Week of May
Re: First Oscars Awarded (1929)

And now the Cityville Library brings you this week's mini-almanac.

Do you have any idea where the name "Oscar" for the Academy Awards originated? The golden statuette took this nickname when an Academy employee jested that the coveted award reminded her of her Uncle Oscar. The awards have been presented annually since May 16, 1929. Remember some of these prize-winning movies? "Gone with the Wind," "Casablanca," "Ben-Hur," "Midnight Cowboy," and "The Godfather"?

The Cityville Library is the place to go when you want to read about movies, learn how to make movies, or find a fact abut an Academy Award winner. The library also has films on a variety of subjects which you can borrow.

Make your motto "Lights, action, camera, LIBRARY!"

This message is brought to you as a service of the Cityville Public Library and radio station _____.

For release: First Week of June
Re: Roses and Their Uses (June is National Rose Month)

And now the Cityville Library brings you this week's mini-almanac.

Did you know that roses are used for making jams and jellies—as well as appreciated for their fragrance and beauty?

June is National Rose Month, a good time to find out more about the flower that is grown in all 50 states. Roses have been pickled, boiled, and potted, and have been used in making cakes, candies, marmalades and even cosmetics. Rose wine was a favorite in many countries long ago and roses have also been used as room fresheners, cures for hangovers and headaches, and a remedy for wounds.

Cultivate an interest in the Cityville Library and you could weed through a whole series of books and magazines on flowers and gardening!

This message is brought to you as a service of the Cityville Public Library and radio station _____.

Quick "fillers" might be useful to your station(s). If so, supply them with a batch now and then, similar to these sent out by the Corn Belt, Illinois Library System:

(5 seconds) Get your mind off the bad weather. Build a boat. Instructions are available at the Public Library.

(10 seconds) So you've lost your address book and can't remember Aunt Margaret's street number. Don't fret. Consult the telephone and city directories available at your local library.

Whether you prepare spots for occasional use or set up a regular series, keep in mind the great range and diversity of radio audiences. If your material is regularly aired at a special time, the station can tell you something of the makeup of the audience that is likely to be tuned in at that time, and you can write scripts to interest those listeners. If spots are used at irregular intervals during the day, they should be varied so as to appeal to many different groups; occasionally pitch a message specifically to students, homemakers, rural people, or business personnel, etc.

You will want to have some record of how and when your PSAs are used; print up a questionnaire such as this, and ask the station(s) to return it to you. Include a stamped, self-addressed envelope.

Cityville Public Library
Main Street, Cityville   April, 1980

Re: Cityville Public Library Public Service Announcements, April series

____ Yes, we will be using the April series of 10 library 30- and 60-second taped PSA's. Frequency ____

____ No, we cannot use the spots.

Reason: _____

Name _____
Station _____
Comments? _____

You can also get some additional feedback by offering something on the air. Many stations like to offer free materials to their listeners who send in postcard requests to the station. Some stations will mail back the items; others simply refer the request to the agency supplying it. The "free offer" serves as an audience measure, boosts the "mail count," and promotes the station image as a public service institution. A book list or other printed piece offered over the air may attract a new audience for the library, and you might design a "free offer" with just this kind of promotion and listener count in mind. The timeliness or appeal of the material will influence the number of requests, of course, but both you and the stations may be agreeably surprised at the response.

Sample Form for Radio News Release

From: Cityville Library   For release: June 1–10
      10 Main St.   Time: 60 seconds
      Cityville

Contact: M. Dewey, Librarian
         233-4343

Re: Special Library Exhibit

A special exhibit of rock samples and gemstones will be on display at the Cityville Public Library from June fifth to June seventeenth. The rocks and gems are from the collection of Mr. John Chuse (Shooz), a noted Cityville rock hound. Mr. Chuse has written many articles about rock collecting. Most of the samples in his collection have been gathered within one hundred miles of Cityville. He will be at the Cityville Public Library on June fifth from seven to nine P.M. to talk about where and how to look for interesting specimens. Anyone interested in rock collecting is welcome to come to meet Mr. Chuse. The Cityville Public Library also has a good collection of books on rock and mineral identification.

News Releases

In most cases, straight news items will go to a different person on the station staff than the one to whom you send PSAs. The news items are timely, such as announcements about exhibits, programs, new services, building plans, etc., similar to your press releases. Event announcements should be sent in one or two weeks in advance of airing time, and if your station has a regular reading of a community calendar of events, provide a separate script for each day you want the announcement read.

". . . go on the air with a call-in . . ."

A radio news release should be written in a different form from a press release. It must be simple, with short words and varied sentence lengths. Write for the *ear* not the eye. Make it easy to read aloud. Write out all numbers, and do not divide a word at the end of a line. Spell difficult names phonetically in parentheses immediately after the word appears. The more "air-ready" your copy is, the better your chance that it will be used by a busy newscaster.

Radio Programs

A regular radio program, anything from 2 to 30 minutes, can take several forms. It can be as casual as a brief chat with the announcer at a specified time each day or week, or it can be a structured 15 minute or half hour feature of interviews, book reports, selected readings, panel discussions, and news. A regular program requires a lot of preparation and effort, definite time scheduling, and may involve other staff members and guests, all of which must be weighed against the exposure benefits.

Some libraries have participated in call-ins. For example, the announcer from a local radio station called in to the Rochester, Minnesota Public Library each Tuesday afternoon to ask, "What's new at the library?" Five minutes were alloted to the response which included announcements of events and occasionally brief mentions of new books or films. In a rural area of Wisconsin, the librarian in the small town of Three Lakes phones the radio station in another community early each morning with a brief report of local news and information about the library; her phone call is taped at the station and included in the station's daily round-up of news of the surrounding towns.

A live or recorded 5- to 15-minute conversation with the station announcer is relatively simple.

You can write out what you are going to say, word for word, if you are a little shaky. If you can ad-lib well or talk easily and casually, just make a few notes, and talk—with an eye on the clock. Give the announcer a clue about the subject for the day, and one or two leading questions, if you wish.

Here are a few suggestions for sources of ideas for daily or weekly chats:

1. Follow up on an interest shown by a group in your school or community, such as a newly formed hobby club, and tell about the materials you have on the subject.

2. Keep track of meetings of clubs and organizations (contact the program or publicity chairperson of the Kiwanis, Rotary, Woman's Club, church group, etc.) and start your radio talk with an announcement of the date of their meeting and the speaker or discussion subject. (You'll make some fast friends this way!) Then mention related materials available at the library.

3. Quote the reactions to new books or recommendations in certain fields of interest of local users—with their permission, of course!

4. Poll your teen-agers, businesspeople, or others for the names of books they find "most useful," "significant," or just "favorite."

5. Canvass the staff for interesting subject matter—what's going on in the children's room? The art and music section? The reference desk? The bookmobile?

6. Keep in tune with the season and holidays, and feature timely material.

7. Most people know that the library has encyclopedias, but what about references and specialized indices?

8. Keep your ears open to casual conversation. What are people talking about or doing, locally? (Example: Farm auctions draw an increasing number of both city and rural people, though possibly for different reasons. Mention books on antique collecting—and on the future of the small family farm.)

9. You might reserve a special time once a week to answer questions that radio listeners send in. Start off by making up a few, to be on the safe side.

A 15-minute program can be built around three to five short book reviews and some brief announcements. A 30-minute program can include interviews with local persons on a wide variety of subjects. To do an interview show, contact your guests well in advance, discuss the subject matter, and send them a list of questions you plan to ask on the air. Then keep the on-the-air discussion informal. If anyone on the staff is good at story-telling or reading aloud, this program format is relatively simple and will often build a devoted audience.

Thirty minutes can be a lot of time to fill, but the libraries in Sauk City and Prairie du Sac, Wisconsin found a relatively effortless way to do this. The local radio station carried a library program at the dinner hour that featured records available from the library, and interspersed the music with brief announcements about new books and library activities.

Sharing air time with schools and other community agencies can be beneficial to all, and you might suggest a "community" format to your local station and offer to organize or MC it. In a few cases air time has been purchased for the library by local businesses or organizations and they sponsor the programs as a public service.

An interesting book review, story hour, or interview that was aired can give you another dividend. Duplicate it in cassette form and circulate the cassettes to patrons.

Don't neglect the publicity about your radio program. List the times in your newsletters, post notices in the library and elsewhere, and include the information in your press releases.

Remember to say "thank you" for the air time you have been given. Forward any favorable comments or reactions, as well, for the station is vitally interested in the response.

Heard and Seen—Using Television

Producing a full-scale broadcast television program on a regular basis is an activity that few libraries can afford. However, television is an increasingly important communication medium that libraries cannot afford to ignore.

Free public service time is available on TV, as on radio, and the subject matter possibilities are much the same. With a little extra effort and some knowledge of requirements, good spot announcements and news clips can be supplied on a low budget. And with a little ingenuity, the library can get frequent mention on the station's regular programs by supplying appropriate materials or background information. No great dramatic talent is necessary to appear as an occasional interviewee, "reporter," or reader. This wide range of opportunities is too often overlooked.

The production cost of a good 20-, 30-, or 60-second PSA on film or videotape runs into thousands of dollars, and anything less than a high-quality spot is unlikely to be aired more than once, if at all. Production of these is necessarily a cooperative project of library systems, state agencies, or associations. But they are often available for purchase by others for a nominal fee. FCC regulations require that such spots carry a tag that clearly identifies the source or sponsor, but permission is usually granted by the agency making the spot to replace the original tag with the library's name—a relatively simple operation, which the local TV station can do if the tag is carried on the end frames. The library press carries announcements of the availability of such spots from various sources, and they are a real bargain that should be snapped up by any library with access to a TV station.

You can also produce your own spot announcements by providing stations with appropriate slides or art work and a script that can be read by an announcer. There are a few important requirements to be considered in preparing these. A television screen is wider than it is high. Slides or art work should be in a 3 to 4 ratio, that is 3 units high to 4 units wide. A 35mm slide should be in a horizontal format; art work, photographs, or cards should be 6 × 8, 8 × 10, 9 × 12, or 11 × 14. In addition, there is some "picture loss" on all four sides of a scanned picture when it appears on a home screen, and so elements of the visual should be kept within an imaginary border amounting to about 10 percent of the area on all sides. Lettering should be kept to a minimum, preferably no more than 10 words or three to four lines. The letters themselves must be as large as possible so that they are easily legible. Ektachrome film is preferred for slides since it has good color saturation, and slides should be submitted in plastic or metal frames, preferably with Newton ringless glass. Photos or art work should not have glossy or shiny surfaces.

It is best to offer a station spots in 10-second, 20-second and 30-second formats. Copy for TV should be timed a bit slower than for radio, no more than 1-2 words per second. A 30-second spot could have 6-8 slides with about 60 to 70 words, a 20-second spot up to 6 slides, and a 10-second spot 1 to 3 slides. In submitting the materials, you can tape the slides down the left hand side of a sheet of paper, in proper sequence, with an identification caption, and the script can be written out opposite each slide. Hand deliver your spots to the station(s). Again, you are up against a lot of competition for PSA time, and your spot may end up on the early dawn or late night schedule. Your creativity in preparing lively visuals, your persistence, and the fact that the spots have a local tie-in to the area are all factors in your favor, however.

Supply stations with stock slides or photos of the library (interior and exterior scenes) and a slide or card with the library logo which can be used when short announcements or brief news items are read. Submit a colorful slide or picture with the suggestion that it be used behind the call letters of the TV station during special periods, such as National Library Week.

An enterprising library publicist will find many ways to relate both local and national TV programing to the resources of the library. Books available at the library, by or about figures in the news, could be featured; cookbooks can be shown or mentioned on homemaking shows; book awards, both national and regional, are seldom covered locally, but might gain a spot on the air if the telecaster is supplied with information and visuals. It is up to you to establish contact at the station, learn the technical requirements, and suggest the variety of materials, relevant to scheduled programs, which you can supply.

News releases should be sent to the TV station(s) routinely, accompanied by good photos, if possible. Keep releases to a page or less, and use the same form as for radio releases. The TV coverage area of a station is larger than the city in which it is located, and items from outlying community libraries will be given consideration if they are newsworthy or of unusual human interest; broadcasters (and their advertisers) welcome opportunities to show interest in activities throughout the viewing range. The news gathering staff of a TV station is often very small, and so submission of legitimate news will be welcomed. In most cases, they won't know about it unless you tell them!

Cable casting is a form of television with which some libraries are extensively involved and with which others have a limited involvement. Whether or not this is the "wave of the future" for library service remains to be seen. Libraries can and do serve as the community broadcast center for the public access channel(s) or take active part in or prepare in-house productions for cable casting. Such activities require a reordering of priorities and a reexamination of the library's service program. The degree of participation depends upon the insight and understanding on the part of librarians, trustees, and local officials of the relative importance of this form of communication and information delivery plus a willingness to budget adequately for it.

Awash in a Sea of Print: The Library's Printed Materials and Publications

First Considerations

The variety and quantity of printed materials that libraries prepare for public distribution is astounding. Whether by choice or by chance, libraries are deep into the business of printing and publishing. Check off, for example, any of the following items that your library distributes or needs to prepare:

- Brochures: general, about the library; how to use the library; rules and regulations; special collections or special services
- Flyers (program, activity, or exhibit announcements)
- Booklists
- Newsletters: for general public; for staff; for special groups (children, senior citizens, etc.)
- Annual reports
- Bookmarks
- Posters
- Schedules, calendars, and directories
- Stationery, bookplates, overdue book notices
- Miscellaneous special purpose handouts (from quizzes, cookbooks, to bumper stickers)

It's readily apparent that some knowledge of graphics, printing processes, and distribution methods is essential if this flood of paper is to accomplish its purpose. But well before any consideration of mechanics, whether the piece is a brochure or a throw-away flyer, there are some questions to answer.

Why are you printing the piece? Is it to inform? Announce? Report? Ask for aid or support? The answer should be specific. If all you come up with is "to let people know about the library," maybe you should consider sky-writing instead.

Whom do you want to read it? If you don't know your potential audience, you are simply "shooting an arrow into the air and where it falls you don't much care."

How will it be distributed? A good many library communications are lost simply because little or no preliminary thought was given to methods of distribution.

Specific answers to these questions are essential because they will determine the textual content and tone, the format, and the number to be printed. For example, a printing project might be outlined in this way:

1. *Why?* To inform a selected group of the availability of program planning aids from the library (films, slides, speakers from the staff, other materials).

2. *Who?* Program planners or the presidents of 130 clubs and organizations in Cityville.

3. *How* distributed? By direct mail, using a list previously compiled by the Cityville Library.

This is relatively simple because the

New ideas

POP·UP overnight... Use the LIBRARY to keep on top

Bookmarks with all sorts of messages are standard library handouts.

DIAL-A-STORY
828-7311

A three minute recorded children's story available
24 hours a day as a public service of the
Bloomington (Withers) and Normal Public Libraries.

A bookmark can be used to call attention to a specific service.

target audience is easily defined. Now consider how you might approach the preparation of a brochure about the library.

1. *Why?* There may be several reasons, but they should be spelled out. (Then it may become apparent that one single piece will not do the job adequately.) Is the brochure intended to inform potential users about the library? Is it essentially a "fact sheet" for reference and reminder? A basic handbook? Has the library recently added new services or become a part of a system? Should it clarify or explain the mission of the library in the community, the purpose and philosophy? Is it a disguised "puff" piece to boost some egos?

2. *Who?* Anybody and everybody? No way. A descriptive handbook, for example, will be useful for reference by present and future card-holders, legislators, community leaders, and others who want in-depth information about the library operation; most libraries of any size may need one such comprehensive guide. But such a handbook or brochure should not be designed for mass consumption, since it would not interest the majority of people.

3. *How* will it be distributed? The answers to the "why?" and "who?" questions will determine the methods of distribution. A library guide or handbook, for example, might be distributed to all new card applicants, and handed out on request. Inexpensive folders should have a wider distribution, with all the possible dissemination methods

considered in advance. The target audience for special pamphlets should be reached in specific, preplanned ways.

Library communications, if they are to be read at all, must be attractive, easy to read, and competitive in appearance with the mass of printed material that descends on the public. The frustrations of time, budget, and occasionally too-many-cooks-in-the-broth hamper many libraries, as evidenced by the materials they produce.

More realistic budgeting may be necessary, but even more important is recognizing the fact that the quality of the printed materials the library produces directly reflects its attitude toward the people who are expected to read them.

Announcements of programs or activities for children and young people are a good case in point. Too often these are crudely printed on one side of a sheet of cheap mimeo paper. Children are attracted by color and pictures, and even very young children respond to good design. If you wish to attract their attention (and that of their parents) you must incorporate these elements into your announcement. (No good librarian buys or encourages the use of poorly designed books or other library materials; why, then, tolerate badly designed information about them?) An amateurish hand-lettered broadside both downgrades the effort put into preparing a program or activity and the importance that is attached to it by the library.

"Oh, children will come to the program. How you let them know about it is not important." Not true. It *is* important, both to you and to them. This is not to say that a children's program announcement—or any other—must be printed in four colors on a letterpress; indeed, it should not. What is needed is skill and imagination in the preparation, by whatever method, so as to reflect the quality of the service or materials offered. Dollars alone are not the answer, and may even be a hindrance if misused; a basic "how to" knowledge of graphics and design is far more important.

In short, you project an image of the library—good, bad, or indifferent—with every printed piece you produce.

Who, then, is going to turn out this properly-designed material? Few librarians have graphics training, or much knowledge of printing. The best answer, of course, is to hire a part- or full-time staff member with such experience. Staff and budget limitations often make this impossible, and so next best is to farm out the work to a free-lance artist on a per-job basis, or to contract with another community agency or other organization to share the services of a skilled person. The libraries in a system usually have access to professional graphics assistance from the system's staff. A community advertising agency or local ad club will often donate services; a talented Friend or volunteer may be available; art students in schools or community colleges may be able to help. One caution: there are some hazards in using "free" or near-free assistance. Deadlines may not be met; the person may be relatively inexperienced or be unwilling to take suggestions or criticism.

In any case, the person responsible for the production of printed materials must know enough about design and techniques to give good direction or supervision to an artist and a printer.

Printing Methods and Graphics Hints

There are some excellent books (see bibliography) which will help to acquire a working knowledge of graphics fundamentals. Familiarity with the advantages and limitations of the various methods of printing, whether done in-house or commercially, and with such terms as camera-ready copy, duotones, offset, etc., is essential. The principles of good layout should be studied. Although the examples given in many references are often done by high-cost printing methods, the principles can be adapted to a simple mimeograph or offset layout when they are understood. A home-study course can be set up by collecting at-

BE KIND

Don't color, mark or tear this book Nor leave it in a damp, dark nook

Don't read while slurping soup for lunch Pick dripless snacks if you must munch.

Washing hands is healthy for you And keeps a book looking nice, too.

To mark your place you never should turn down the corner. No, not good.

Beware of Baby Bob or Sue

You never know just what they'll do.

Should books get damaged let them be Leave fix'n to the library.

A bookmark can give some gentle instruction (Saint Paul Public Library).

REMEMBER There are others waiting ...

Please return this RESERVE BOOK as soon as possible

Squirrel Hill Branch
Carnegie Library
of Pittsburgh

A bookmark can be a gentle reminder.

The Fond du Lac City-County Bookmobile Gets the Show on the ROAD!

tractive materials from any and all sources, analyzing their appeal, and using them for models.

The major printing and reproduction processes are:

1. Commercial letterpress: This is most suitable when you want a large number of copies, and is relatively expensive.

2. Commercial offset lithography: This is usually less expensive, and is suitable for both long and short runs. Plates are made from photographs of the material to be printed. A considerable saving can be effected by supplying camera-ready copy.

3. Silk screen: This can be a do-it-yourself process or can be done commercially, using handmade or photographic stencils. It is best for short runs, for posters, signs, covers for booklists, etc.

4. Offset duplicating: This is an in-house process, using machines manufactured by such firms as A.B. Dick, Addressograph Multigraph, etc., and employs a photographic process. There is a wide range of models and prices.

5. Mimeograph: A stencil duplicating process.

6. Spirit duplicating: The familiar, unimpressive, and inadequate ditto process.

A bookmark can be a handy schedule reference (Fond du Lac Public Library, Wisconsin).

The choice of a printing process is determined by the purpose of the printed piece, quality desired, use of color and/or photographs, number of copies needed, as well as by the funds and equipment available.

If you can afford or justify the use of commercial printing for certain publications, you can effect economy in many ways. The more work you do yourself, the more you save on the final bill. Whether it is in the form of a layout and accompanying text for letterpress printing, or pasted-up, ready-to-go camera copy for offset, good, clean, *exact* copy is a must. Make any change before copy is set in type or photographed by the camera; any changes made later, other than printer's errors, are very expensive. Keep the amount of type that must be set to a minimum; 99 times out of 100, your text will be vastly improved when it is cut, simplified, and cut again.

You may want to get price quotations from several printers initially, but if you plan to have much printing done, you will find that constantly shopping prices is unduly time-consuming. Once you have found a printer who does good work at reasonable cost, you will be better off working with that person. When s/he understands your needs, s/he can also give you good advice on how to cut costs; for example, s/he will tell you about leftover paper that may be sufficient for a short run, similar to or better than what you may specify. Learn about down-time when business is slack, and plan ahead so that you can send in material during this period, for better service and a possible discount. Learn the printer's lingo, so that you can talk the same language. Use stock paper sizes so that you do not pay for waste. Order in standard quantities.

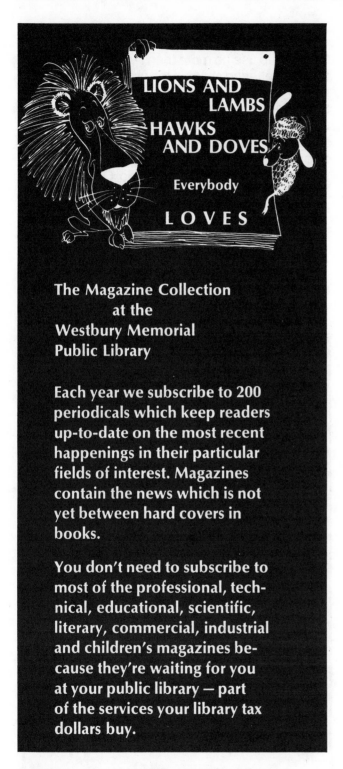

Sample Bookmark: Westbury (NY) Memorial Public Library

The text on the bookmark reads:

LIONS AND LAMBS
HAWKS AND DOVES
Everybody LOVES

The Magazine Collection at the Westbury Memorial Public Library

Each year we subscribe to 200 periodicals which keep readers up-to-date on the most recent happenings in their particular fields of interest. Magazines contain the news which is not yet between hard covers in books.

You don't need to subscribe to most of the professional, technical, educational, scientific, literary, commercial, industrial and children's magazines because they're waiting for you at your public library — part of the services your library tax dollars buy.

going back on the press for another run is an added expense. Quantities are important in another respect, because there are price breaks in a print run. The first 100 copies may cost $25, but the next 400 may only add $10 to the total. Will the piece be out of date soon? You can often lengthen the life of a brochure or other informational piece by eliminating names that may change (such as trustees or staff) or specific dates.

Using more than one color of ink will add to the cost, because this means that the paper must go through the press twice. However, it is frequently worth the small additional expense, and by imaginative use of colored paper stock, with black (which counts as one color) and a colored ink, you can achieve an effect that looks like much more. Another trick to cut costs of two-color printing is to standardize a format that you may use often, such as that for newsletters, notices, etc., and have a quantity run through the press in the color you want for standard headings, design motifs, etc. Stockpile this (the printer will store it) and use the stock as needed for later one-color runs.

Most libraries own or have access to a mimeograph or multilith machine, and it is probably safe to say that 95 percent of all library printing is done on these machines.

The results are not only frequently poor, but often this process is not suitable for the purpose of the printed material. Poor results cannot be helped if the machine is old and cranky, but a vast improvement is possible if the processes are exploited to their full extent. With some knowledge of the possibilities, more care and imagination in the preparation of stencils or plates, and greater attention to design, the results can be reasonably attractive. It does not take a great deal of skill to learn to run the machines, but it does take time and thought to prepare a good master.

Line drawings and halftones can be reproduced by both mimeograph and multilith processes, and two-color printing is possible. If you are not familiar with the mechanics of this, contact the representative of the manufacturer for advice and assistance.

The range of price for these office copiers is wide, from $500 for a new mimeograph up to thousands for a versatile offset duplicator. Unless you need a large number of copies of many different publications, it would be difficult to amortize the

Spend some time carefully estimating—not just guessing—your needs, so that you order no more than you can use. But remember, too, that cost of a new machine plus the time of the operator and the cost of supplies. For most medium and

---

". . . some printing no-no's . . ."

---

small libraries, it is far better to have a few good pieces printed commercially, and spend your time and energy on the design and layout that will do the job adequately.

Unless it is done very well, you really can't afford in-house printing for anything but routine pieces. It is wasteful if it is not adequate for the purpose and more costly than it appears on the surface in terms of staff time, maintenance, and materials.

The most common mistakes found in library printed materials (all of which can be avoided with a little care) are as follows:

1. *The body typeface is too small.* Eleven-point type is the most legible, and ten-point is acceptable, but smaller type is a strain, and most readers will simply skip the text. Typewritten copy prepared on a poor machine prints unevenly, and even illegibly, particularly when mimeographed. Copy written on a typewriter with a script face, a favorite with amateurs, should be outlawed! Italics should be used very sparingly; although they are intended for emphasis, they are lighter than the regular body type and fade into the page.

2. *The lines of body type are too long.* Use no more than 1½ to 2 alphabets (40 to 65 characters to a line or about 2½ to 3½ inches in width). Copy, particularly for newsletters and brochures, should be set in narrow columns.

3. *There is a lack of white space.* Crowding the text results in a loss of readership and thus imparts less, not more, information. Long blocks of copy should be broken up with spatial divisions, subheads, etc.

4. *The layout is too busy.* The eye is confused by a jumble of cuts, cartoons, inserts and other odd elements that distract from the message. To be on the safe side, use only one graphic element to a page.

5. *Too many different styles of typefaces are used, in either heads or text, or both.* A good rule of thumb is to use no more than two different typefaces or lettering styles in the heads and body of a piece. There are thousands of different typefaces, but 25 kinds do 75 percent of the work. Avoid using those fancy or esoteric typefaces for anything but an occasional special piece. (A flyer from a library public relations group, of all things, was a startling example of what not to do. On a single 8 × 10 sheet there were six different typefaces used, including serif faces, nonserif faces, blocks of copy written on a typewriter, and blocks of set and justified body type, plus a mishmash of drawings and graphic elements!) If you are making your own stencils or masters, learn about and use good lettering guides, leroy sets, and press-on letters.

This poster is the exception that proves the rule about not mixing type faces; here the variety is an integral part of the graphic design.

Freehand lettering or script is disastrous unless it is done by an expert.

6. *The copy is wordy, contains involved phrases and over-long sentences.* This tends to demonstrate a librarian's love of words, but it impedes communication. Write less and say more.

The following are some additional hints that do not appear in most standard printing and graphics references:

If you are using colored paper, avoid pale or washed-out tones, since they are no more effective than white paper. Orange, scarlet, or yellow-

---

". . . some printing do's . . ."

---

orange are exciting colors that will attract attention. Dark-colored papers do not read well because the contrast between the print and the paper is too low. Colored ink on white or light-colored paper can be effective if the difference in brightness is strong enough.

Always justify (make even) the left hand margin of textual material, but the right margin can be ragged in a one- or two-column layout. There is a method for justifying both margins of typewritten copy, which involves counting spaces and retyping each line; it is not worth the effort and frequently distracts the eye with strained spacing.

Boxing (drawing a line around) a block of copy is a graphic element that helps to break up a page, but it does not ensure greater readership; therefore, use it for design, not attention-getting purposes. Typographical devices, such as arrows, fancy underlines, and odd inserts and gimmicks (such as a Christmasy combination of red ink on green paper) lessen the readability and usually detract from rather than enhance the overall appearance.

Caps and lower case letters for heads are more legible and are preferred to all caps.

Check and recheck your copy for spelling and punctuation, and then have someone else read it. Despite your best efforts, an occasional misprint will creep in. Take heart from the story that columnist Sydney J. Harris tells. In the 18th century, some English professors attempted to pub-

A two-faced bookmark makes a "friendly" point.

lish a perfect specimen of typographical accuracy. Six experienced proofreaders were employed, who spent hours checking every page. After it was believed to be perfect, the text was posted for two weeks at the University and a reward was offered for anyone who could find an error. When it was finally printed, it was discovered that several errors had been committed—and one was on the first line of the first page!

Do not cut a line of type into a photograph. Place captions on every photo, directly below the picture.

Pictures or photographic illustrations are never too big, they are usually too small. Use fewer pictures, if necessary, but make them big enough to tell the story adequately. Photos with many people, such as at banquets, conferences, or board meetings, should not be used unless you have sufficient space for all the details to be seen and understood. If possible, organize photos into a picture story, or capture a moment that tells the story.

Illustrations can be secured from many sources. "Clip sheets," commercially prepared art for reproduction, are available from several sources. There's a wealth of material on your

Sample Bookmark: Purdue University Libraries (IN)

shelves in old magazines, catalogs, and books. Be careful of copyright, but if something you would like to use is still protected, you can usually get permission to reproduce it by writing to the proper source.

The size, shape, and format of a printed piece will be determined by several factors, one of the most important being the method of distribution. Is it to be mailed? A desk handout? To be kept for reference? Posted? Filed?

A flat 8½ × 11 inch piece of paper is pretty straightforward (and dull), but there are many attractive ways to cut and fold this standard size for brochures or flyers. Tricky overlaps, outsize sheets, and cutouts will add substantial costs to production; therefore, use these with great care. Discuss paper stock sizes with your printer or paper supplier before designing your printed piece: 8½ × 11 inches, 11 × 17 inches, and 17 × 22 inches are the usual standard bond and offset stock paper sizes for small pieces. Certain proportioned multiples will cut most economically, such as 5½ × 7½, allowing for trim. The amount of paper wasted by odd cuts in large runs can be very expensive; it is not a big factor in the total cost of a small run, however. Design all large pieces (posters, flyers, etc.) to fit the paper stock size, since waste in this case will add greatly to the total cost. Consult the printer, too, about folds, since these must be made in the direction of the grain of the paper, which in turn will determine the most economical cut size. Again, a

good collection of folders, flyers and brochures will give you ideas for future use.

Establish an identity for the library by using distinctive and consistent graphics. The recognition factor is important, and can be reinforced by choosing and using a unified style for similar materials.

This should not preclude variations and experiments, of course, because if everything you turn out looks the same, it will tend to be overlooked. At least once a year spread out all of your printed materials and take a good look at them. Has consistency turned into monotony? Do you need to revise, update, or brighten up the format of newsletters, flyers, or whatever?

Deadlines have a habit of creeping up and causing last-minute flurries and less-than-best results. This seems to be endemic with publicists but it can be avoided, at least most of the time, with a little forehanded backwards scheduling. If you fill in the following list and follow it as best you can, you will sleep better at night:

Date due for piece to be in hands of readers

_____

Date must be mailed, if applicable _____

Date material must be assembled (for collating, stapling, mailing, etc.)_____

Date printing must be completed _____

Date material must be completed for printing (artwork, layout, copy) _____

Date graphics and copy must be started _____

Date to initiate discussion, ideas, and outline of project _____

Test and evaluate the response to a proposed printed piece, especially an expensive one that will have a large print run. Don't just ask your co-workers or devoted patrons; try it out on a cross-section of the intended audience, wherever it may be. For important pieces, prepare as complete a dummy as possible, including sketches; you can photocopy this, color it by hand, and paste in duplicates of photos so as to closely resemble the finished product. Then be guided by the reactions of readers to the *clarity* and *effectiveness* of the message. (But don't try to revise to suit everyone's taste!)

Your distribution plan is a major factor in the effectiveness of your printed materials. It must be specific and understood at the very beginning of the project. Half of your work goes down the drain if the method of distribution is dismissed casually, "Oh, we'll hand out some at the desk, send a few to our mailing list." (That "hand it out at the desk" routine is one of the reasons for the poor results of many library promotional efforts.) If you make up a list of all possible distribution channels, both standard and innovative, you will have a quick reference for each new project.

The major categories for general public distribution are (1) by handout at the library, (2) by quantity deposit in other areas in the community, (3) by deposit with other individuals and organizations for hand distribution, (4) by posting in community areas, (5) by direct mail, and (6) through the mailings made by other agencies. Note all possibilities in your community under each category. Have you thought of waiting rooms, lobbies of office buildings, beauty shops, bookstores, racks at factories and large businesses, churches, schools, Welcome Wagon, local realtors, all civic, social, and special interest organizations?

Delivery of materials for distribution to various outlets will take time and personnel; make sure the method is planned in advance and build in the cost as part of the project, *since it is every bit as important as the cost of printing or mailing.* Who will put up the posters in the community? How will the flyers be delivered around town? Don't print them until you know!

Direct mail is a business, and you are undoubtedly part of it. Keep up-to-date on the frequent changes in postal regulations, and consult with the post office about ways to cut costs. Learn how to use nonprofit bulk mailings, and learn the current rules and costs for the various classes of mail.

You will want to compile your own mailing list for such regular publications as newsletters, annual reports, special flyers, etc. Develop categories for your list, if possible, because not everyone should receive all of the material you may be mailing throughout the year. Your list would likely contain the names of government officials, both local

and regional, trustees, Friends, heads of various community agencies or organizations, editors, individuals who have requested mailings, and exchanges with other librarians, local or state publications, etc. Mailing lists can also be compiled from various resources for special purposes—city directories, library card-holders, tax rolls, membership rosters of certain organizations, or the yellow pages of the telephone directory, for example.

Names on a mailing list are not set in concrete, although it often seems that way, and your list must be revised from time to time. One way to avoid too frequent changes is to use titles rather than individual names (President, Cityville Civic Association, rather than Mr. John Smith, President, Cityville Civic Association). After a period of time you may find it worthwhile to send out self-addressed postcards to those on your list asking if they want to continue receiving your publication or notices, or you can include a return form in your newsletter or announcement.

Large mass mailings such as to "rural box holder" or "resident" are best handled by a mailing service which has the facilities, lists, and equipment for this. There may also be occasions when you will want to buy or borrow the mailing lists of other organizations, such as the Chamber of Commerce, the School District, or the League of Women Voters.

Don't overlook the possibility of having a piece inserted with the bills or mailings made by others; utility companies, banks, telephone companies, community water companies, and large department store chains have all included library promotionals at one time or another.

WE HOPE YOU'LL SOON

MAKE TRACKS FOR

THE EAST SYRACUSE FREE LIBRARY
to return the materials you borrowed
several weeks ago!

A gentle reminder to return overdue books.

Checklist for Printed Materials

1. *What* is the objective of the piece, what do you want to accomplish?

   a. Inform a general group of a specific fact? (Announcement of a program or activity? A new service? A display?)

   b. Supply information about the library for general use? (A brochure describing hours and resources? An annual report? A newsletter for the public?)

   c. An attention-getter? (A reminder of the library's existence? Image-builder? A throwaway?)

   d. A piece to be used and referred to by a specific group? (A book list? A film catalog? A teacher or student manual?)

   e. A call to action? (Plea for financial support or donations? Formation of a Friends group? Formation of a citizen pressure group?)

2. *To whom* will this go? (General public? Selected general audience—i.e., walk-in patrons? Specific group—i.e., homemakers, business personnel, children?)

3. *How* will it be distributed? (Through a general or selected mailing? As an insert in someone else's mailing? As a handout in the library? As a handout in selected places— i.e., banks, group meetings? As a handout by other members of a group? Through community organizations? As a mass handout— i.e., supermarkets, shopping centers, fairs?)

Only after the previous questions have been answered, should you consider the following:

4. What *tone* of the piece will be most suitable for what you want to accomplish and for those who are expected to read it? (Dignified? Sophisticated? Folksy? Straightforward? Humorous? A flashy "grabber"?)

5. What is the expected length of time this will be usable? (One month? Six months? Two years?)

6. What will be the most suitable format? (A broadside—a single sheet flat or folded? A leaflet or folder? A poster? A brochure or booklet?)

7. Are the illustrations, proposed layout, and copy suitable to the tone and format?

8. What printing method will you use, and is it adequate and suitable for the purpose?

9. What will be your print run (number of copies)?

10. Will the format size you have chosen cut economically from stock paper?

11. Is the amount you plan to spend commensurate with the purpose?

12. Will you print this one color on white paper, one color on colored paper, two colors on white, two colors on colored paper?

13. After the general decisions have been made, possibly by a committee, is *one* person assigned to supervise or do the layout and copy?

14. Is the language and writing style of the copy appropriate?

Library Brochures

Library brochures range from simple folders giving facts about the resources, activities, hours, and regulations to elaborate booklets explaining the organizational structure and the philosophy of library service. Indeed, many libraries prepare both types for use with different audiences. Inasmuch as they are intended for referral over a period of time, they should be done in a format that will be kept, and not thrown away after a casual glance.

Preparation of a brochure must start with a determination and understanding of its purpose. Is it to be an introduction to the library to promote

Sample Brochure: Atlanta (GA) Public Library

usage and for easy reference? Or is it essentially a guide, with an explanation of how to use the various resources? It is almost impossible to combine the two and achieve both purposes effectively.

A folder or brochure is the mainstay of your printed output, and as such, it deserves careful thought, good graphics, and attractive printing. If there is no way to squeeze the printing cost out of the budget, this is surely a legitimate occasion to seek funding from Friends, business organizations, or other sympathetic groups.

The following basic information should be included:

- Name of the library, sponsoring agency (township, city, or county, etc.), affiliation, if any, with a regional library system
- Location, including street address, and telephone number
- A concise statement of the purpose and aims of the library
- Days and hours of service
- Materials and services available locally
- Regulations regarding use
- Extended services available through any regional unit of which the library is a part

Sample Brochure: Iowa State Traveling Library

Beyond these essentials, you may want to include additional information about major collections, special rooms available, number of holdings, bookmobiles or branches, a brief history, special features or services, names of the director, staff members, and trustees. A sentence or two about how the library is governed and financed should be included; community surveys have revealed that an unconscionable number of people have no knowledge of these matters.

Beware of trying to include too much or complex information, since this will deter the average reader or intimidate the potential user. Floor plans, instructions on how to use the card catalog, information about the classification system, indices, etc., are more properly included in a handbook or orientation guide for selected distribution within the library. The basic brochure need answer only the major questions: What and where is the library? What can it do for me? When and how do I get access to the materials and service?

A brochure will need periodic updating, particularly if schedules and names are included; revisions can be minimized if those items subject to change are grouped on one page or section. Then only one part needs to be reset when reprints are ordered. Annual or current material can also be included as a loose insert.

The tone of the copy should be positive; you are, in essence, issuing an invitation. The content is organized in decreasing order of importance, and headings should be selected for clarity and to attract attention, with emphasis on the reader's interests.

Watch your language and eliminate the negative. This applies especially to that necessary bugbear, statements about the rules and regulations imposed by the library. Too often it seems that the librarian-designer is more interested in spelling out what the potential user can't or must do to enjoy library privileges than in persuading the user of the advantages. Keep all regulatory information to a minimum and don't feature it conspicuously. These typical statements, culled from actual brochures, could be tactfully rephrased:

"Books are charged out for four weeks. No renewals." Try, *The Library has a liberal policy of loaning books for a four week period for your convenience. Because of this extended loan period, books cannot be renewed for the sake of others who may be waiting for the material you borrowed.*

"No encyclopedias or reference books may be withdrawn." Try, *Numerous encyclopedias and reference books are kept in the library, available for your use in the bulding at all times.*

"Only four records can be borrowed at one time." Try, *Up to four records may be borrowed for your listening pleasure for a week at a time.*

Eliminate such phrases as "Any breakage or damage shall be the responsibility of. . . .," "The patron bears full responsibility for. . . ." Take out

the words "no," "only," "must," and rephrase the sentence.

Use a light-hearted heading, such as "Some Rules that Keep This Place Running without Spoiling Your Fun" or "Sharing Is a Must and We Need Your Help. This means bringing books back on

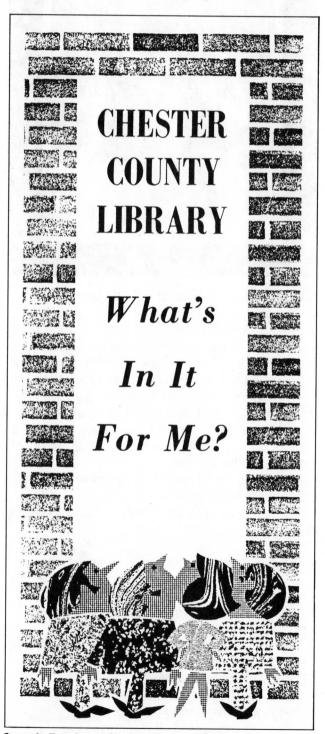

Sample Brochure: Chester County (PA) Library

time. If materials must be kept beyond the due date, a fee of 5¢ per day is charged."

If you have a long list of rules and regulations that you feel you must spell out in detail, it is far better to list them on a separate card or sheet for distribution within the library to actual users and new card applicants.

Eliminate any professional jargon from the text; "interlibrary loan," "audiovisual," "stacks" and similar terms make a reader wary of trying to use something new or different. A personal or conversational tone will often increase interest,

and a little humor will go a long way to relieve necessary but dull information.

The appearance and overall character of your leaflet or brochure portray an image—lively, inviting, contemporary, or staid, forbidding, indifferent—to the reader. The common practice, for example, of using a photo or sketch of the library building on the cover simply emphasizes the image of a building rather than a service. Inasmuch as some library buildings are undistinguished architecturally and only the very near-sighted have difficulty finding them in the community, this choice of illustration subconsciously reflects a storehouse orientation, or undue pride in brick and mortar.

There is no single format that is preferred, and folders, leaflets, or brochures may take many shapes and forms. Methods of distribution are an important consideration, so many are designed as self-mailers or are sized to fit a standard envelope. Clarity and simplicity are the keynotes to a good piece; with the addition of a little color, a theme or attention-getting caption, and a good illustration or attractive graphic, the piece will fulfill its purpose.

Many libraries supplement a general brochure with one for special groups, such as children, teenagers, the home-bound, government officials, etc., with more specific information directly related to the interests and needs of those groups. Most library systems or cooperative units also prepare a brochure that explains what a system is, the area it covers, and the activities and services undertaken. Although the concept of networking and cooperation is well understood by the profession, it is a relatively new idea to the general public, and must be described in terms that relate to the individual and the local library if it is to be meaningful.

Booklists

Preparing booklists is such a traditional library activity and so dear to a librarian's heart that to question the value and function is rank heresy. Nevertheless, booklists are generally ineffective as a promotional tool and the preparation of them often takes a disproportionate amount of time, effort, and money at the expense of other public information activities. A bit of soul-searching is in order so that their production receives the proper

Baltimore County Public Library

is
PEOPLE
and
SERVICE
and
YOU

Sample Brochure: Baltimore County Public Library

priority and there is a clear understanding of the purpose beyond that of tradition and habit.

The designation "booklist" is something of a misnomer, because a good list should include

---

". . . three ways to use booklists . . ."

---

nonbook materials (cassettes, newspaper and magazine articles, films, pamphlets, or filmstrips) when appropriate.

Booklists can be useful in three ways:

1. If they are of wide and timely interest, presented in an attractive format, and brought to the attention of the general public through planned publicity and distribution.

2. If they meet a measurable and recurring patron demand.

3. If they are made up for specific groups, either on request or as a means of demonstrating the library's resources to nonpatrons or influential members of the community.

In choosing the subject matter, the following advice appeared in the article "Creative Booklisting," by Rose McGlennon Best in *PNLA Quarterly,* Summer, 1971, Volume 35, Number 4:

1. Will enough patrons care? In small libraries it is easy to note what people ask for, books on dogs, disasters, lawyers, and crime, for instance, and supplying the answer is guaranteed to be a happy choice. (An interest may exist, though unexpressed. No one ever asked us for books on eccentrics, but "They Dared to be Different" proved to be our most popular list.) A large library means a large clientele with a great variety of interests and the books to satisfy them. Even if you do a list on mushroom culture or Japanese inro you may fill a need, but you had better wait for a hint from your public. On the other hand, don't underestimate your readers: there may be an Eric Hoffer among them. Consider the enormous sales of worthy nonfiction paperbacks.

2. Is the subject so popular that all the books about it are usually in circulation? Then they don't need advertising. Furthermore, it irritates a reader to have his appetite whetted, then frustrated. Post the list of the current best-sellers from the Sunday papers, but make your selected list of them after they have become "Great Books of the Century." Current controversial issues must be regarded in this light. No subject could be more timely than Vietnam, but unless books are set aside for adult use, students will have borrowed every available item.

3. Consider the life expectancy of a list. It is economical to choose a subject which will not go out of date too soon, as new editions with minor changes and additions can be made from time to time. The timely interest of books for Mother's or Father's Day, however, is guaranteed to recur.

4. Does a good, readily available list cover the subject? National organizations prepare excellent lists dealing with brotherhood, mental health, child development, etc., which can be checked against your holdings and offered to the public with no further effort on your part.

5. Could a patron get the same list by using the card catalog? There is no use in duplicating the cataloger's effort at considerable trouble and expense, and the non-selective compilation of everything listed under one subject heading makes a very dull list, as it removes the elements of creativity and enthusiasm that make a list fun for compiler and user alike. You will enjoy choosing a theme, e.g., Courage or Women, that takes you thru many classifications, challenging your knowledge of books in many areas.

Some booklist subjects are standard and seemingly inevitable, but the major purpose of a list—an invitation to read about something (or listen or view)—is totally lost in the ubiquitous "New Books" or "What's New" listing, or the bland and pointless "Did You Miss?" or "Old but Good." If these were dispensed with entirely, it is very unlikely that they would ever be missed by 99 percent of library users. The truly significant list is likely to be a challenge to the reader to learn something new or will contain references on both sides of controversial questions, the life-related issues and concerns of Everyman. The subjects chosen are a fair indication of what the library thinks is important to call to the attention of its present and potential clientele, and anything on the order of "Books for Building Birdhouses" hardly qualifies. (So, OK, type up one copy of a list of such titles for quick reference within the library if you must, but save your printing efforts for the 500 or 5,000 copies of something that could or should interest that many.)

The format of the booklist should be in keeping with the subject matter, with a title or caption to intrigue the reader. The number of titles to be included will vary with the subject, but remember that a booklist is *not* a bibliography. It is a sampling at various levels to interest someone in a particular subject, to indicate the variety of materials available on the subject, and to suggest additional sources for the reader to pursue. If the list is long and exhaustive, it may discourage or confuse; if very short, it indicates a paucity of resources on the subject or causes an undue run on a few titles. Small libraries with limited holdings can often issue very useful lists by including materials available on interlibrary loan, with an explanation of the procedure.

A list that is expected to serve as a standard reference over a period of time should be prepared in a substantial form that will encourage users to save and file away; others may be "quickies" designed to capitalize on a current interest that may soon fade.

Annotations are a must, whether a brief line or two or a short commentary. Fiction titles, particularly, are seldom a clue to content. Many libraries, for example, issue an annual updated list of Newbery Medal or other winners, but if only the title, author, and date of award are listed, it is relatively meaningless to the average reader, and if a book must be sought out on the shelves to determine what it is about, interest will wane rapidly.

Booklist cover designs or illustrations can often be taken or adapted from the books listed (with permission, of course, if copyrighted) or from book

===

"... more than a 'book' list ..."

===

jackets. Color, photographs, striking graphics, and abstract designs are important points to consider to attract attention.

Some recently-issued booklists have incorporated ideas worth considering. Several from the Elgin County Library (St. Thomas, Ontario) carry

this message in the front: "USE THIS LIST AS AN ORDER FORM! If the book you want has been borrowed by someone else, put a mark or underline it on the list and print your name, address, and telephone number on the bottom of the page. Tear out the page and give it to the librarian. She will either send you a card or phone you when your book is in."

A list compiled in conjunction with a library program on gems and minerals at the East Meadow (New York) Public Library went beyond a simple title listing by including definitions and explanations of various related terms. A Baltimore County Public Library folder, "The Tale of a Comet," contained facts about comets and a diagram, with a short suggested reading list. "Scary Tales" from the Buffalo and Erie County (New York) Public Library was a large striking poster.

When the Metropolitan Opera came to Memphis, the Memphis/Shelby County Public Library prepared a folder that was much more than a booklist. The cast for each performance was named, and a synopsis of the story prepared. Then books about the Metropolitan Opera itself, books and magazine articles about the starring singers, and related recordings, scores, and librettos were listed. The booklist "Buyer Be Aware," prepared by the Burbank Public Library, was an information list as well; in addition to useful book, magazine and newspaper titles, there were sections on telephone numbers to call, suggestions on how to make a complaint, addresses to write, and volunteer organizations to contact. A miscellaneous list of books in various categories was printed on one side of a large 22- × 16-inch sheet by the Enoch Pratt Free Library (Baltimore), and the other side was designed to be folded into a book cover, with the caption, "We protest the loss of books from library shelves . . . GO PLACES WITH BOOKS BUT BRING THEM BACK."

Although booklists should contain information about nonbook materials related to the subject, separate folders or brochures with a sampling of titles or categories of holdings of cassettes, films, slides, records, framed art, sculpture replicas, group play reading scripts, music scores, or periodicals and newspapers are useful if the collection warrants them.

Many good booklists never get off the counter because they are not publicized or distributed outside the library, and it is difficult to justify their production for the faithful few. Gauging the amount of potential interest, and thus the number you should print, is not always easy, but if it is based solely on a standard (500 copies) or the number you got rid of last time, you may be underestimating the value or usefulness simply because enough people never learned about it.

Publicize the availability of new lists in your releases to the media and in your own publications; make selected mailings; post a sample in well-trafficked areas in the community. Some lists are suitable for distribution by community agencies; banks, for example, for a list on money management, supermarkets for a cookbook list, children's clothing or toy stores for a children's reading list. This helps to justify the time and expense that goes into the preparation—which is far more than the actual printing cost.

Limited interest lists, in smaller quantities and inexpensively reproduced, can be both a service and a good form of library promotion when distributed directly to specific groups. A booklist on baby care, for example, can be sent to new parents whose names appear in newspaper notices, or a suitable folder can be sent to prospective brides. Check your community events calendar and prepare a list of related materials that could also be inserted into the program that is handed out at a concert, circus, play, dance performance, or opera, as the example cited from Memphis. A colorful "Booked for Travel" brochure, issued by the Gilbert M. Simmons Library in Wisconsin, listing the dates and suggested readings for each of the 12 lectures in a series at the Kenosha Public Museum, was a good example of interagency cooperation.

A sample copy of a booklist and a request form for additional copies should be sent routinely to all agencies or organizations with an interest in the subject, as an aid in reaching a target audience.

Library Newsletters

Following the lead of other agencies, more and more libraries are producing newsletters for in-house distribution and for public communication. One wiseacre has pointed out that, when four people "organize," one sets about writing a newsletter, one reads it, and two use it for a laundry list.

The challenge, then, is to produce one that is so interesting and informative that it will be read avidly by more than the editor, the people whose names are mentioned, and the compulsive types who read anything, including cereal boxes.

A newsletter is neither newspaper nor letter, but combines some of the features of both. It contains news, but the news is limited to information about a single agency. Like a letter, it is informal in tone, and assumes a reciprocal interest. "The basic function of a newsletter as a public relations vehicle is to inform a special audience in a special way. It is strictly an on-target medium," according to Richard Toohey, President of PR Aids, in a recent company newsletter.

Library newsletters fall into two classifications; those intended for internal distribution (library-associated personnel) and those for external distribution (selected or general public). They are two distinctly different publications.

The purposes of both types are similar in that they are to provide information about the institu-

". . . staff newsletters . . ."

tion's philosophy, policies, and activities, to ensure understanding, and to enlist support.

Internal or staff newsletters have a very specialized audience and a high level of readership if the editorial material is interesting and relevant, because reader interest in any publication increases with the amount of personal involvement. A local newsletter will usually be read before that of a state association, a state before a national. This built-in motivation is blunted, however, if the writing is pedantic or the material simply a miscellaneous jumble of unrelated items.

A staff newsletter plays on the desire to be in on what is going on. For good or bad, it is a major vehicle for communicating administrative policies—communicating, that is, not laying down the law. It can also be a forum for discussion of the pros and cons of policy decisions from the staff viewpoint, and should try to bring out the topics discussed soto voce in the staff lounge, with the questions raised and the reactions. It should contain reports of board meetings, and news of local, state, or national library legislation which affects individuals and the library.

Sample Newsletter: Prince George's County (MD) Memorial Library System

Sample Newsletter: Queens Borough Public Library

Feature material, such as reports on various aspects of library service, interviews, or biographical sketches of trustees and staff members with special responsibilities helps to build a better understanding of all aspects of the library or library system. A summing-up of the number and type of meetings held in the library, number of news releases issued, publications prepared, new materials received, and other statistics can be useful information for all library personnel. Succinct reports by attendees of professional meetings or workshops are valuable for the stay-at-homes.

Most internal newsletters report on staff changes and activities, both personal and professional. A word of warning on "social notes": don't try to beat the grapevine. Assess the amount of interest in that too-typical item, "Mary Jane spent her vacation in California, visiting her parents. Welcome back, Mary Jane." But human interest items are essential—the news, comments, anecdotes that help to make the staff feel like part of the organization.

Occasionally the editor should take a survey to determine staff readership and interests. It may come as a surprise to find, as one such survey did, that the staff was most interested in more information about board and administrative actions and policy, about employment or promotional opportunities, important future dates and meetings, all in the form of features or news, and not as editorials disguised as "Memos from the Director."

Regular reports about activities in the branches or system member libraries, or other libraries in the area, are often included for an exchange of ideas.

A little humor and some occasional trivia help to keep the reader going. Newsletters have included recipes from the staff, crossword puzzles, reprints of letters received from patrons, a question-of-the-month ("Which library in the system keeps a jigsaw puzzle on the front table so patrons can work at it at their leisure?"). When one library system newsletter threw out the challenge, "How many words can you make from the letters in

CLASSIFICATION?" the response from member librarians was solid evidence that the issue had been read.

Brevity, regularity of issue, and a recognizable format are additional ingredients of a good newsletter. The number of essential, relevant, and interesting items should determine the number of pages, from one to eight. (If it is very long and wordy, it usually goes to the bottom of the in-pile!) The newsletter should come out at regular intervals—biweekly, monthly, or bimonthly. Less frequent issues lose both immediacy and identification.

Staff newsletters are usually printed in-house, and are not elaborate productions, nor need they be. A simple format, a few discreetly used graphics to liven the pages, headlines to help readers find the sections or items they are most interested in, and a judicious use of white space will be sufficient. Teacher and graphics consultant Edmund C. Arnold summed it up, "Form is far less important than content. If your publication carries information that the reader is interested in, that can be used to achieve desirable goals, that is friendly and sprightly in tone, that is brief, and—above all!—is accurate and dependable, then the reader will forgive all your typographic sins."

". . . external newsletters build good will . . ."

External newsletters—those intended for the public—can be a potent public information aid. They supply information and news about services, programs, materials, policies, and problems to a target audience, material which is often too specialized for other media. They can build goodwill and an expanded vision of the library as a vital community resource. Success depends on three factors: good editorial content, attractive format, and effective distribution to a selected readership.

Defining the target audience is more difficult than for an internal newsletter, but the failure to do so results in an uneconomical communication process. It must get into the hands of people who are or will be motivated to read it. It must contain information of interest to them, presented in a form that encourages them to read or at least scan the material.

What is the target audience? It might very well be all the residents or households of a small community. It could be all present card-holders. Or it may be a selected group which includes interested patrons, Friends, community opinion leaders,

Sample Staff Newsletter: Baltimore County Public Library

Sample Newsletter: Plainedge Public Library (Massapequa, NY)

Sample Newsletter: Arlington Heights (IL) Memorial Library

organization officers, government officials, trustees, donors, and media representatives.

Its function is akin to the purposes espoused by other organizations or businesses—to keep membership or "stockholders" informed about what is going on and foster the feeling of getting inside information.

Most newsletters carry schedules of programs, activities, displays, bookmobile stops, and a listing of branches or member libraries, as a ready reference for the reader. In Massapequa, New York, a survey of the readers of the Plainedge Library newsletter, which is mailed to every household in the community, indicated that 85 percent of the respondents learned about library programs and activities from the newsletter, and only 26 percent cited the newspaper as a source.

News from and about Friends, photos and blurbs about staff members and trustees (the "inside stuff"), and a discussion of selected new materials are often included.

A special issue of the newsletter can serve as an annual report, and is a good place to explain the proposed budget. Statistics can be handled with a light touch and still retain meaning. An occasional list of memorial or gift donations is a subtle hint to others and recognition of the donors. Highlights of significant programs sponsored by the

library can be reported, and news of local authors' publications may be of interest.

A newsletter can be a good vehicle for editorial comment (your side of the story). The Queens Borough Public Library (New York) *News,* for example, issued a special edition in the summer of 1976, with a big bold 60-pt. headline, "LIBRARY STRUGGLING TO SURVIVE $$ CUTS." A photo of a board meeting was captioned, "A grim Library Board of Trustees, faced with crippling budget cuts, ponders how best to serve the entire borough."

A newsletter offers an opportunity to blow your own horn, subtly or blatantly. For example, *Voices,* the Mobile (Alabama) Public Library publication, took a pat on the back with, "We continue to help the advertising agency which is handling the Sunday 'Historical' ads for the American National Bank. It has been reported to us that John Doremus, well-known announcer . . . will make use of the material and *credit will be given to the library."* (More inside stuff.)

The Whatcom County Library (Bellingham, Washington), among others, has reprinted short articles from other publications that are of possible interest to the readers of "Going Places with Books." Use this ploy sparingly, if at all, for there may be a temptation to cut too wide a swath in your coverage.

The textual format can be varied occasionally with a piece written in the form of a conversation or question-and-answer with the library director, a staff member, or a board member.

Fillers that are made up, picked up from other sources, or contributed by staff (possibly under duress!) help to break up blocks of text and catch the reader's eye. Here's part of one that appeared in *Library Lines,* from the St. Clair County Library, in Mississippi:

How Well Do You Know the Best Sellers?

Clues

1. I can't believe I ate the whole thing!
2. When the sirens weren't squealing, they were singing.
3. Title of a novel that appeared on TV.
4. Looking for __ ___.

Answers

1. Jaws
2. The Choirboys
3. Rich Man, Poor Man
4. Mr. Goodbar

BOOKNEWS

BURNABY PUBLIC LIBRARY   **VOLUME 8 NUMBER 1**

DID YOU KNOW . . .

...that it may be illegal to set your suitcase or packsack down on a public sidewalk in Kelowna?

...that people on welfare in B.C. can't receive compensation under the Criminal Injuries Compensation Act without jeopardizing their welfare payments?

...that one section of the Criminal Code makes it illegal to entice someone to commit an act that is not illegal? (Although prostitution is not illegal, soliciting for prostitution is.)

The obviously criminal character in our photo was collared by the law several times every week for six years. He is Paul Soles of "This is the Law," an entertaining panel show of CBC-TV that ran weekly from 1971 until it was cancelled last year. Do not fret. Now you can get any legal information you need from Burnaby Public Library.

THIS IS THE LAW

Photo: C.B.C.

EXPANDED LEGAL COLLECTION IN THE BURNABY PUBLIC LIBRARY

One of the more beneficial outcomes of the turbulent 60's was a growing concern for citizens' access to the law which resulted in the 70's in a host of self-help programs and activities. The Legal Aid Society was established in 1970, followed closely by the Vancouver Legal Assistance Society in 1971 and the Vancouver People's Law School. At that time, a private firm, Self-Press, publishing...

result in a major expansion of our legal information capabilities. The Commission made funds, advice and training available to Burnaby Public Library for purchase and use of complete and up-to-date statutes and regulations from both federal and provincial governments. In addition, several comprehensive guides to specific legal topics and government publications have been purchased and a fascinating and useful "case law" available.

cases, some going away back to the earliest period of British jurisprudence — perhaps even to the Magna Carta. In other words, the outcome of a case you are involved in may be affected by a decision made a few months ago or years ago, perhaps even in another province.

We are gathering materials will be of interest to Burnaby in such matters as credit, tenant relations, family industrial relations, business employment benefits, rials v...

Sample Newsletter: Burnaby Public Library (British Columbia, Canada)

All of the suggestions about graphics and formats described earlier also apply to your newsletter. If you are starting a new one or redesigning one, it will pay to get an experienced graphic artist to design a standard masthead, standing heads, and suggested page layouts, since you will be using them for a long time. A stock of blue line layout sheets can be printed or hand-drawn in advance to facilitate copy-fitting and dummying. Most newsletters are 8½ × 11 inches in size, and they run from 4 to 12 pages. An eye-catching title, preferably with some relevancy to the library, can be composed with a little effort; "Ad-Libs," "Read-Out," "Et Cetera," "Bookings," "Branching Out," "The Insider," "Update," "Sum and Substance," "The Imprint," and "Footnotes" are some that various libraries use.

There is an ongoing argument about whether it is better to write copy at a sixth- or twelfth-grade reading level. Some experts claim that sixth-grade writing is resented by readers; others that twelfth-grade level is not understood by the majority. It would be a mistake to assume that all readers of your newsletter are college-educated library users, and, in any case, simple language does not offend educated people. Brevity of writing carries the most weight, and that requires clear direct sentences.

Evaluate your newsletter from time to time, and get some feedback in various ways. A survey of the readership, by mailed questionnaire, by phone, or by insert in the publication, will give you valuable reaction to the contents, length, and format. A publications advisory group, composed of staff representatives, reader representatives, and one or more professional journalists, can be very helpful. Solicit their frank comments, and take criticisms and suggestions with an open mind. Be willing to give up your favorite gimmicks if they are questioned or receive a negative response.

Workshops on the subject of newsletter production are offered occasionally by schools or library associations and are worth attending. If this is not feasible, a professional journalist might be approached to give you a critical evaluation for a small fee.

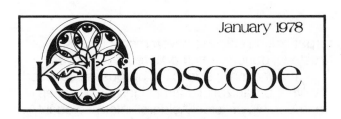

January 1978

Kaleidoscope

Sample Masthead: Memphis/Shelby County Public Library

A good program for distribution is essential, as always. A selective mailing list can be compiled, if one does not exist. It's a good idea to send a letter, with a personal signature of the library director or a trustee, with the first issue mailed, or to someone new to the list to assure the interest of the recipient. The mailing list should be examined periodically, so that it does not become static. A good list will grow substantially and change over a period of time; if it does not, it is missing the mark. Additions to the list should be sought out in various ways. With each issue, send marked copies of stories that would interest people who are not on your regular list, concerning exhibits, special collections, program highlights, etc. A copy of your newsletter might be inserted in the mailing of another organization, with a subscription return reply card or blank. Sample copies can be put in a conspicuous place, both in the library and other

Sample Newsletter: Evansville/Vanderburgh County Public Library (IN)

places, with a large sign saying "Take One." Ask other people to suggest names for a sample mailing.

Some libraries in small communities mail copies of their newsletters to all community residents. This is not a clearly defined audience and interest in the library cannot be assumed; therefore content coverage must be broader in scope. The newsletter of the Plainedge Public Library includes information about other community agencies, educational opportunities in the community, and short features on consumer information. The Salem Public Library, in Massachusetts, mails its bimonthly newsletter to families of all library cardholders in the community, and estimates that it reaches 60 percent of the homes. The Library reported that attendance at programs increased dramatically and hundreds of calls were received after the first issue was mailed, with the end result that more people made greater use of all library facilities.

Mass distribution of the monthly newsletter of the East Islip Public Library, in New York, was accomplished by placing copies in all supermarkets, three post offices, four banks, and six other businesses. Copies were also given to all library

program attendees. In addition, a children's edition goes out ten times a year to all school children in the district through the interschool delivery service. The Library bundles the copies for each classroom and labels them with the teacher's name.

The cost of printing a newsletter for public distribution is a substantial budget item, but if it is to be done at all, it should be done well. In Peach County, Georgia, the "Peach Poster" was printed as a public service of the Blue Bird Body Company, and this was prominently noted on the front page. In some communities the library "piggybacks" by using a section of a newsletter distributed throughout the area by the city, county, or the school district when it cannot afford to produce its own.

Annual Reports—Playing the Numbers Game

A detailed, statistic-filled administrative report and/or audit for the use of their governing bodies is a legal obligation of almost all public libraries. But an annual report to the public and tax-payers is both more and less than that. It is an opportunity to explain and justify the expenditure of tax money and contributions, an increasingly important task in the face of greater demands for accountability. An annual report intended for the public is more than a financial disclosure; it is a picture of the library's nature and activities. It should be readable as well as informative; it should be good promotional publicity as well as an accounting. This is especially important if the library does not issue a newsletter or if media coverage is poor.

To produce a truly useful piece that will be widely read requires some hard thinking about content and considerable imagination in designing a format and approach to catch the public's attention.

The annual report should be a factual record of the library's accomplishments and activities in the year past; a record that is only partially revealed by figures and statistics.

Don't play the numbers game. When you do only that, you force readers to play their own game—to see if the totals are ahead of last year's—and they draw conclusions which may not

Sample Annual Report Cover: Glenview (IL) Public Library

be justified. If, for example, circulation statistics show that juvenile circulation has dropped (as it has in many libraries across the country), the reader may simply conclude that kids aren't coming to the library any more. But what about all those who attended story hours, watched films, joined the Summer Reading Program, or just came in to browse? The library's thrust of service to youngsters may be changing, and this needs explanation, perhaps even justification, to those who hold a traditional view of the library's role. Figures may also be meaningless to the average reader. Is the fact that the book collection now numbers 120,000 volumes good, bad, or indifferent for a community of your size? Or a circulation of 271,000 volumes? Compared to what? Last year? Ten years ago? A comparable community elsewhere? What *does* it prove? Obviously you need some well chosen words as well as numbers.

As a beginning, discard the title "Annual Report." As a matter of fact, your report to the public need not be an annual January 1st affair. Perhaps

you will find it possible to issue a substantial, well-planned report only every two years, four years, on a special occasion or anniversary, or when there have been some significant changes and developments. If so, either design it so an insert can be added yearly, or supplement the long-term report annually with a simple one-page sheet that briefly summarizes the past year's budget and expenditures.

There is no hard and fast rule as to the time to release such a report. If it is an annual summary, you may get better news coverage within a few weeks after the close of the fiscal year. On the other hand, National Library Week is a good time to issue a report; or you may hold off until a few weeks before budget time to bolster and reinforce public support.

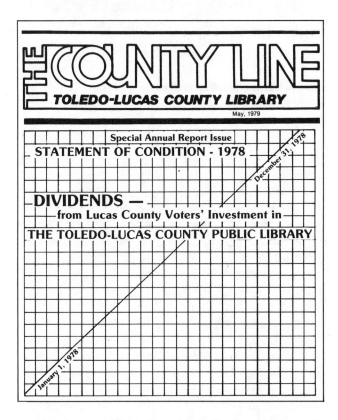

Sample Annual Report Cover: Toledo-Lucas (OH) County Public Library

Gather and assemble material for your report throughout the year, not in the month or last weeks before it is due. Keep notes of significant activities and events, and ask for memos and suggestions from department heads. In fact, as soon as your current report is issued, decide on a tentative format and theme for your next, to ease the chore of collecting material and to avoid the trauma of last minute decisions.

The content of your report is no problem when you have facts and figures available from records, minutes, newspaper clippings, etc. The *real task* is to "sift and winnow" for the material that is significant, important, and interesting.

As Claudine Smith pointed out in the December, 1971 issue of *News From the State Library* (Ohio), "One of the major reasons some annual reports fail to stir much interest is that all items are treated equally. The result is that nothing sticks in the reader's mind. Each year's report does not need to cover every aspect of your services. It is far better to pick a few items and give them more detailed attention than to try to cover everything." And, "The report should spell out accomplishments to benefit the reader . . . in terms of the reader's own experience."

A simple theme will help to give your report cohesion and interest. If you wish to stress growth, or improved service through interlibrary cooperation or systems, or to point out facets of community involvement through special activities or outreach programs, choose this for major emphasis on your cover, in illustrations if any, and in the headings and text.

Your theme need not be original; a good idea that has worked for someone else can often be adapted. For example, the idea of presenting the library as a money-saving institution has been picked up and used by many libraries. One year the East Meadow Public Library in New York showed that an individual starting a library at home (by purchasing one popular book, a record, a super-8 film, and a dictionary) would spend 83¢

more than the average cost per family in taxes for access to *all* the library's materials and services.

The Huntsville-Madison County Library in Alabama phrased it this way:

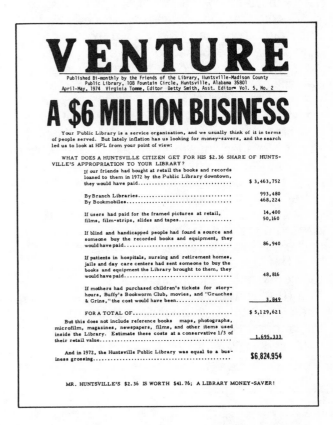

The Pickens County Library (South Carolina) adapted this theme. With a heading, "We saved these people $1,181,295.16," the report itemized the costs of the books borrowed or services used if they had been purchased by individuals. The Massena Library (New York) followed the same format, concluding with the statement, "We gave you a $83.65 dividend on a $7.24 investment."

The East Baton Rouge (Louisiana) Parish Library asked, "What can you get for $2.94? A ticket to a ball game? A small piece of meat? A necktie? $2.94 was the per capita cost of operating the East Baton Rouge Parish Library in 1973." Other highlights of its annual report pointed out, in dollars and cents, "your $2.94 made you a part-owner in 8 branch libraries, 1 bookmobile. . . . You could not take your $2.94 and buy a new book or subscribe to a magazine. Your $2.94 that went to the library added 26,564 books to your collection, which now numbers 292, 736. You own 1,773 microfilmed periodicals of which 455 were added in 1973. You

Sample Annual Report Cover: Orlando (FL) Library System

received 11 newspapers and 343 magazines with your $2.94. . . . Your $2.94 made you a stockholder in a business with a budget of $886,559. You've got a good thing going!''

The Cahaba Regional Library (Alabama) report asked, ''Are you getting your money's worth?'' and pointed out that, if the system libraries had sold all the items loaned to people, they would have grossed over two million dollars in retail sales. If patrons had purchased the items loaned to them, they would have paid $1,005,295 for books, $63,395 for recordings, $738,000 for films and filmstrips. Using a stock report form, headed Public Libraries, the ''report'' was that each dollar invested brought back $27.56 in goods and services in the fiscal year, adding, ''You probably never thought of it, but the tax dollar investment grows in value because library materials are borrowed and returned to be used over and over. Sort of like having your cake and eating it too.''

The Adult Information Department of the Evansville and Vanderburgh County Public Library (Indiana) did a study of the cost of answering a reference question and reported that the figure that surfaced was $4.33 per question. Let your community know that there is $4.33 worth of service for the asking. Library service does not lend itself easily to per-dollar interpretation, and gathering and justifying such figures may be a mind-boggling experience, but the impact of the approach seems to justify the exercise. Figurative price tags may enhance the value of the library and its services in the eyes of present and potential users.

Sample Annual Report Cover: Carnegie Library of Pittsburgh

Sample Annual Report Cover: McMillan Memorial Library, Wisconsin Rapids (WI)

Many notable library reports have used pictorial themes. The Public Library of Youngstown and Mahoning County (Ohio) featured Sherlock Holmes in ''One for the Books,'' and headed various report sections with appropriate quotes. The 1975 report of the Great River Regional Library in Minnesota admitted in the foreward, ''Annual reports are customarily dull affairs seldom read by their intended audience," and then proceeded to enliven the report with reproductions of classic Doré illustrations from Dante's *Divine Comedy* and tongue-in-cheek captions that were bound to lead the reader on.

The library-loving character, Hollyhock, from Al Vermeer's strip, "Priscilla's Pop," graced the pages of a report from the Evansville and Vanderburgh County Public Library (Indiana); each page had an appropriate cartoon across the bottom, with a heading that tied in the cartoon content with the library's message about circulation, book stock, budget, etc.

When the Fresno County Library (California) marked a 52nd year anniversary, a handsome report was issued, illustrated with symbols from the Aztec calendar, which has a 52-year cycle. An 18th century almanac style was used by the Madison Public Library in New Jersey, complete with signs of the planets and stars and appropriate art.

A calendar theme in other forms has been used by many. A simple "diary" report might be carried out this way:

● January 1—	Library starts year with budget of $150,000.00 (Give brief statistics of operating funds and sources.)
● March 3—	Scout troop visits library. (Give details of other group visits, tours, etc.)
● June 26—	416 children swamp library for story hour program. (Give details of other activities for children.)
● September 3—	Library answers 1,000th reference question. (Discuss telephone and other reference services.)
● December 18—	4,113th new book added to collection. (Give details of books and other materials acquired.)
● December 31—	Library ends year with $.53 in petty cash. (Give summary of expenditures.)

Other references can be tied to dates: number of interlibrary loan requests filled; confer-

ences, workshops attended; new staff hired; trustee appointed. Some dates can be fictitious or even facetious to keep the reader going or as an excuse to mention a service or statistic.

Statistics are necessary in a report, but the inherent dullness can be overcome by presenting them in various forms. For example:

IN 1976 HOW DID WE HANDLE

102,710 requests for information?
85,433 registered card holders?
23,456 new materials added?
866,765 materials circulated?

ONE AT A TIME!

The Waterloo Public Library in Iowa put it this way: "The number of books borrowed by Waterloo people would make a pile 39,000 feet high, 10,000 feet higher than Mt. Everest."

The Cincinnati Public Library pointed out that more people use that library than the total number of persons "attending the Reds and Bengals games, the Opera, the Symphony, Playhouse in the Park, and the Art Museum in a year's time." You could put your own figures into a local context that makes the volume of activity meaningful.

Statistics can also be fun, as an eastern library proved some years ago. In addition to some straightforward figures, they added some with tongue in cheek:

Number of persons who offered to donate books from their attics	14
Stray animals entering building	22
Stray animals leaving building	22
Number of wailing children found in adult section	57½
Ruly teenagers entering building	9,280
Unruly teenagers entering building	17
Persons who complained that we charge fines for Sundays	6
Teachers who sent students to library for books we don't have—and which are out of print	5

The text should be tightly written, with specifics that the readers can apply to themselves and with statements about activities that are little known to the average citizen. Avoid library jargon.

Make use of illustrative anecdotes and/or comments to interpret bare facts. List a few of the more interesting reference questions answered, special requests filled, describe unusual programs or activities beyond the simple in-and-out of books and money. Stress the new materials added—not just the number of new books added, but name one or two unusual references or titles, or give the number of copies purchased of one book for which there was a great demand; mention a new journal or magazine as an example of this kind of addition to the collection; give the title of a film that was popular or a cassette; refer to a typical or atypical gift received. Under that often-buried statistic "books withdrawn," point out that this included a moldy copy of an esoteric science manual with a 1927 copyright that had not circulated in 45 years.

Reprint a facsimile of a heartwarming letter you have received, or condense some phrases from the library's fan mail.

A brief acknowledgment in the annual report of gifts and assistance from individuals and organizations is in order. (Don't overlook mentioning the media, as well, with a line or two about the number of inches of space or hours of time.)

The Lorain Public Library in Ohio added a gimmick to their report entitled "Saga of '76." On the 75th anniversary of the Library, voters passed an increased mill levy. In return, the Library put 5¢ coupons totalling 75¢ into the report which could be redeemed for fines, photocopying, film fees, etc.

Sample Annual Report Cover: Youngstown and Mahoning County (OH)

If your library is in a county or regional system, point out (by example, if possible) the values and benefits to the local community, but not just in terms of interlibrary loans. Why not use a figure that shows the total resources of the system, with an explanation, "We don't have '(Title)' handy, but we can get it for you promptly"? Systems headquarters reports could be included as part of, or inserted with, the reports of participating libraries.

Sample Annual Report Cover: Tulsa City-County Library (OK)

Discuss some of the library's problems and tell how you are working on them. You might quote some actual criticisms and answer them forthrightly; you could use the phrase "Our business is an open book" for your theme.

Your report should look to the future as well as the present; it can contain a summary of goals and how they are being achieved, and a statement about the on-going philosophy of library services; people are interested in where you are going as well as in where you are now.

Although 8½- × 11-inch pages, mimeographed and stapled, are a fairly typical format for library reports, it can take many more interesting forms.

The 1974-75 report of the San Mateo County Library in California, titled "Matchless Services and Information," was presented in the shape of an oversized matchbook. The 1974-75 report of the Toledo-Lucas County Public Library (Ohio) had colorful graduated pullout sheets with various headings tucked into inside pockets. The Mobile Public Library in Alabama sported a gold seal on the outside flap of a brilliant orange cover folded to make a self-mailer.

The Public Library of Cincinnati and Hamilton County (Ohio) used a large poster format, enlivened with clever drawings and graphics, and a report of the Tulsa City-County Library System (Oklahoma) was also a single large sheet that folded down to a 4 × 9 mailing piece.

The Denver Public Library issued an annual report in the form of a note pad. The first ten sheets were the report; the remainder, useful notepaper. The Northland Public Library in Pennsylvania prepared an annual report as an alphabetical address book. The Nassau Library System in New York has issued its report in the form of a monthly engagement calendar, with pictures, text, and figures on the overleaf of each month's page.

Possibly a record of some sort was established when the East Brunswick Public Library (New Jersey) annual report turned up in *The Guinness Book of World Records*. On the paperback cover, under the title, is the modest statement "1976 was the Library's greatest year ever. Turn to page 1 for details of this record breaker." A one-page review of the library year was neatly pasted inside the front cover, and the slightly altered paperback was handed out as the library's annual report. (Complimentary copies of the book were supplied by a generous library supporter.)

Visual elements—pictures, graphics, and layout—are important factors to assure readability. A rule of thumb says that, for each unit of text, an equal amount of space should be given to graphics, and that includes plain white space! If photos are used, they should be dramatic and imaginative, not routine group shots. Good candid pictures showing people in action can replace a lot of type.

Use no less than ten-point body type, and resist the temptation to reduce typewritten copy for offset printing. The gain in extra words will only result in a loss of readership, which is no bargain.

Newspapers in many communities have published the library's annual report as a full- or half-page sheet. A report of the Michigan City Public Library in Indiana appeared in an eye-catching graphic tabloid page. A local bank made a special donation which was used for preparing the design and layout professionally; reprints were purchased for distribution. (In a pitch for new cardholders, the report said, "One of the little-known benefits of owning a library card comes from an unsubstantiated research report on the Giant Rat of Sumatra. The report shows no known cases of the rat ever attacking a person carrying an unexpired library card. The choice is clear, get a card . . . avoid risks with the Rat."

A report of the Orlando (Florida) Public Library was published in the magazine supplement delivered with the Sunday newspaper, and reprints were also used. (This report was headed, "How much do you know about OPL?" with a question-and-answer test with questions such as the following: "1. More males than females use the Main Library. True. False." The answer is true, 57 percent male.

In Lincoln Township (Michigan), the Library purchased the centerfold of the local newspaper on a date when the newspaper sends a sample copy to every household in the community as a special promotion. The reported cost to the Library was less than three cents a copy.

Not all readers are (or ever will be) library patrons, but they are helping to foot the bill. A well-designed message about the service provided for the tax dollar will help to make even nonusers believe that the library is a very good thing to have—if only for other people.

One other possible format for an annual report is a colorful slide show, supplemented with a

Sample Annual Report Cover: Bridgeport (CT) Public Library

Another way to get public feedback is to add a tear-off section or include a self-mailer in the report, asking the readers to list books that they would like to purchase, indicating their special interests, and asking for other suggestions or questions.

The information gleaned from the responses, both positive and negative, will be an invaluable guide for your next report. If there is little or no discernible reaction, you are forewarned that a reassessment of your procedure must be done before more time and money is invested in a no-return activity.

Miscellaneous Printed Library Materials

A tremendous variety of other materials is printed and handed out by libraries. Bookmarks, of course, are traditional, cheap, and easy to produce. Whether handed out as a convenience to the reader (and to avoid turned-down corners on books) or as a reminder or announcement, they are easily associated with the library and are, therefore, a useful promotional item. Those which simply promote the library or give general information, such as the examples here, should be dis-

printed sheet using some of the photos from the show and brief pertinent statements and statistics. The slide program can be booked throughout the community (beginning with the governing officials) and can be shown often in the library.

The task of preparing and distributing your annual report is not completed, however, until you make an evaluation of its effectiveness. The simplest way to do this is to ask a sampling of recipients, either in person, by phone or mail, about their reactions. These are sample questions to ask:

1. What is your general opinion of the library? Its strengths? Weaknesses?

2. Was there anything you did not understand in the report?

3. What is your impression of the library personnel? Can you name some of them?

4. Did the report tell you all you want to know about the library operation?

Sample Bookmark: Anaheim (CA) Public Library

one of a these days a librarian is going to punch you into her computer file

libraries are changing — for you!

the public libraries / Fairfield County, Conn

Sample Bookmark: Fairfield County (CT)

tributed *outside* the library, not to present patrons, who are, presumably, aware of the library. Inasmuch as they are inexpensive, bookmarks make good giveaways or inserts in mailings. Other kinds of information can be carried on bookmarks for distribution both to library patrons and to others.

Many library publications, flyers, or brochures are designed primarily to meet a current interest or demand, and are only incidentally regarded as promotional pieces. Nevertheless, identification of the library as "author," "publisher," or "source" is a reminder that it is the center for many informational services, and the publications may be justified for that reason.

Among the more typical examples are community calendars of local events, directories of community social service organizations, and listings of local resources and agencies to aid program planners. Some libraries have compiled local histories of their communities, drawing on both their own archives and contributions from the public. Others have issued "where to go and what to see" listings for the local area. Pamphlets for and about children's activities, booklets of prose and poetry written by children, young adults, or senior citizens, and compilations of favorite recipes of staff or patrons have been published by libraries. Occasionally these are sold to cover costs, or done with special funds from Friends or other groups.

Inexpensive broadsides or flyers are occasionally issued as handouts on a timely topic. Examples: "How to Save Water" (San Mateo County Library, California); "How to Write Your Favorite Pro Football Team" (Iowa City Public Library, Iowa); "Know your Public Officials" (Mead Public Library, Sheboygan, Wisconsin); "Bird Feeding" (Fairfax County Public Library, Virginia); "Dutch Elm Disease; Don't Pass It On" (Hennepin County Library, Minnesota).

The growing number and variety of such library publications is indication of a debatable trend toward regarding the library's function to be one of actively disseminating and printing miscellaneous information, as well as collecting and making it available on request.

Some pieces, such as overdue notices, are essentially business communications, but they need not be stereotyped or dull. A gentle reminder is often better than a straightforward statement or a veiled threat.

Library stationery letterheads should employ modern graphics to help foster the image of an up-to-date institution, and should incorporate a good logo or symbol. The use of an old-fashioned engraving or even a photo of the building is passé.

The logo can also be used on press release forms, mailing labels, annual reports, brochures, memorial book plates, newsletters, the bookmobile, van, or delivery vehicle, stamp meter, signs, book bags, posters, name tags, seals, and library

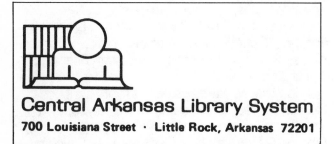

Sample Logos for Letterheads

DISCOVER LIBRARIES

Sample Logo: Coordinated Library Information Program (CLIP)

cards. In addition, you can have it made up as a rubber stamp and as a special typewriter key. A 2-3 frame lead of the logo in color could also be added to your films or filmstrips as additional identification.

Once your logo is designed, use it consistently and uniformly in the original form. Do not vary the size or placement of the elements except as it may be necessary for horizontal or vertical arrangement, and reduce or enlarge the logo proportionately so that the relative size and shape of all elements remain the same. Use the same typeface wherever the logo appears.

All libraries use posters, an historic and traditional way to call attention to a special message. They range from simple announcements of events or programs to graphic, dramatic, or whimsical reminders of the library's existence and services. To be effective, a poster must embody the principles of good design, be simple, and convey a clear message. Beyond these basic requirements, the possibilities for illustration and text are limited only by the

Sample Postmarks

Interlibrary Loans

Another service of your Dane County Library Service

Discover Libraries

This bookmark, calling attention to an important library service, originally designed by an Illinois library system, has been widely copied.

imagination of the designer. One-of-a-kind posters are hand-drawn, but multiple copies in small numbers are most often made by a show-card or silk screen process.

Gift of
Madison Lions Club

Gift and memorial book plates take various design forms, from traditional to decorative; this simple plate is from a New Jersey library.

Posters can be decorative accents for a library, and too often they end up as only that. There's very little point in posting a National Library Week poster—or any other urging use of the library—inside the building! Ninety percent of the effectiveness of good library-oriented posters is lost because of placement, but a good poster in a heavily trafficked area or in a single unusual or unexpected vantage point can be profitable and pennywise publicity.

There are innumerable locations in any community where posters can be placed if an effort is made to seek them out. In addition to the usual outlets (store windows, community bulletin boards, bank lobbies), there's the post office, town hall, movie house lobby, bus depot, airport, laundromat, staircases in buildings, elevators, shopping centers, meeting rooms of other organizations, community centers, and employee coffee-break areas of businesses and factories.

Permission may not be given for posting in all these areas, but you won't know until you ask! Suggest the inclusive dates you wish to display the poster, and then be sure that it is removed at the end of the period. An outdated or faded poster is very bad publicity and an annoyance to those who gave you the space.

Some libraries have indicated reluctance to post materials outside the library because of the problem of pilferage. Losses can be minimized by (a) stamping on the front and back "Property of the Cityville Library. Do not remove"; (b) indicating that copies are for sale or for loan at the library; (c) attaching the poster to the display area in such a way that it would tear when removed; or (d) displaying it in a "safe" area that is supervised in some way. (Meanwhile, satisfy the demand for wall decoration, particularly by teenagers, by starting a loan collection of posters.)

The "biggest" print job you may ever undertake may be a billboard, assuming that you do not object to the existing state of "visual pollution." If you want to go this route to advertise, the following pointers should be kept in mind. On a highway, you have about 3½ seconds to "pitch" your message, so obviously it must be simple and succinct. Seven words is the maximum for effectiveness. Use a very large and legible typeface (such as Helvetica), and a strong visual or graphic. Billboard companies will often donate space to libraries when it is not otherwise rented, but you will usually have to pay for the production of the billboard and the labor for pasting it up. Use of this print medium is most often employed in a concentrated campaign or for special observances, but keep some art work in reserve for "space available" notification so that you can take advantage of an unexpected opportunity.

The Library on Display

Using displays in the library is a time-honored and traditional activity, and there are some very good reasons to do so—and some very poor ones. Before embarking upon a program of planning and preparing exhibits, consider the justifications for this activity and the relative priority it should receive in your promotional scheduling. In-library displays, per se, rank relatively low in promotional value to the general public unless they are of unusual or widespread interest and well-publicized. They may, however, have quite another purpose which can justify the time and effort needed. The reasons and the expected end results should be carefully weighed against the estimated expenditure of hours and money to avoid undue emphasis on this activity. Too frequently there are little or no funds budgeted for displays, and librarians are prone to pride themselves on their success in scrounging materials and "making do." This may take an inordinate amount of time that would be better spent in more productive ways.

The first and foremost question to ask—and answer honestly—is "Are we doing this simply because we have empty wall space, an exhibit case, or bulletin board to fill, or does mounting displays have sufficient significance to our func-

This display, prepared by Erie Community College, Buffalo (NY) was designed to illustrate the ravages wrought on library materials by careless users. Ragged black cloth was draped across the front, and inside the case examples of maimed and dismembered books, magazines, records, cassettes, filmstrips, and microfilms were displayed. A scroll, "Missing in Action," listed titles that have never been returned. The deliberate clutter and disarray help to convey the message.

tion as a library to warrant doing so?" This is in effect a policy question, and should not be determined solely on the basis that space is available, that it is a traditional activity, and "we have always done it." There are better reasons, and one or more should be clearly understood and accepted as the basis for planning and scheduling.

Displays and bulletin boards are one form of advertising. They are used for the following:

1. To lure people into the library. This applies particularly when the materials are displayed outside the building or when a significant exhibit is mounted within and properly publicized. In addition, if a schedule of well-organized displays is maintained, both present and potential patrons may form the habit of dropping in regularly to view them.

2. To project the image of the library as a valuable community source of culture, knowledge, and information.

3. To motivate people to use the library and its resources with attention-getting devices or displays of materials linked to the viewer's needs or interests.

4. To inform both patrons and nonpatrons about the variety of materials and services available and to introduce them to subject matter outside their usual interests.

5. To encourage circulation of little-used or little-known materials.

Exhibits also serve in the following ways:

1. To educate or entertain viewers through display of selected materials from the library's collection or from other sources; to stimulate intellectual or cultural interests; and to communicate worthwhile information through visual presentation.

2. To offer an outlet for the display of materials or collections from others. This has the very real value of making new friends, establishing relationships with other community agencies and groups, and involving individuals in the library's operations. In serving this function, the library must guard against the attendant risk of abuse through displays of trivial interest or poor quality which are simply ego trips for individuals or organizations at the expense of the library. In order to avoid contention or misunderstanding, a policy statement should be developed and some minimum standards established (see sample policy statements at the end of this chapter). Signs or announcements on bulletin boards, perhaps with some cut-out figures or a cliché caption of the "Hey, it's Halloween" variety, are not "displays" in this sense, but are frequently used in libraries as decoration or to brighten a dull corner; they often make the interior more inviting, but they are of minimal significance, and preparation can, or should, be left to students, pages, or volunteers.

A full-size bicycle, enlarged photos as a background, and a selection of appropriate books make an arresting display by the Virginia State Library.

Many library displays do not go beyond the common or simple book display on a single subject, such as humor, Gothics, hobbies, or of some seasonal interest, such as sports or Christmas materials. These, of course, have some value in encouraging use of particular titles or as aids in a patron's selection.

Display space is where you find it. Display areas inside the library range from wall space, counter tops, stairways, and hallways, to streetside windows, exhibit cases, and glass-topped tables; exhibits can also be free standing "constructions," or can be hung from the ceiling. Outside the library, displays can be set up in store windows, building lobbies, meeting rooms, shopping centers, or incorporated into the exhibits of others.

The built-in space, particularly in older library buildings, can be a frustration if it is poorly located, ill-lighted, or inadequate in spatial dimensions. Often some minor remodeling will correct the situation.

Permanent exhibits, usually the well-meaning bequest of some benefactor, belong in museums, not libraries, but if you are burdened with one or more of these, rotate them in and out of storage, add something new, or display related books, clippings, or articles about them from time to time to change the scenery.

Some basic principles apply to all displays, for whatever purpose. Two of paramount importance are (1) the display must communicate something worth saying and worth the viewer's attention, and (2) it should be visual communication that is not too dependent upon written words.

The following pointers and a checklist are adapted from material used in a course taught by Professor Peter V. Willoughby, Agricultural Journalism, University of Wisconsin—Madison.

Know your audience; be specific about the group you want to reach. (Will they see the display where you intend to place it?)

Decide what you want the display to accomplish, including what action, if any, the viewer should take. The facts presented should be useful; the more immediate the use the better.

Edit your ideas to the essentials so that they clearly answer the viewer's question, "What's it to me?"

Don't attempt to warp content to fit a clever gimmick. (Gimmicks and clever captions may be fun and attract attention, but be sure you have a message that is reasonably worthwhile.)

Keep exhibit or display elements in a logical sequence so that they are easy to follow.

Plan your display to fit the viewing situation. The story-at-a-glance is the rule for street windows, fairs, and moving crowds. More detail can be used in in-house displays or at meetings or conferences.

A life-sized clown at the Tippecanoe Branch of the Milwaukee Public Library encouraged children to enjoy books; the balloons held the names of those who joined the library club.

This checklist will be helpful:

1. The object of any good exhibit is to communicate factual worthwhile information. Have you?

2. Have you picked out the significant to emphasize?

3. Are all your facts accurate?

4. Have you said your thing, and then quit? (Remember, an exhibit is a visual experience.)

5. Have you chosen the best possible visuals to illustrate your message and objective? (Real objects? Photographs and pictures? Projected visuals? Models and miniatures? Diagrams, charts, or maps? Drawings?)

6. Have you considered using the real thing before making a final decision? You should!

7. Would it be desirable to use more than one type of visual? Have you included related media as well as books?

8. Are you thinking visually? One picture or graphic element replaces a lot of words.

9. Does the design look like a supermarket window—chaotic, cluttered, too busy? Start over!

10. Did you give thought to the elements of line, shape, form, color, and texture? (Bone up on this in an elementary art book, if necessary.)

11. Is the background really a background? Avoid overpowering designs, textures, or colors.

12. Is the overall design spotty? Organize and relate all the elements.

13. Is the title short, to the point, eye-catching?

14. Is the lettering size related to the distance from which it can or must be viewed?

15. Have you included too much copy? Edit! Then edit some more.

16. Have you used more than two lettering styles or type faces? Don't, unless you are an expert.

A library is . . . a listening place.

A library is . . . a picture place.

A library is . . . an enlightening place.

Enlarged photos, such as these samples, of the action in and around the library, are a quick and easy resource for exhibit in various areas in the community. Size them 11 × 14 or larger and mount on sturdy mats.

It is well to keep in mind that exhibits are seen best at eye level. Table tops or horizontal glass cases require the viewer to bend over, and many won't; objects or text high in a wall case or low near the floor require neck craning or stooping, and are disastrous for those who wear bifocal glasses!

Big is beautiful, and photostats are an inexpensive way to "blow up" elements of a display, whether it is a caption, photograph, or reproduction of a printed piece. Negative stats (white on black) can be an eye-catching element.

Motion attracts attention, and an inexpensive battery-operated turntable with a revolving exhibit of books and related objects will have more of an impact than a static display. (Many of those elaborate moving seasonal displays in liquor stores and supermarkets are tossed out after use; ask to have them saved for you and redesign to suit your needs.)

You can also create motion or animation with a fan to flutter streamers or other elements, with flashing lights, and mechanical devices (such as automatic slide projectors, computers, microfilm readers, video sets, or tape recorders). Animation is useful to catch the eye but should not be an end in itself or be allowed to unduly distract attention so that the point of the display is lost.

A blank wall in the library or a rear view projector can be used for a continuous showing of slides or film. The slides can be art reproductions, pictures of book jackets, library scenes that show services, even candid shots of people who have visited the library.

====

". . . good displays take time and advance planning . . ."

====

Change displays at regular intervals. Even a well-conceived and well-designed exhibit "fades" into the case or wall and fails to catch the eye again in a short time. When displays are changed, make a *big* change so that it is immediately evident that it is different. Change the color, the size, the shape, and change the type of display.

Good displays and exhibits take time to assemble and mount. The less time there is to do this, the more important it is that some of it be used to

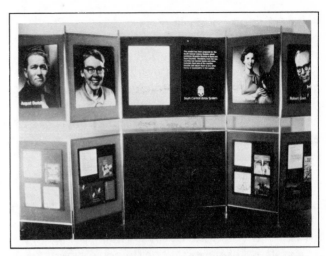

This circulating exhibit prepared for the South Central Library System (WI) with pictures and information about local authors featured enlarged photographs and photostatically enlarged textual material, with some text blocks reversed to white on black.

plan ahead, as much as 6 to 12 months at a time. A monthly calendar can be made up. A large Wisconsin library, for example, has nine display areas, ranging from exhibit cases to the tops of bookshelves. (You may have only a bulletin board or table top, but the principle is the same.) A typical month's schedule lists each of the display areas, indicates the theme or caption to be used (a single one for all or several), the construction materials or objects needed, and notes about the particular books, colors, etc.

Such a schedule need not be rigid. If an unexpected opportunity arises for an unusual loan collection to be displayed or a very timely subject is being cussed and discussed, you can make shifts in your plans. But the long-range outline lets you collect necessary materials and make arrangements in advance. It will help to avoid the last-minute panic that seems to result in that very uninspired catchall entitled, "New Books."

Consider the possibility of using a single unifying display theme for all or part of the year. This can be coordinated with a planned program series, chosen to highlight some aspect of library service, or used to add impact to a planned year-long promotional message. For example, the Manor Branch Public Library in Portsmouth, Virginia, chose a year-long theme of "Travel by Armchair," and exhibits and programs were planned around this. Displays were not limited to artifacts and related materials from single countries, however. A Snoopy and Friends exhibit, designed primarily to promote a special story hour, also included Spanish and French editions of the Schultz books in keeping with the overall theme. In addition, attention was attracted to the displays by placing selected related objects at the checkout counter, where they could be handled and closely examined.

Responsibility for exhibit and display planning should be assigned to one person. S/he need not be artistic, but should be familiar with the library and with what interests local people, be imaginative, and above all, a good planner. Actual art work can be done by art students, volunteers, or a staff member under one person's direction.

Build up an idea file; this may be your most valuable resource. Make notes about themes and slogans from many sources; advertisements of all kinds are useful. Note the subjects that people are talking about and that newspapers and magazines are playing up.

Translate themes into visuals by modifying the designs you find in advertisements, book jackets, pamphlets, and in store windows and merchandise displays. If you spend a few hours or a day or so just thinking about this, you will suddenly see an infinite number of possibilities, perhaps in unlikely places, such as the billboard that you pass twice a day. You will get fresh ideas and ideas with greater impact from the many visual variations you come in contact with daily—"now" ideas. Use the instruction books on displays and exhibits for the "how" of putting your ideas together visually, not the "what."

". . . cooperate and share exhibits . . ."

Many libraries have found it valuable to take color pictures of displays for future reference. Major components or art work can be packaged and stored for reuse. Library system headquarters can file duplicates of the photos to assist member librarians looking for ideas, and note whether the exhibit elements are available for loan.

The Nassau County Library System in New York, one of the pioneers in circulating exhibits for system members, uses the resources and assis-

Life-sized mannequins, whether borrowed, purchased, or donated, make eye-catching elements and add interest to displays, as in this example from the Briggs Lawrence County Public Library, Ironton (OH).

tance of local museums, Hofstra University, and private collectors to prepare and book outstanding exhibits that few libraries could assemble alone. The Eastern Massachusetts Regional Library System has paid the rental fee for traveling exhibitions from a commercial source and books them within the system for periods up to two years.

There are special libraries in many large and small communities—libraries associated with businesses and industries, hospitals, museums, service and government agencies, etc. These can be valuable sources for exhibits and exhibit loan materials. An exhibit exchange arrangement will be useful to both public and special libraries, and will help to publicize both to many in the community.

Public libraries and area school libraries can also share exhibits and displays to the benefit of both. If there is no established channel of communication, appoint a volunteer "coordinator" to

The Cleveland Public Library used a vacant store window in the downtown area of the city to promote the use of the library's films and the theater and movie collection of literature. The old movie camera and spotlight were borrowed from a local company.

canvass all libraries in the system or area; inventory display space; list exhibits or exhibit sources used by each library in the past; and, if possible, get each cooperating library to assume the responsibility for preparing one display or exhibit that can be circulated to others.

System headquarters libraries can serve as both a clearinghouse for and an originator of traveling exhibits. The Nassau Library System publishes an annual "Library Hang-Ups" booklet that lists the exhibits circulated by the Public Relations Department, plus a comprehensive listing of exhibits available from other sources, with the name of the person to be contacted, any special conditions, and a list of libraries in which the materials have been displayed.

The library exhibits that generate the most public interest are usually those that are either very timely or that relate to local interests and activities. For example, when interest in lunar exploration was at its peak, the Shawano City-County Library asked the Northeast Wisconsin Geology Association to arrange an exhibit that included the Wisconsin flag that went to the moon and some moon chips that were brought back. Between 4:00 and 8:00, over 800 persons came in on an April day that year. The arts and crafts of students or townspeople, and unusual local collections will often attract many. The library is a good and natural place to inform residents about the community, both past and present. For example, the Joseph Mann Library, in Two Rivers, Wisconsin, has displayed local products manufactured in the area.

One way to judge the significance of a display is to ask yourself if it is worth preparing a handout—a related booklist, flyer, special invitation for preview, or a small brochure. If so, you probably have a winner. For example, a handout prepared for an exhibit of Tolkien-related material at the New Carrollton Branch Library in Maryland included a biography of the author, a bibliography, and some interesting commentary. A descriptive folder, "The

Artists on Art," for an exhibit of works of local artists at the Westbury Memorial Library in New York had succinct statements of viewpoint or philosophy from each of the artists represented. The attractive brochure for the Japanese Scroll Painting exhibit prepared by the Nassau Library System contained a brief explanation of the history and purpose of the scroll paintings in the display, and the brochure design was repeated on a bookmark, which listed both books and films on Japanese art.

For maximum value from an exhibit, the amount of time spent assembling it should be matched by time spent in publicizing it in newspapers, on the radio, in flyers, posters, and notices that are sent to special groups. If the exhibit warrants, the mayor, a sponsor, or a dignitary can appear for a brief opening ceremony. It is better to do a few exhibits well and get maximum exposure than to attempt a constant stream of new ones, seen only by chance.

The display that will pay the biggest dividends in terms of promotion is likely to be the one that is viewed from or placed *outside* the library. Street-side library windows are excellent vantage points. In lieu of this, the store windows in other establishments can often be used for an occasional exhibit, or elements can be incorporated into the display of others. For example, a selection of related books and materials could be put into a back-to-school display of a clothing store, in a window featuring a sale of cooking equipment, or in a sporting goods store. If there is a home show or model home "open house," books and records could be placed in appropriate areas—cookbooks in the kitchen, art books in the den, storybooks in a child's room, current fiction and magazines in the living room.

An alert publicist can seek out the officials planning such events as garden shows, and travel and sports exhibitions, and offer to display related library materials.

A compact, well-designed portable display unit can be an invaluable outreach aid that will enable you to exhibit materials on short notice and in many situations—club meetings, union meetings or halls, study groups, church-sponsored classes, etc. An all-purpose background and some changeable captions will enable you to key the display to the subjects under discussion or projects of interest to the particular group with a minimum of effort. Just your presence (or the presence of a Friend or Library Trustee) will go a long way to indicate the library's interest in serving those in attendance. The money spent for constructing or purchasing an easily erected unit may be the best display investment you can make, and the off-site hours may be far more valuable than those spent in the library arranging exhibits of books and objects.

"Contemporary Eskimo Art" is an example of a traveling exhibit prepared by the Nassau County Library System in New York for use of its member libraries.

A library is . . . a children's place.

Sample Display and Exhibit Policies

Yuma City-County Library (Arizona) Display Policy

The Yuma City-County Library welcomes the opportunity to allow community groups, organizations, or individuals to use the various display areas of the library. Space is provided for displays of an educational, cultural, civic, or recreational nature, rather than for commercial purposes. The final decision as to the suitability of a display will be made by the Display Committee and the Library Director. Acceptance of a display by the Yuma City-County Library does not constitute an endorsement by the library of the group's or individual's policies or beliefs.

Areas available to the public for display are: (1) the entrance hall, (2) the stairway, (3) the arts services room, and (4) the glass display cases.

The Display Committee is responsible for the displays in the above four areas. The displays must be judged appropriate for a given area by the Display Committee. The Display Committee will coordinate displays in other areas of the library. The Children's Department will be responsible for displays and exhibits in the Children's Room.

The Display Committee will meet regularly and will be responsible for approving displays, establishing and maintaining contact with community organizations, and for resolving any display conflicts. Displays will be scheduled through the administrative office of the Yuma City-County Library and will be on a first-come first-serve basis.

It is the responsibility of the displayer to set up and remove the displays. Displays and exhibits will be scheduled for a period of one calendar month to begin with the first working day of the month and end with the last working day of the month. Exceptions must be approved by the Display Committee. Publicity for a display is also the responsibility of the displayer.

The library does not carry insurance on, and is not responsible for, any items owned by the displayer. The library will not provide storage for the property of organizations or individuals displaying in the library. All displayers are required to sign the attached form which releases the library from any responsibility for displayed items.

EXHIBIT RELEASE

I, the undersigned, hereby lend the following works of art or other material to the Yuma City-County Library for exhibit purposes only. In consideration of the privilege of exhibiting them in the library, I hereby release said library from responsibility for loss, damage, or destruction while they are in the possession of the library.

Exhibition to be held in the _____

During _____

Description of materials loaned: _____

_____

_____

Signature _____ Date _____

Permanent Address _____ Tel. _____

Madison Public Library (Wisconsin)

AVAILABLE SPACE

1. Main Library space includes first floor exhibit and second floor lobby. Suitable exhibits may be approved for Children's Room and other public service areas.
2. Limited space is available in each branch and exhibits in these units must not interfere with normal Library use of these spaces.

BASIC POLICIES

1. Exhibits are an extension of the Library's cultural and educational services and, as such, there is no rental charge. The Library reserves the right to decline any exhibit or to schedule any exhibit in accordance with the Library's best interests.
2. The Library is not responsible for the arrangement, care, supervision, or dismantling of exhibits, but reserves the right to approve or disapprove of the handling of any exhibit. All exhibitions are at the risk of the sponsors, although the Library carries normal risk insurance.
3. There should always be something in the Main Library exhibit areas to enrich the Library's programs and the Library may rent appropriate exhibits to provide a rounded schedule.
4. No permanent exhibits or gifts or museum materials will normally be accepted, although the Library itself may solicit exceptional materials if available without conditions.
5. Hours of exhibits must coincide with hours that the Library is open unless special permission is granted by the Library Board.

RULES

1. All exhibit requests and schedules must be approved by the Assistant Director. At the Main Library, such requests and schedules shall be channelled through the Art and Music Division.
2. No show shall last for more than one month.
3. All exhibits shall be sponsored in writing by an appropriate organization to minimize difficulties over the appraisal of a one-person exhibition.

Getting Your Act Together: Library Programs and Special Events

In-House Library Programs

On the surface, sponsoring library programs, whether performances, classes, lectures, demonstrations, film showings, or concerts, would appear to be a logical extension of library service, and this has long been a traditional and recognized function.

The program schedules and reports from libraries across the country, large and small, reveal a program subject array from A-Z, Admirable to Zany. There appears to be little discernible pattern, and there are several schools of thought on the value and importance of such programing.

One holds that anything goes—from a rock concert to a sewing bee—as long as it attracts people to the library. This philosophy is based on the assumption that such programs have a publicity and promotional value which will, in turn, lead to a greater awareness and support of the library by the public at large.

Another school questions the value of "packing 'em in" if those who come leave with no better idea of what the library is or of what it has to offer other than a good meeting room. This group finds programing justification in such precepts as "enriching a child's or adult's cultural background," "directly stimulating interest in the library's resources," or "providing information in other than the printed form."

And then there are those who do no programing on their own, but believe that their responsibility is simply to provide the program materials and resources for other groups and agencies, and, on occasion, to support them with special book displays, lists, or exhibits. The Vigo County Public Library (Indiana) explains it this way:

> Here at VCPL we believe in programs and we believe libraries can be a vital part of programing. We just do not believe that the library itself needs to provide the 'ready-to-wear' program as its service. Rather, it is the function of the library to see to it that its materials, equipment, and human resources are used by community groups as those groups plan and produce their own programs. . . . Programs offered by libraries can and do make headlines, and, in the short run, are certainly more visible activities than library service which only supports programs given by others. The latter, however, has much greater impact on the community, and over the years generates more public support. The VCPL, after fifteen years of giving this type of supportive program service, is now a recognized place to go for program help.

Despite the divergent opinions, libraries across the country have demonstrated that increased public support and usage result from sponsoring programs that meet the needs and interests of their communities. These institutions, large and small, have defined their service role in terms of educational, instructional, cultural or recreational programing, as well as in terms of books and media materials.

Whatever the program subject or format, the key to success has been a clear objective, a sound knowledge of the community, and sufficient resources to meet local needs or interests adequately. The range and diversity of programing reflects the diversity of libraries themselves, although there appears to be undue or unwarranted overlap and duplication of the program areas of other agencies and community groups on occasion. This can and should be avoided by cosponsorship and cooperative scheduling of events.

In the past, book reviews, book discussions, story hours, and film showings were standard fare, but in recent years there has been a rush to schedule programs ranging from microwave cookery to karate demonstrations. The latter have brought people into the library for the first time, and may aid in extending the image of the library as an information and resource center.

What Kind of Programing Should You Do?

There is no simple answer to this question, because it varies with each library. Shortage of suitable space and staff may be limiting factors, although both can and have been overcome when there was sufficient desire and motivation.

There is a distinction between library programs and special events. Programs are continuing efforts, usually on a regular schedule; special events are single focus affairs on a one-time, all-out basis, usually intended to attract a diverse group or to give promotional exposure to a large number of people. One poor example of such an event is the "library open house." Long popular as a National Library Week activity, it has outgrown its usefulness, if it ever had any. An open house is a social affair, not a program. It may be required or appropriate on the occasion of opening a new building, but the library presumably holds open house every day, albeit without coffee and cookies. You may be able to justify an invitational open house on some special occasion, but without a special focus or attraction of some sort, it will very likely be a dismal failure or attended only by the old faithfuls.

The best-attended programs are usually those with a local tie-in, either because of the personalities involved or because of the subject matter. Programs that are timely because people are discussing or concerned about a matter, or those that appeal to a latent or growing interest, usually will attract many. There are also certain "need-to-know-about" subjects of perennial or recurring interest which will bring in a sizeable audience. Audience size is not the sole or basic consideration, however, because in some communities the library may be the only agency that could or would put on programs with a limited appeal. (Nevertheless, a performance of baroque music that attracts only six people, including staff, is a bit too limited in its appeal to warrant the effort.)

In determining types of programs, it is essential to know your community—all segments of it, not just that part with which you have daily contact—and to assess the needs and interests of the people whom you wish to attract.

Programing should never be done (although it often is!) on the basis of the fact that there is an expert on Chinese calligraphy in the community who is willing to give a lecture. Picking a program subject simply because it is easily scheduled is putting the cart before the horse.

In short, first know whom you want to reach and why.

". . . program with an objective . . ."

The next step is to assess your resources and limitations. Some libraries can afford to offer such varied programing that there is almost literally something for everyone.

For example, the monthly calendar of a Minnesota library included these offerings: a talk for parents on coping with teenagers, a discussion of books made into movies, a three-week session on needlepoint, a demonstration by a home economist, a lecture on choosing books for children, film showings, travel slide-talks, a concert, and a workshop on how to use the library effectively. During a fall month, a Pennsylvania library programed movies, book and travel talks, plus cardiopulmonary resuscitation training, an afternoon "entertainment," and a young adult reading club. Book reviews and films, a genealogy program, and a demonstration on self-defense for women were the programs offered in one month by a Tennessee library. Each program offering is intended for a particular target group.

Libraries that must limit their programing activities will find the choice of subject matter and target groups more difficult and more crucial if the intent is to extend service to other than regular patrons. The Everett Public Library in Washington solved this dilemma by what was termed "cooperative programing," created for and with other city departments, community agencies, businesses, and institutions. This is an invitational approach, which aims at involving a wide variety of community groups and individuals in an informal network closely aligned with the library. Director Gary Strong reported in *Idaho Librarian,* July, 1975,

> The key to this type of planning is not to become locked into any program or relationship with another agency. The library must be open to work with any group in the community. Business relationships are particularly sensitive. The entire business community must realize you will work with them. An association should not continue so long that you become identified with only women's groups, or certain civic associations, or only that you program in one area of service. When the program has met its objectives, we evaluate its effect and move into another area where we have not worked, attempting to seek a new audience or identify another aspect of library resources.

Some libraries have found a solution by adopting an annual theme and relating all programing efforts to this. "The Festival of Nations" theme used by the Bloomfield (New Jersey) Library in 1978 is an example that involved many disparate segments of the community. Each month of the year was devoted to the heritage of a different ethnic group. A heritage committee of local residents was formed for each culture. During the scheduled month, craft and cooking demonstrations, concert and dance performances, travel talks, films, lectures, displays and guided tours were all related to the honored nationality.

Library systems occasionally offer packaged programs to aid member libraries in putting on programs of broad contemporary interest, using resources which would otherwise be beyond the reach of smaller units. These have included selected films, speaker lists, display materials, booklists, and discussion outlines in a flexible format, which could be adapted to local situations. Some systems have contracted for a program series from other organizations, which are then offered to member libraries for individual booking, and aided with system-wide promotion. Successful programs developed by individual libraries can also be shared and sent on the system circuit.

Hints for Producing Programs

In determining program subjects or series, an advisory council of representative lay people and staff members can be helpful for suggesting subject matter, for assessing potential interest, and for aid in securing speakers and other resources.

Seek a balance, if possible, between those matters of perennial interest (health, money management, retirement) and those of current interest. Monitor the media for the latter, and watch for trends indicated by subject requests in the library.

Plan all programs well in advance, preferably on an annual or semiannual basis. Tentative dates can be established and possible conflicts with other events avoided. Speakers or program participants can be contacted early, offering alternative dates if necessary. Make up a checklist and calendar of all necessary prior arrangements.

Publicity can be planned and released at the proper time when details are established well in advance. It is inevitable that at some time a speaker or performer will fail to show up or cancel at the last minute; prepare for this by keeping a backup program in reserve—a talk by a staff member, a demonstration of materials on the scheduled program subject, or a substitute all-purpose film.

". . . may I present?"

Discuss the subject to be covered by a guest speaker in person or by telephone, suggesting the possibilities you have in mind. Explain the interests or type of audience you expect so that the speaker or performer can tailor the presentation. Explain the physical setup (large meeting room; stage or podium; informal space in basement or classroom; small around-the-table space for demonstration), the date and time, and the length of presentation that you prefer or that the speaker is prepared to deliver. If a fee or honorarium is not involved, offer to pay mileage or travel expenses for anyone who must come a distance, or arrange transportation. Follow up the initial contact with a letter restating the arrangements.

Make sure that you have good speakers or reasonably competent performers, even if they are free local talent. A dull, rambling, or poorly organized speaker or program will be too costly in terms of the library's image. Check with others and get at least two unbiased opinions first, if possible. Cope with over-eager volunteers tactfully and in a businesslike manner.

Schedule programs for the maximum convenience of those for whom they are intended. Know your community and the pattern of activities so that you avoid conflicts with the meetings or programs of others which may appeal to the same group. Keep attendance records as a guide for future changes in the hour or day of a program series. A seasonal pattern of ups and downs may appear in time, and this should be kept in mind for future scheduling. If there is a steady decline in attendance, reassess your plans. Either the quality of the offerings has deteriorated or the audience is surfeited. Never continue a program series just because it is customary, traditional, or expected. Give a new program series time to build up interest, though, for often a well-conceived series

that gets off to a slow start will acquire a growing and enthusiastic audience when the word gets around.

Estimating the potential audience size is tricky, particularly for program subjects or formats that have not been tried before. It is better to underestimate the number than to have a lot of empty seats. If you think you have a block-buster in the works and there may be insufficient space, request preregistration, use the lobby or a reading room in off-hours (Sunday, or an evening when the building is ordinarily closed), or, weather and subject permitting, use the lawn or parking lot.

Promote and publicize your programs effectively. Use newspaper and radio releases, newsletters (your own and those of others), mailing lists,

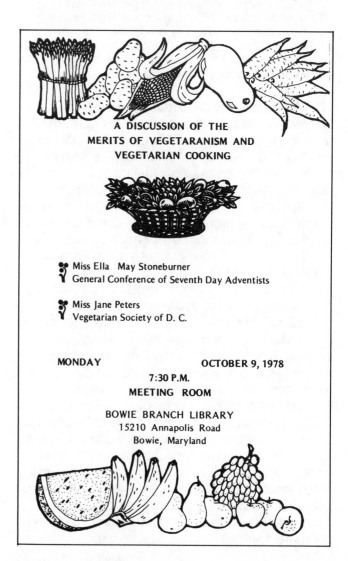

Publicity flyers are produced for branches by Maryland library systems.

program flyers, posted schedules, special invitations, or announcements to selected individuals and groups. Give the program an intriguing title; use catchy phrases, fresh, provocative words, or feature names of well-known persons. If you send out a regular schedule of program events on a monthly or quarterly basis, add a few explanatory phrases or sentences to each listing to pique interest. Use varied and imaginative flyers and program schedules. The Danbury Public Library in Connecticut, for example, printed the "Lunch at the Library" schedule on a small brown paper bag.

Capitalize on the interests and energies of community groups for aid in publicizing programs. For example, when the Mead Public Library (Sheboygan, Wisconsin) cosponsored a program entitled "Where Should We Grow from Here? How Shall We Plan Our Land?" with the League of Women Voters, the staff feared very low attendance at such a discussion. The League members beat the bushes, persuaded the news media to attend, invited town and county officials, and turned out a large number of interested participants.

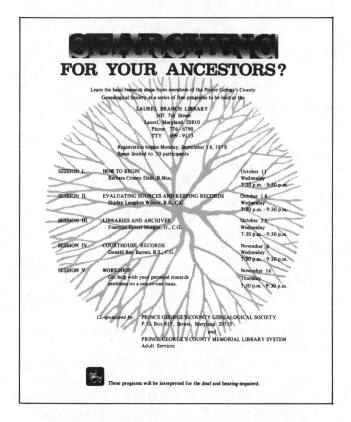

Publicity flyer for a Maryland library-sponsored program.

Flyer for a Greenville County (SC) library lecture series.

You could get additional mileage from a good program by videotaping it and showing the tape in the lobby of the library during the following day or week.

Keep records of your programs, both for future reference and as an aid to evaluation. At regular intervals, evaluate the overall scope of your programing, in terms of target groups and numbers served, objective, community reaction, and cost. The question to be answered, ultimately, is "Have these activities helped to achieve any of the long range goals of the library, improved public relations in the community, and filled some identified needs?" And remember, everyone bombs once in a while. Learn from failure. For example, an Illinois library agreed to take part in a town "Home Tour Day," and Friends and board members prepared refreshments for the expected influx, but only six made the pilgrimage to the library. Obviously those making the community tour were interested in houses, home decorating, and how people live; a visit to the library didn't fit into this category.

If, as one library reported, a family film series turns into a baby sitting ordeal, a toy safety program draws only the expert who was speaking and four patrons, and a program on "Occupational Planning for Students Not Attending College" attracts only one who came on the wrong day, ask these questions. Was there enough good promotion and publicity to the right groups? Was there a conflict with other community events? Was the weather or season bad and did this offer an unforeseen (or foreseeable) obstacle? Was the program title dull? Was there any evidence of local interest in the program or did you just make a poor guess based on a program that worked for someone else? Has the subject been worked to death by others? Have past library programs been so poorly organized and presented that the reputation lingers on?

A Sampling of Successful Library Programs

Book reviews and discussion are traditional library program staples, and they continue to draw a select audience. Lunch hour sessions variously billed as "Booked for Lunch," "The Brown Bag

*For parents of registered story program participants and other interested adults

THURSDAYS   1:00 - 1:45 P.M.
SEPTEMBER 21 - OCTOBER 26, 1978
EASY SECTION

Laurel Branch Library
507 Seventh Street
Laurel, Maryland

Program for parents sponsored by a Laurel (MD) library.

Bunch," and "Books Sandwiched In" have proved popular in many areas. Book reviews are frequently offered as a program feature for meetings of other organizations; in Arlington Heights, Illinois, for example, clubs can select the book titles they would like reviewed from a list the library prints and distributes.

Programs featuring authors and illustrators are always of interest. They take the form of panel discussions, interviews, individual talks, or reception-and-autographing parties. Local or regional writers are usually featured, but touring writers are available on occasion.

It's quite a distance, in format and philosophy, from book reviews or author appearances to a "road show" put on in Iowa; "How to Make the Best Car Deal" was one topic covered in the program series, with a car salesperson giving pointers for measuring used car values, followed by a showing of a color film, "How to Buy a Used Car."

The broad range of out-of-the-ordinary programing, timely, significant, or simply entertaining, is illustrated by the following random examples from both large and small libraries.

The Brewerton Free Library in New York brought in divers from the Volunteer Fire Company to explain the techniques of scuba diving and to show some of the recovered articles.

In New Mexico, the North Las Vegas Library sponsored a "Powder Puff Auto Mechanics Workshop" that attracted so many women they had difficulty finding room for all. The classes were held on Tuesday and Thursday mornings, and were conducted by a high school faculty member.

A North York (Canada) Library sponsored a three-part panel discussion series entitled "Citizen Involvement, Myth and Reality." An alderman and several citizens discussed "Citizen Involvement in Politics" in the first session. The second discussion, "Citizen Involvement in Education," was led by a Board of Education member, a school superintendent, a member of the Teachers Federation, a recent graduate, and a parent. The third session was entitled "Citizen Involvement in Community Affairs," with representatives of various agencies, including the Library Board.

The Ortega Branch, San Francisco Public Library held a one-day program, "To Experience Life in a Teepee." The announcement said,

> You can begin by helping to put up the 20 foot structure, and then go inside to learn how the tepee figured in the life-style of the Plains Indians. Besides Indian tools and other artifacts to look at, there will be special rocks for you to crush into paint, as the Indians did.

Several people were on hand to talk about Indian culture.

Some "dog-gone" good ideas have been used elsewhere. Sled dogs were featured at the Chisholm Public Library, Minnesota as members of the Sled Dog Club demonstrated dog sleds and hook-ups, and described the difference between Siberian and Malamute Huskies. The Canine Corps has been shown in action at the Fort Worth Public Library and Salt Lake County Library. Other animals have been in the act; the Morwell Public Library (Victoria, Australia) had two live ponies in attendance for a program on their care and the

use of riding gear; a Hennepin County Library (Minnesota) had a live model for a demonstration on horse grooming, and in Virginia, at the Fairfax County Library, a blacksmith shoed a pony and handed out free horseshoes. Misconceptions about such endangered species as wolves and cougars were dispelled in a program at the Mead Public Library in Sheboygan, Wisconsin, which featured two live wolves, on tour with the North American Association for the Protection of Predatory Animals. At the Maude Shunk Library (Menominee Falls, Wisconsin) and Bayport Public Library (Minnesota), a cub and an adult cougar from Cougars Unlimited made friends with enthusiastic audiences.

The Cambridge Public Library (Massachusetts) sponsored "An Evening in Greece" to honor

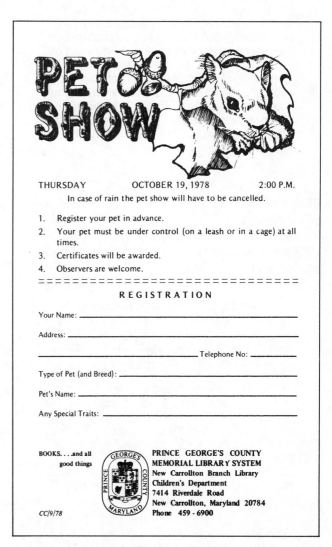

Registration form for a Maryland library's pet show.

the Greek Orthodox community. The program consisted of a film about Athens, past and present, folk songs and dancing, an exhibition of the works of a Greek artist, displays of Greek books, recordings, sculpture, etc. The response was overwhelming, and, according to the *News* (Eastern Massachusetts Regional Library System):

> As a result of this evening the Cambridge Public Library became the recipient of gifts not envisioned in the initial planning. The first gift was in the form of a pleasant happening. Half of the people in attendance were non-Greek . . . this was perhaps the greatest gift—the bringing together of two cultures in a warm and friendly manner. The second gift came as a result of the City Manager, City Council members, and School Committee being in attendance and their recognition of the needs of the library. The day following the event the Mayor readily agreed to the purchase (of needed equipment). . . . The last but far from the least was a gift of an original drawing by the artist who had exhibited that night. . . . The Cambridge Public Library offered to the community a simple evening of Greek culture and was rewarded threefold with gifts that made the members of the library staff proud of their efforts and grateful for a response beyond their expectations.

On the theory that you can learn from the imaginative programing of children's librarians which draws enviable audiences, an Adult Services Librarian of the St. Charles City-County District in Missouri tried a taffy pull. Reports Anita Haller:

> It worked. A total of 39 adults pulled, yanked, and fought with taffy in its various stages. What made it a success were the pauses. While sugar, water, and corn syrup bubbled, we talked about the library's latest books. As busy fingers stuck to tables and chairs, I plugged the bookmobile. And amidst contented munching, we discussed the reference service. Or rather I discussed. No one else could get their mouth open. . . . To children the library is a fun place to be. Shouldn't it be for adults, too? What if we borrowed a little 'fun' from the Children's Room and put it in our book reviews and informational programs? It might attract more people. . . .

The Des Moines Public Library scheduled a special program directed mainly to local mer-

chants; two color films, rented from the Small Business Administration, Washington, D.C., on burglary and pilferage were shown and a question and answer period was fielded by a member of the Des Moines Police Department. A short commercial was given at the start of the program on materials at the library of special interest to businesspeople.

A late summer program on bus safety especially for children about to start school for the first time was planned in cooperation with local school officials and held at the Hannibel Public Library in New York. The safety lessons were capped with a ride on a real school bus.

A workshop to instruct participants in the use of both camera and tape recorder to create program materials, sponsored in New York by the Manlius and Fayetteville Libraries, had a covert purpose—to encourage additions to the libraries' local archives.

One of the least structured programs occurred in Depauville, New York, when the teacher

Christmas program promotion for a Utah library.

of a class in chair caning failed to appear; the librarian, a member of the class, invited the others to the library for a "teach yourself—learn as you go" session using some good instruction books. Perhaps a selection of instruction books and a scheduled time for a group of interested people to get together informally are all that are needed for small libraries to sponsor how-to-do-it programs or classes!

And these program titles, culled from recent announcements, reveal additional diversity reflecting both general and special community interests:

"The Individual in the Growing Bureaucracy" (a talk by a member of congress)
—*co-sponsored by the Greenville County Library in South Carolina and Clemson and Furman Universities*

"A Jaundiced Look at Today's Press" and "Condominiums—Shall I Buy One?"
—*Carnegie Library of Pittsburgh, Pennsylvania*

"A Sing-In" (for anyone who could play an instrument, wanted to sing, or just listen)
—*Musser Public Library, Iowa*

"The Loch Ness Phenomena: New Evidence"
—*Mead Public Library (Sheboygan, Wisconsin)*

"Calculator Power" (how to figure sports statistics, money matters, even do crossword puzzles)
—*Milwaukee Public Library, Wisconsin*

"Songwriters' Workshop"
—*Bryant Library (Roslyn, New York)*

"The Joys and Pitfalls of Starting Your Own Small Business"
—*East Meadow Public Library, New York*

"Maple Sugaring" (how-to for the hobbyists)
—*Hennepin County Library, Minnesota*

"Ventriloquism" (six-week series)
—*Laurel Branch Library, Maryland*

"Genetic Engineering"
—*Port Washington Library, New York*

Program for a family film series from Prince George's County Library System (MD).

The bulk of library programing, however, is presently focused on topics in such categories of lasting interest as:

money management	plants-gardening-land-
consumerism	scaping
energy-conservation-	nature study
pollution	food-cooking-nutrition
self-help	alcoholism-drugs
hobbies-crafts-collec-	pet care-training
tions	astrology-ESP-UFOs-
health-first aid-safety	outer space
retirement	child care
sports	local history
genealogy	job-careers
home maintenance	

Few libraries could fail to attract attendance at an up-to-date program or series on any one of these subjects.

Much library programing has a seasonal or holiday emphasis, or is based on a special week, month, or anniversary. The intent of such observances ranges from an effort to focus attention on a particular group or subject through demonstration and instruction to using a date simply as an excuse or theme for an entertaining promotion.

The following are examples of such programing. Black History Week, in February, was observed at the Milwaukee Public Library with a concert featuring music written or made popular by Blacks, a "Latest African Styles" fashion show, a gospel evening with church choirs, and a slide program on Africa. The Chinese New Year was celebrated by the Rochester Public Library (Minnesota); over 800 children and adults attended special events which involved high school students, a local Oriental restaurant and an import shop. April 23 is St. George's Day, and the Laramie County Library System in Wyoming observed this little-known anniversary with a display of British souvenirs, British publications, and a dragon. (A little Shakespeare was included, too, since that is also his birthday.) The staff made roses to wear and to give to patrons on that day, and sent out news releases and radio spots. (St. George was martyred in about the year 300, and became a warrior hero of the Middle Ages and the ideal of the Christian soldier. St. George's Day was once famous for its fairs, and some are still held today in England. He is, of course, best known by children of all ages for his encounter with the fabled dragon.)

When April 8 was designated Food Day, a Des Moines branch library sponsored an informational afternoon to educate the community on participation in breakfast programs, food stamp eligibility, and nutrition, with displays demonstrating the available services. The Nashua (New Hampshire) Public Library went all out for Country Music Month in October, with live concerts and special broadcasts on local radio stations.

In Wyoming, the Laramie County Library turned a calendar notation into a weeklong activity. The report, from the *Wyoming Library Roundup:*

Our librarian, board and the public were amused when we first suggested Unicorn Hunting Week, but it proved particularly suitable for us since we have a very fine collection of art books. Unicorn Hunting Week enabled us to feature these.

The project was first presented to the staff in early August. Contact was made with the coordinator of the city school elementary teachers so that those who wished to make mythology come alive for their pupils could begin the school year with this project. We next contacted the coordinator of library service, the art and music supervisors, and the principals of the special schools, such as our parochial schools. The Artists Guild was alerted and asked to sponsor a project to secure some art for an exhibit.

The library staff became excited over hunting . . . unicorns in the various fields. [The staff decided] to put out a hunting license for students who came to the library during that week. These were used to promote the week. Radio and TV made use of special spot an-

nouncements. A feature story in our Sunday Magazine was talked about widely throughout the community.

Teachers were asked to have students hunt the unicorn in their school libraries, and in our library, and then to prepare some type of material to show what they had found. These items were brought to the library during Unicorn Week for display, and a Certificate of Award was given each school room which had the most interesting and unusual display. Our Friends of the Library group agreed to act as judges.

One of the local gift shops loaned us two Haviland plates which featured the tapestries of the Hunt of the Unicorn. These with an open art book showing all the tapestries were placed in our display case. Pictures in our newspapers picked up the interest in viewing the exhibit.

Unicorn Hunting Week proved to be such an interesting promotion, teachers are already asking if it can be observed again next year.

Birthdays of authors or other characters are often an excuse for a one day "party"; Edward Lear's birthday on May 12 was the occasion for a limerick contest at the Moscow-Latah County Library in Idaho. Libraries have named their own

". . . name-your-own-week . . ."

successful "weeks": the Thurston Library in Ann Arbor, Michigan invented "Be Kind to Possums Week" and coordinated displays, story-telling, and other activities; the Library at the University of Texas at Austin declared a Campus Library Week, and held a countdown to the acquisition of the four-millionth volume, adding one important book each day to the goal; the Port Washington Public Library in New York declared January the month of the future, and offered programs and displays on the future of Long Island, the use of holograms, the everyday implications of computers and data storage banks, outer space colonization, energy alternatives, and a discussion of the skills and philosophy needed in a changing world.

Programing for Children

Children represent a special target group that is easy to identify, and some of the best and most imaginative programing is done for them. Perhaps because librarians have readily accepted the responsibility for interesting children in reading, there has been far more substantial and structured exchange of information about how to plan and conduct activities and programs for children than for other groups. Summer reading clubs or special summer library programs, often designed around a theme, are undertaken by most libraries, and local efforts are frequently aided and abetted by regional or state agencies, or such national organizations as the Children's Book Council. Workshops for children's librarians proliferate, children's programs are featured in the news media and professional journals, and many books and other aids are available.

Planning a Special Event

Although the distinction between the type of library programing discussed and a special event may seem a little fuzzy, a special event is usually an uncommon activity for a special promotional purpose. It is primarily an attention-getting device, in an attempt to reach new people, although it may have other purposes, including that of fund raising. It can involve a large crowd or a small select group. The term covers a multitude of activities from book fairs, festivals, anniversaries, dedications, imaginative "happenings," to contests or ceremonies involving citations and awards. The one thing that all have in common is the need for a lot of planning and a lot of people to help!

Before deciding to stage a special event, you must consider whether it is special enough and on a sufficient scale to secure the attention and publicity you need, and if the requisite time and energy warrant it, because it may be at the expense of more routine or on-going programing activities. But, if so, full speed ahead! As stated by Lawrence O. Aasen in a seminar on Public Relations Practices in Non-Profit Organizations, "Special events are the most fun you can have in public relations work."

The lead time necessary for staging a special event may be six months to a year or more; in any

". . . take plenty of time . . ."

case, it is apt to take an extraordinary number of hours and careful organization to be successful.

The following formidable list of considerations, adapted from "Checklist for Planning and Staging Special Events" prepared by Reymont Associates, is offered as a guide in preparing a list for your particular event, and it should be tailored to fit the scope of the activity you are planning.

Checklist for Planning and Staging Special Events

1.   A committee of staff and appropriate persons appointed; chairperson or project director selected. Objective of event determined and proposed plans assessed in terms of appeal and potential crowd.

2.   Budget prepared and funds secured.

3.   Date of event and tentative hours selected:

Sufficient lead time allowed for adequate preparation?
Possible conflict with other local events?
Speakers, important guests, and site for event available on proposed date?

Alternative date selected if event must be postponed?
One person designated to make cancellation decision?
Checklist prepared of all persons to notify or arrangements to change in this case?
Substitute of an indoor program planned if weather interferes with outdoor program?

4.   List of speakers and/or other participants prepared and individuals contacted and briefed:

Fees, honorariums, or expenses understood and in writing?
Amount of program time allocated to each clearly specified?

Checklist for Planning and Staging Special Events (Continued)

Copy of speeches available for advance distribution to the press, master of ceremonies, or other speakers (to avoid duplication) or to be made available after event?

Arrangements made for transportation and housing of speakers or other participants?

Bibliographical information, photos secured in advance for publicity?

Person(s) selected to MC event or to make introductory remarks?

5.   *All necessary facilities and physical arrangements listed and checked:*

Seating arrangements or crowd flow pattern determined?

Floor plans or site plan drawn up? Platform seating chart?

Speaker's stand erected and decorated? Water and glasses on hand?

Microphone, PA system, tape recorder, slide or film projector(s), screens, easels needed and tested? Repairperson available?

Lighting facilities adequate?

Electric outlets located? Additional power lines needed?

Directional signs necessary? Directional maps needed with invitations, announcements, or at the site?

Tickets needed, printed?

Registration table(s) required? Name tags?

Adequate restrooms available?

Food service arranged (refreshments, sit-down meal, buffet, concessions)?

Adequate parking assured and clearly marked, including "no parking" areas? Special parking passes or areas for program participants, VIP's?

Municipal officials, including fire and police chiefs, briefed on scope of event? Special permits needed?

First aid arrangements needed? Additional security advisable?

Waste receptacles handy?

Decorations, flowers arranged?

Personnel assignments made for staffing booths, displays, greeting special guests, etc.?

Post-event clean-up, arrangements made?

6.   *Promotion and publicity planned and scheduled:*

Mailing list prepared for special guests and VIP's? (Mayor, city officials, heads of civic, fraternal, women's organizations, media executives, labor union officials, leading business and professional persons, educators included?)

Special invitations mailed well in advance?

List of acceptances and regrets compiled?

Welcoming escorts and transportation arranged for VIP's? Special passes or tickets necessary and mailed?

Publicity about VIP's and press interviews arranged?

Program copy and layout prepared and printed?

Advance releases scheduled for media? Program and photos mailed in advance?

Releases sent to internal and special publications?

Leaflets, brochures, promotional displays, and posters prepared? Distribution method planned?

Congratulatory or promotional messages obtained from VIP's, local merchants? Proclamation by mayor advisable?

Paid media advertisements solicited from local businesses or other groups?

Additional promotional gimmicks considered— main street banners, flags, bumper stickers, decals, buttons, car-top placards, billboards, bus signs, sound trucks?

Press interviews of participants before or after event arranged?

Personnel assigned to assist reporters at the event?

Event recorded for local archives and future picture needs?

7. *Follow-up and evaluation procedure established:*

Financial accounting and report compiled?

Thank-you letters sent to all program participants, volunteers, and contributors?

Follow-up publicity or additional information made available?

Press coverage summarized?

Comments of VIP's and others recorded?

Review of problems and oversights accomplished?

Steering committee's subjective appraisal of success or failure in relation to original objective recorded?

Here are some additional caveats, hints, and niceties to keep in mind.

Seek professional advice concerning the need for proper insurance coverage; unexpected mishaps can occur which could lead to financial disaster.

"... and consider too ..."

To enlist the appearance of a celebrity at your nonprofit event, it may be advisable to contact the person directly, not through his/her agent. The initial approach should be made by someone with clout (e.g., library board chairperson, community or political leader) or through a friend with a contact, however nebulous. Agree in writing about fees or lack of them, expenses to be covered, and responsibilities of the celebrity at the event. Explain the type of program and the reason for it, and be honest about the arrangements; a celebrity may be reluctant to risk public image in a low budget or restricted exposure activity, or may expect more than you can provide in the way of expenses, facilities, or sophisticated equipment. Give the person a simple, thoughtful gift afterward. Be aware, too, of the possibilities of embarrassment over a celebrity's lifestyle that may not be in tune with your community's mores. Many big names may be willing to appear on your behalf, for personal or altruistic reasons, and you won't know until you ask!

Have back-up speakers, and schedule rearrangements and substitutions for every aspect of your event; just in case—and so you can avoid a total nervous breakdown.

Arrange for a standby vehicle for emergency transportation of missing guests, missing or malfunctioning equipment, accidents or illness.

Include a personal letter or make a phone call to key people along with your printed invitations.

Provide souvenirs or giveaways, if only informational brochures or bookmarks, to increase the promotional and good-will impact of your event.

Tape informal comments of attendees to aid in your follow-up publicity and evaluation.

Secure post-event publicity by reporting interesting human interest anecdotes or as a "letter to the editor" in the form of a thank-you, naming all contributors and volunteers (including the newspaper for the publicity coverage).

Form as many committees as necessary but be sure that each one clearly understands its duties and function; write out an assignment sheet with a timetable and check regularly to be sure that the schedule is maintained.

Appoint and brief a back-up project director.

Keep staff and board members informed of progress and as enthused as possible.

Prepare advance "teaser" displays to be put up inside the library, in banks, stores, Y's, chamber of commerce, other available and appropriate places.

Enlist the aid of outside organizations (the garden club for flowers, Boy Scouts or other youth groups for distribution of flyers, and other tasks.)

If you are rash enough to plan a parade:
- Select a route and check with city authorities.
- Determine number of potential units and confer with groups or organizations.
- Appoint a parade marshall.
- Determine order of units and location of reviewing stand.
- Designate an assembly point.
- Arrange traffic direction and closed area.
- Prepare timetable for assembly, starting hour and review stand passage.
- Prepare review stand with public address system, chairs, decorations.
- Appoint judges if entries are to receive awards.
- Sing "Please Don't Let It Rain on My Parade" daily for a week in advance.
- Paste a smile on the face of everyone involved.

A Few Typical and Atypical Events Libraries Have Staged

National Library Week is often the major excuse for library special events, but they can and do take place at any time of the year. The Orlando (Florida) Public Library sponsored an all-out youth night with eight continuous activities and eight special shows scheduled during the evening. Attractions ranged from handwriting analysis to a fashion show, exotic dancing demonstration to "moods" of surfing. The program announcement included floor plans of the three levels of the library, with a key to the location of each activity. In a similar carnival vein, the Madison County-Canton Public Library (Mississippi) set up booths throughout the building, with each booth featuring books, materials, and demonstrations on a different subject.

In New York, the East Meadow Public Library chose "Carousels, Coney Island and Cotton Candy" as a theme for a three-day affair that featured the author of a book about Coney Island, a display of antique carousel figures, nostalgic films, midway games, a "paint-in," merry-go-round music, and, of course, cotton candy.

"Author Festivals" are ambitious undertakings that often draw sizeable, enthusiastic crowds. One such event, planned by a California library and shared with over 70 county schools, overcame the formidable odds of an isolated area and little funding to do "more to promote reading and interest in the library and its use than anything that's ever happened before," in the words of one of the librarians involved. An account of this, "The Pied Pipers of Humboldt," by Ann B. Elliott, appeared in *California School Libraries*, Winter, 1977, Vol. 48, No. 2, and this report of the planning and promotional procedures would be a helpful guide to anyone considering a similar event.

Library tours for special groups at specified times are frequently scheduled by libraries, particularly during National Library Week; the Osterhout Free Library (Wilkes-Barre, Pennsylvania), for example, declared Senior Citizens' Day, Business People's Day, Educators' Day, Governing Officials' Day, and held twice-daily tours specifically aimed at these groups.

Contests are special events and are always of interest. The purpose—to attract the attention of a large number of people and to involve them in a library-sponsored activity—is relatively easy to attain through good publicity and the solicitation of donated prizes. Properly conducted, a contest has the additional virtue of a good return, in terms of participants, for the amount of staff time needed, as compared with many other pro-·

". . . anyone for a contest?"

grams. Some contests also have a secondary purpose, and can produce something useful for the library itself, such as a new logo, a design for the bookmobile or van, a slogan, or good quality photographs of the library suitable for use in publications. If contests prove popular in a community, it is even possible to reap a greater reward by requiring a donation or "entry fee" to be applied toward the purchase of some specific item needed by the library and to offset any expenses.

Rewards, in the form of recognition and/or a tangible item (certificate, plaque, ribbons or prizes of more or less value) are important for motivation, and the greater the promised reward, the greater the participation. Prizes, in whatever form, should be commensurate with the amount and type of skill required and the age or particular group that you wish to interest. Some contests lend themselves to classification according to age or to amateur/professional status.

Judging should, of course, be fair and impartial, and in the case of value judgments about quality, the judges should be people with expert knowledge or backgrounds, preferably from outside the staff itself. Picking persons with well-known names in the community will also have additional publicity value. The contest rules should be clearly stated and all possible contingencies considered in formulating them according to the nature of the contest. If children are involved, it is wise to see that every entrant receives a token of some sort.

If the primary purpose is to get people into the library, the contest can be staged in-house, require a trip to the library to pick up an entry blank, or require a library card for participation. This is somewhat self-limiting, but may be of value if combined with a pitch for library usage in the form of a smiling welcome, a library brochure handout, or a sheet of winning hints.

Quiz contests are frequently used as a sugar-coated approach to teaching library usage by requiring that answers to questions must be found in the library's resources. Trivia contests have been highly successful. The Oshkosh (Wisconsin) Public Library sponsors one as an annual affair. The contest runs for a week, and contestants can sign up individually or as a group. The librarian may suggest books or types of materials to aid in finding the answers, but cannot research questions. Two separate sets of questions are used, one for adults and one for young people in grades three through eight. (See Appendix III.)

The Queens Borough (New York) Public Library offered a prize of a 10-volume home reference library for answers to a quiz about the Library itself, entitled, "The Fun Way to Find Out What's New at the Library."

Crossword puzzles are popular with young and old, and a subliminal message can be included in book or library-related clues. The puzzle can be printed in the local newspaper for wide dissemination, in a regular newsletter, or as a handout and distributed from various community outlets. In New Jersey, the Mercer County Library held a crossword puzzle contest. An original was prepared by the puzzle editor of *The New York Times,* a one-hour deadline was set, and dictionaries were made available. This event drew extensive media coverage and crowds of people. Libraries have staged other in-house game contests—chess, checkers, backgammon, bridge, and others.

Contests or shows that feature such skills as cooking, art in various forms, hobbies, and crafts appeal to a select group of entrants, but the event or resulting display engenders interest on the part of a more general viewing public. The series of photography contests sponsored jointly by the Central Kansas Library System and the headquarters library at Great Bend is a good example of how one such competition was handled. Several photo categories were chosen, at different periods, including travel, people, and animals. Sometimes the contest was held for two divisions, amateur and professional, and/or in two classes, adult and junior; others were "open class" with no distinctions. Only black and white or color prints were accepted. Judging procedure has varied: the

travel category was judged by a professional photographer and the head of the art department of a neighboring college; the animal category by a photographer, zoology professor and an artist; the people category by vote of library visitors. Each event was publicized several weeks in advance by releases to all media resources in the four counties involved. The contest was featured for four or five days on the daily library radio program, bookmarks describing the contest were distributed by all of the libraries in the counties, and flyers were prepared for various outlets, including photo shops. Gretchen K. Ford, Public Information Officer, reported, "We have had outstanding entries, lots of positive comments, a great deal of traffic through the building during the shows, and an increase in interest with every category."

A good contest that has sparked a lot of comment and attention is often worth repeating, such as this series of photo contests. In time, a certain amount of anticipation can be built up, and the number of entrants may increase, particularly when considerable lead time is needed for preparation of entries.

Many contest are just for fun—limerick contests, original jokes, write-the-end-of-this-story, pet shows, guess-the-number-of-whatever, and so on. The small Cedarburg Public Library in Wisconsin sets its sights high and turns out a large following with an "Annual Great Balloon Race"; participants are eligible if they have, or apply for, a library card, and the person whose tagged helium balloon travels the greatest distance receives a book gift certificate. In Mellen, Wisconsin, the Legion Memorial Library sponsors an annual and amusing frog-jumping contest. The library reports that the annual contest has become so popular that people in the rural community start catching frogs early in the season to "train" them—and occasionally lose them in the house. On the big day, youngsters line up with their entries in jars, boxes, and bags, and enter the roped-off area one by one. The frog is placed by the child on the starting line, and "encouraged" to jump. The librarians mark the distance of each of three jumps and the total is recorded. Excitement runs high; frogs have been known to pass out on the starting line and some jump to oblivion into the crowd!

Libraries are occasionally asked to participate in fairs, festivals, expositions, or shopping mall promotions, and others actively seek such opportunities to display their wares and promote their services. Such forays into the outside world can and have been successful, but many library "promoters" have learned from experience that it takes more than a willingness to set up a backdrop, table, and some books to get attention from a crowd in a holiday mood or intent upon shopping.

First, if you are one of many exhibitors, find out what space has been allocated to you, and what competition you must contend with on either side or across the aisle. If you have been relegated to the boondocks you may not want to participate, because you may sit in splendid isolation without a brass band or some noisy hijinks to lure people far afield.

Design your booth or arrange your space so that the setup is simple and dramatic; avoid clutter and the urge to include too many messages. Pick a theme or focus on one or two resources or services to feature so that those passing by get the message quickly, whether or not they linger to learn more. (And most will not!)

". . . Do something! Don't just sit there!"

Identify the library in large bold letters and repeat the identification as often as possible so that it can be seen clearly from all directions.

DO something! Don't just sit there. Have some sort of activity going on. This can be a film, a slide show, or a demonstration. You could air music from the library's collection, tapes of an old radio program, sound effects, whatever. Hold brief story-telling sessions or put on a puppet show—dress up in an imaginative way. Sell used books or let Friends sell craft or library-related items, such as book bags, stationery, or postcards. A static display will interest very few, and you are in the midst of this hubbub to reach the masses.

The challenge to "Stump the Librarian" is an activity that some libraries have found worthwhile. This is an opportunity to demonstrate the reference resources of the library by producing the answers to questions submitted by the public. Usually a small reference collection is kept at hand at the booth, and a direct telephone line is set up to the main library. Rules vary, but generally librarians are required to answer a "reasonable"

question within 30 minutes or consider themselves stumped and award a prize.

Staff the booth at all times and *stay on your feet*—no matter how they ache. A person sitting passively, awaiting attention, will get only a brief glance from bypassers.

Curiosity is a motivating factor in a crowd, and it is apt to flow where people are congregated. Keep a few onlookers around, even if you must prevail upon friends or co-workers to mill about when there is a slack in the tide.

Distribute a giveaway. If this is only a bookmark, booklist, brochure, or announcement, make it as dramatic or unusual as possible. Roam the area with your hand out, if necessary, and buttonhole individuals.

If this kind of hustle and bustle goes against the grain, then fairs and malls are not for you. Additional good advice and suggestions can be gleaned from the reports of libraries that have taken the plunge.

The Portsmouth Public Library in Virginia sought exhibit space for three days in a local shopping mall to prove that "Librarians Are Lively." Films and demonstrations were interspersed so that there was continuous activity, and one of the key aims of the project was achieved when 355 new borrowers were registered. They coded the registrations to find out how many people actually used their new library cards within a three-month period, as an additional evaluation of this objective. Although they tried to circulate books, they found that this did not get enough response, since people were in too much of a hurry to select a title. In the course of circulating about the mall and talking to people, one staff member, to her surprise, learned that many persons were not aware that library cards were free—the free aspect was subsequently emphasized to attract the shoppers. Six weeks later they restaged the event in the same mall, and registered another 383 patrons; this would indicate that the potential for attracting new friends is by no means exhausted one time around.

When several Connecticut libraries cooperated to put on a three-day extravaganza at a shopping square, they learned that activity at each table (film, filmstrips, video recording) was necessary to make people pause long enough for the staff to tell them what it was all about. They found that busy shoppers did not stop to pick up the flyers that were available, and resorted to handing them out in an aggressive manner. They also benefited from the expert advice on publicity and traffic flow that was provided by the staff at the shopping center. (Others would do well to remember to seek this assistance if it is not volunteered.) When the shopping square personnel called this "the most active and exciting event ever staged by a community group," the librarians attributed the success to the fact that it was a cooperative venture on a scale that no one library could handle alone. Cooperative funding kept the cost per library low but enabled them to engage professionals for signs and posters. The consensus was that the librarians learned something about what people thought libraries were, which was, perhaps, as valuable as showing others what libraries really are and do.

Although the Connecticut group decided to focus on common library services rather than on individual libraries, in Pennsylvania, 31 libraries cooperated for a "Salute to Montgomery County Public Libraries" and opted to highlight each library or library association individually. Each exhibit displayed or demonstrated one single aspect of the varied library services of all. Thus, one library exhibited rare books, another a vertical file collection, one displayed recordings and cassettes, another children's materials.

When the Brown County Library in Wisconsin had a display at a Home and Garden Show, they learned some lessons that they applied to a subsequent participation in a Sports Show. A liberal use of balloons on the backdrop proved to be effective as an eye-catcher and was used again, but an extensive display of books did not attract much attention and was cut to a small selection related to the subject of sports the second time around. Recognizing that a handout of a dull booklist could not compete with the free yardsticks, carnations, and drawings of others, they designed and handed out a special "Sports Quiz," in keeping with the theme of the show. The library name appeared alone on the backdrop in very large letters and was repeated on two table-top signs. A staff member reported, "We discovered that the theme—any theme—was relatively unimportant, but that the words "Brown County Library" and the smiles of the librarians outweighed everything else in importance."

The Birmingham Branch Library of the Toledo-Lucas County Library System in Ohio used the occasion of a neighborhood festival to promote the fall programs planned at the library, and people were encouraged to sign up in advance at the library's booth. Children sporting decorative and informative cardboard cartons mingled with the crowd as "walking book boxes" to advertise various scheduled events. A large and effective banner simply said "Birmingham Library—Sign Up for Fall Programs." In addition, the Friends of the Library gave additional exposure by staffing the festival's information booth, and at the same time sold balloons and novelty hats.

When the Onondaga Library System in New York participated in Syracuse's annual Festival of Nations, a lively demonstration of folk dancing was chosen as their exhibit feature. With the theme "Your Public Library Has the Know-How," a large sign admonished festival-goers to "Step to the Music—Learn Folk Dancing Here." Dances from a different country were taught every half hour, and a bookmark list of folk dance recordings was distributed.

Festival-goers were taught folk dances from many countries when the Onondaga Library System (NY) participated in the city-sponsored "Festival of Nations."

Anniversaries and Centennials

A milestone in the library's history—10th, 25th, 50th, or 100th anniversary—offers a timely opportunity to remind the public of the library's long service to the community and to call attention to present and future activities. The observance can be a many-faceted festivity or a simple ceremony.

Although centennials are the big ones, you needn't wait until you are 100 years old to celebrate. The Salt Lake City Public Library System marked the tenth anniversary of the move into a new main library building with a "rededication ceremony" that capped a month of exceptional programing which demonstrated and reflected the type of programs sponsored throughout the year.

The all-day "75th Birthday Bash" of the Plainfield (Indiana) Public Library, on the other hand, was a rollicking celebration inside and outside that involved local artists painting at easels, quilters working at a quilting frame, folk singing, a bluegrass music group performing, a "birthday tree," animals from the zoo, a book review, film showings, homemade ice cream, a reception honoring former trustees, staff members and long-term patrons, all climaxed by the release of 1,000 balloons.

The Oshkosh Public Library observed its 75th anniversary with an intensive five-day series of demonstrations, music, film, slide and lecture programs, highlighted by a flag-raising ceremony that included the first display of the library's own flag, produced from the winning entry in a flag designing contest for children.

For the "Diamond Jubilee" of the Manitowoc Public Library in Wisconsin, the staff dressed in turn-of-the-century costumes, and four special days were designated: Heritage Day, Yesterday's Crafts, Senior Citizens' Day, and Young People's Day, with appropriate activities. A newspaper release read,

> If you get to the library only once every 75 years that once should be Wednesday, Thursday, Friday or Saturday—or preferably all four days, when the Manitowoc Public Library is celebrating its 75th birthday anniversary. . . .

and seven area radio stations, a TV station, and numerous daily and weekly newspapers gave the event extensive publicity.

The Memphis Public Library and Information Center elected to observe its 80th birthday with a more traditional ceremony, featuring a speaker, recognition and presentation of a book to the holder of the oldest library card, and tours of the Main Library. The program was printed as part of an attractive history, "The First 80 Years."

A centennial occurs only once-in-a-lifetime, and is often the excuse for a major production which may extend throughout the year and which involves a long lead-time for planning. Although few libraries are the size of the Milwaukee Public Library, the following account of a centennial observance offers some interesting ideas and suggestions that others might adapt.

The celebration was scheduled to start in February, 1978; the first planning meeting was held in March, 1977, almost a full year in advance. The budget was established at $5,500, but this was augmented many times over by the donation of materials and services. A 25 member Centennial Committee was named, chaired by the chief of publications and exhibits of the Library. Each committee member was assigned to one of the seven working subcommittees. Staffwide participation was considered one of the main goals of the centennial celebration, and volunteers were encouraged and—on occasion—recruited. To aid in keeping the staff of 500 both informed and involved, a series of special staff newsletters, "Sneak Preview: the Library at 100" was published at intervals, in addition to the regular bimonthly issues of the staff news publication "The Booktruck," which previewed or recapped all events.

A slogan contest for the staff members was held in December and a $100 prize was awarded for the motto "Source of the Past, Resource for the Future." A new logo was designed and adopted:

The kickoff activity was a community open house at the Central Library, but it was preceded by a staff preview party the night before, which was designed both as a salute to the library staff and a rally. There was wine donated by an anonymous friend, plus cheese, door prizes, and entertainment.

Over four thousand people attended the official opening affair the next afternoon. After a brief program in the Library rotunda at 2 P.M., tours were started and continued all afternoon; refreshments, including a cake made in the shape of the Central Library and mounds of staff-baked goodies, were served; the player-piano entertained people, using player-piano rolls from the Library's historic collection; children's films and the library's multimedia show were shown over and over again. Over 6,000 posters and 2,000 buttons were distributed. People browsed, ate, drank, toured, watched, and became reacquainted with their library.

The final noting of the February 7 anniversary came in the form of a resolution from the Wisconsin Senate congratulating the library on its centennial.

Announcement of Centennial Celebration.

ONE GOOD CENTURY DESERVES ANOTHER

photo exhibit of the library
First Wisconsin Center -
Galleria
thru Sept. 8

Announcement of the Library Photo Exhibit for the Milwaukee Public Library Centennial.

An entry in the slogan contest, "One Good Century Deserves Another" was used as the caption for a photographic panorama of the library's past. Numerous special events were scheduled throughout the year at the Central Library, including a concert series that featured all types of music, from bluegrass, rock, country to Renaissance, woodwinds, and choirs. The Central Library also shared the centennial with its neighbors—downtown Milwaukee—on Downtown Day, one of the periodic special "sale days" sponsored by the Downtown Association. A variety of activities, billed as "The Downtown Association Salutes a 100-Year-Old-Neighbor—The Milwaukee Public Library," included a library used-book sale, children's story-hours given by librarians at various stores, and film showings. Library information, posters, and pamphlets were distributed by members of The Bookfellows-Friends of the Milwaukee Public Library System at three downtown banks, and the Business Information Services added its special materials to tables at four more locations. Exposure was provided in display windows at three bookstores and through a special historic display in the J.C. Penny Co. Store—an early site of the Milwaukee Public Library. Ronald McDonald distributed free Library balloons, Library flags with the new logo were flown from several locations, and the Electric Company sign touted the salute to the Library.

Each branch library participated in the celebration by scheduling special events on its own birthday, i.e., the day it opened its doors to the public. The citywide children's summer reading program took both a centennial and a sports theme, based on the tenth anniversary of the popular Milwaukee Bucks basketball team, with the slogan "Score with Books." Children received a special Bucks folder, T-shirt iron-on, team picture, and button.

In addition to new flags, banners, buttons, and book bags, a series of commemorative posters was issued. In a mutual recognition of shared centennials, a large printing company printed a four-color poster for the Library, and in return, the Library displayed samples of the company's production through the years, from turn-of-the-century checks to an Elvis Presley poster.

The weekly library newsletter, "Milwaukee Reader," carried many centennial related features, including a history, a series of human interest vignettes about various patrons, an article on what they were reading in '78, and a history of the "Reader." Few promotional or publicity opportunities were overlooked during the year to call attention to the centennial of a valued community resource—even the passes used on the bus wished the Library a happy birthday for a week.

Finally, the Library planned a lasting "birthday gift" to the city. A communitywide fund-raising effort was initiated to renovate the beautiful old Central Library lecture hall, a large, accoustically sound theater, which had fallen into disuse and needed remodeling to bring it to building code standards so that it could be made available freely to community groups.

Grand Openings and New Building Dedications

The dedication and opening of a new library building is a very special event, and one that is eagerly anticipated by staff, trustees, and many members of the community; a successful one is bound to leave many in a state of both euphoria and exhaustion! Planning and scheduling an opening are frequently plagued with uncertainties about structural completion dates and delays in delivery of new equipment, compounded by unforeseen glitches and last minute hitches. Forewarned is not necessarily forearmed.

A long-term media publicity program should proceed any planning for publicity about the actual dedication or grand opening ceremony. In many cases, community awareness has been raised to a high level through the bond issue or fund raising campaign waged to secure a new building, but it must be sustained during the months (or even years) that it takes to complete the structure.

A ground-breaking ceremony can be staged and pictures released. This should be followed, at intervals, with pictures and releases as the building progresses. In New Brunswick, for example, the Fredericton Public Library managed to catch the attention of the media by staging a "paint-in" at the construction site of the new building. Children from the school district submitted picture entries on the theme, "People, Places and Events from Books We Have Read," and 100 were selected to

One issue of the Milwaukee Public Library's newsletter reprinted the various heading styles that had been used in the year preceding its centennial observance.

be painted by the original artists on the wall at the building site; local drive-in restaurants donated hot meals and the library provided hot chocolate as the youngsters worked on a cold day. There were front page pictures in the newspaper and interviews on the radio as a result.

Moving day can be a newsworthy event in itself. Pictures of staff and volunteers aiding with the move or a long "bucket brigade" passing books from hand to hand will often be printed. One newspaper even ran a picture of a stack of empty boxes, donated by a local firm, that were to be used for hauling books to the new location. The director of a library in a small community garnered

". . . move those books!"

some good publicity when he tried to solve the moving problem by issuing a plaintive request for everyone in the area to come in and check out a large quantity of books and then return them directly to the new building when it opened!

Publicity about an unusual activity helped to make the residents of Jefferson City, Missouri aware of the impending move to a new building. The library held an auction of all items that were not suitable for the new quarters or were being replaced. A huge crowd jammed the structure and over $5,000 was bid for old desks, shelving, and file cabinets, as well as for a few antiques such as wall fixtures and oak armchairs.

In Salt Lake City, plans for a progressive advertising campaign were made as soon as ground was broken for the new Whitmore Library; before the grand opening, ads were placed in the daily and local weekly newspapers, posters and handouts were distributed through the schools, and a grocery store used the handout as a bag stuffer. Space on an electronic flashing light sign at a busy intersection was purchased for a month to invite everyone to the open house. Television and radio interviews were arranged, and news releases were sent out regularly.

The opening of a new library building is often the occasion for a special newspaper supplement, usually underwritten by firms involved in the building and civic-minded businesses.

Institutional ads or flyers, designed to call attention to the occasion, need not be in the usual staid picture-of-a-new-building format. For example, a small folder announcing the new library building in McHenry, Illinois was a light-hearted piece:

PREMIERING OCTOBER '76
THE STORY YOU'VE
BEEN WAITING FOR!!!
THEY SAID IT COULDN'T BE DONE
not a musical . . .
not a disaster movie . . .
not x-rated . . .
but thrilling!
IT'S
LIBRARY '76
NOW SHOWING ON THE CORNERS OF
MAIN AND GREEN STREETS, McHENRY,
ILLINOIS

The enclosed invitation gave the date of the grand opening and the "curtain time."

Special brochures are often printed up when a new building is completed. When intended as tour guides or as introductions to new services, arrangements, and resources, they will have a longer life as a handout if the dated dedication program is a separate, loose insert. The descriptive brochures issued upon completion of a new building traditionally contain a list of credits, special donors and other acknowledgments, building data and statistics, sketches, photos, or floor plans, and a list of officials of the town or city and the library board. Sometimes a brief message from the mayor, board president, and/or library director is given along with a history of the library. They are of limited interest to the general public, and the press run should be estimated accordingly.

The Broward County Library in Florida used a very different kind of handout on the day of opening of the new building; key officials and the news media representatives were given library cards and cassette tapes which described the Library's resources.

The actual dedication ceremony usually follows a standard pattern. A typical program would read:

Fanfare by band
Presentation of colors
National Anthem
Invocation
Welcoming comments by Library Board President
Official greeting
Introduction of dignitaries
Dedication address
Musical presentation
Benediction
Ribbon-cutting
Tour of facility and reception

Many libraries have chosen to keep the mandatory ceremony to a minimum and have added innovative twists to attract public interest. In Green Bay, Wisconsin, the new building, which occupied an entire city block, was wrapped around with a wide ribbon, and everyone who came on opening day was given a pair of scissors to help cut the ribbon on signal. In Door County, Wisconsin, attendees at the brief dedication ceremony registered for a commemorative gold key to open the new building, and the governor of the state drew the name of the winner. In Washington, at the North Spokane Branch of the Spokane County Library, Indians from a nearby reservation did a tribal dance in the center of the new building on opening day to put their stamp of approval on the affair.

The Onslow County Public Library in Jacksonville, North Carolina reported that their dedication was a smash.

> One of the library's oldest patrons and one of its youngest helped cut the ribbon. The magician performed magically. . . . The rock band that performed in the evening didn't arouse one complaint from nearby residences. The goateed sculptor, unperturbed, chipped away at a bust of George Washington, and politicians showed up en masse. . . . People milled about the library browsing through books and magazines, listening to records and signing up for library cards. Staff members feel that they were able to get the people out and show them the library and what it has to offer. The day was such a success that the library is considering hosting an annual rededication event.

In larger libraries, opening day festivities are frequently followed up by several days or a week of special activities, often of a gala nature. When the Carnegie Library of Pittsburgh opened a new downtown branch, primarily serving business personnel, five large companies sponsored a series of continental breakfasts for local merchants and executives, and a week of special noontime talks was scheduled on subjects of interest to this select group.

The Brown County Library (Wisconsin) held one of the most successful grand openings on record. Several key factors contributed to the success: the staff was enthusiastic and actively involved in the planning; assistance was sought and received from hundreds of people in the community; and an executive with public relations and promotion experience was "loaned" by a local savings and loan association to head the steering committee, coordinate the planning, and work with numerous committees and key staff personnel.

Detailed planning commenced four months in advance of the opening date, and reports were regularly submitted to the Library Board for its approval and information. Several events before the formal grand opening were designed for special target groups. The first was a Civic Club Night; 150 invitations were issued to organizations throughout the county, suggesting that this event might replace a regular meeting, offering a tour of the facilities, and a room for the group's business session and regular program if desired. The following evening was designated "Business and Industry Open House," and the Chamber of Commerce invited top management personnel to attend. On the night immediately preceding the Sunday public opening, a Founder's Night reception was held for local, state, and federal dignitaries and officials. The official Sunday afternoon grand opening, highlighted by the spectacular ribbon-cutting ceremony, was attended by over 2,000 people, despite a cold drizzle. Each day of the week following featured a different theme: Senior Citizens' Day; Fashion Day; Arts and Crafts Day; Drama Day; Home and Garden Day; and finally, an all-out Sports Day with members of the Green Bay Packers, school athletic teams, and the local snowmobile club. There were daily events for children, and continuous musical performances. Refreshments were served and door prizes awarded daily. Tour guides were selected from schools and various civic groups and given special training. A local technical institute produced a pretour slide program for visitors to watch. The principals of all of the schools in the county were contacted and participation was solicited for exhibits, student performances, and school visits. Every possible community organization was involved in some facet of the event, from garden clubs and senior citizen centers, to the American Association of University Women.

Friends of the Library raised funds to help defray the costs, and about $500 was allocated from the library budget, primarily for printing, stationery, and postage.

A media blitz was mounted that resulted in a barrage of publicity. The planning committee initiated this with a Press Corps Wine Tasting Party at the new building two months before the formal opening to acquaint media representatives with the facilities and the plans for activities and special events. This was followed with regular news releases in the ensuing weeks as plans were finalized. In addition to this coverage, a series of nine special feature articles, "The Library Story," was published weekly. Subject matter included snippets of history, including speculation about the

fate of the old building, a recounting of the political activity that led to formation of a county system, vignettes of the staff, articles about special services and resources, and information about library costs and financing. Full page photos of the interior and shots of patrons and library activities appeared in the local newspapers, and a special newspaper supplement was published on the Sunday of the opening. The ribbon-cutting ceremony was given prominent space, and there were follow-up stories about the first customer, and a report on the number of materials loaned and new registrations received.

Congratulatory editorials also appeared in the newspapers, local radio stations agreed to conduct live remote broadcasts from the new Library, and an original TV drama, starring a former Miss America, was taped on location by a local station and aired just before the formal opening.

This cumulative, aggressive promotional effort, plus detailed and imaginative planning, left few Brown County residents unaware of the new facility or apathetic about the enlarged service opportunities available to them.

Promoting the Library to Special Publics

The importance of establishing objectives for promotion and public information programs has been stressed frequently in the preceding chapters. In most cases this includes defining the "target audience" so that publicity and other activities can be pinpointed effectively. Although there is a certain amount of spill-over effect from any publicity and promotion on some members of a defined group, this may be only marginal and cannot be counted on to inform or influence the majority. At some time, a concentrated campaign to reach a specific group, be it legislators, businesspeople, or senior citizens, should rate a high priority in planning. Such a campaign might be a subprogram of the annual plan, carried on concurrently with all other activities, or it may require the bulk of available time and resources for a period. Any initial all-out effort must be continued in some form if it is to have any long-term measurable effect.

". . . most libraries have a great deal of valuable material for special interests . . ."

Designing a special campaign simply means adapting the usual tools and techniques in ways that will reach and interest a designated group of people. Effective promotion of special services and/or resources can, of course, only be carried out when these are adequate. For example, it would be useless to expend much effort in interesting businesspeople in better usage of the library for reasons related to their work if reference tools and aids in the field are extremely limited. On the other hand, most libraries have a great deal of valuable material, and even most small libraries have access to this through their system or network membership; it is seldom used simply because this segment of the public is unaware of its existence.

Top Priority, Reaching Out to Legislators and Governing Officials

Establishing good relations with legislators and governing officials and keeping them informed and aware of the library is not a matter of much choice; it is essential to survival, because these people hold the purse strings and make the decisions that affect library operations.

The hopes of librarians and concerned patrons for strong support and backing rise when those elected to office—local, state, or national—have a known library interest or background. The hopes and expectations frequently fade as more vocal groups receive attention and desired actions through their aggressive activity.

Lobbying *is* promotion, and it is "special group" pressure even when it is in the interest of the general public. It takes two forms: so-called crisis lobbying, when forces are marshalled to influence pending legislation; and, equally important, activities to keep local and state decision makers informed about the library—its role, services, and needs.

Much of the blame for the failure to secure sufficient funding and constructive legislation can be laid at the door of the local library for its failure—or, more charitably, oversight—in initiating and maintaining an active communication program with governing officials and legislators.

A great deal of information on how to mount a crisis lobbying effort is readily available, but there is much less attention given to the more mundane and regular political contacts that are essential underpinnings of any lobby campaign—contacts that may, in fact, help to avoid the all-too-frequent necessity for crisis lobbying.

Some honest answers to the following questions will give a clue to the state of your political relations:

When was the last time an individual contact was made with one or more governing officials? (By the library director, the board chairperson, public information staff member—in person, by phone, at lunch, or his/her office?)

How many local officials have been in the library to use it or by invitation in the last six months? In the past year?

How many actually own, use, or have been offered library cards?

How many receive regular written communications, other than board meeting minutes and the budget request? When were these last sent?

". . . isn't it time to beef up your efforts?"

A plan to establish or improve working relationships (and the relationship already exists, for good or bad) should have two major thrusts; (1) to interest individuals in personal use of the library by serving their needs and interests, and (2) to keep them *directly* informed about how the library serves the public.

Individual contacts are the cornerstone of the relationship. The number and kind of officials involved and the size of the community will determine the type and frequency of contact that is appropriate or possible, but it is the one-to-one contact that will count most, even if this is nothing more than a personalized note attached to printed material. There can be no hesitancy or necessary justification for giving special attention to a small, select group. In many libraries the effort expended by an outreach librarian to give special service and attention to a small number of people, whether blind, homebound, or an ethnic minority, far exceeds that accorded legislators and governing officials.

If you are not now familiar, at least by name and office, with local decision makers at various levels, start by compiling profiles. In addition to the standard data—addresses, phone numbers, office hours, key aides, etc.—find out as much as possible about their personal interests and activities.

It will be easier to establish a friendly personal relationship, if it does not exist, through mutual friends or a member of the official's family; the social contacts of board members, Friends, or staff will also help to open some doors. Try to arrange occasional face-to-face meetings,

". . . hang around city hall!"

whether informal, by appointment, or on a regular schedule with key persons, and use the time to discuss problems and report on activities and plans. Ask advice. A periodic, personal update can be invaluable, and the official with the "inside dope" is more apt to be a sympathetic ally in the future.

Attend meetings of the city council and other government agencies. This has a twofold purpose: it keeps the library representative, and thus the library, visible as an interested member of the governing authority, and it offers an opportunity to learn firsthand about current concerns. You can then be prepared to offer information and references relevant to the topic, and thereby demonstrate your services at the level where it may count most. (It might not be out of order to establish a "hot line" from council chambers or meeting room directly to the library for instant input.)

In addition to visitations to city hall, get officials into or involved with the library in some way. An open house, which may be more or less well-attended, is one method frequently used. It will be more successful if there is a good pretext, a special inducement, or if it is planned as an informal family night, in which case adults will be brought in by their children!

For this event, issue individual invitations two or three weeks in advance, and follow up with a personal reminder a day or two beforehand. Then write a note thanking the official for coming, or, in the event of a no-show, express regret that s/he could not attend and enclose any information or handouts that had been prepared. If you have held such an affair in the past, repeat it for newly elected or appointed personnel, to acquaint them with your facility, resources, and needs.

A Friends group can be particularly helpful as a sponsor; the Friends of Adriance Memorial Library in Poughkeepsie, New York, for example, invited local government officials from the city, county and adjacent towns to a tour of the library, followed by a buffet supper. In Harnett County, North Carolina, an annual luncheon is held which brings together staff, trustees, Friends, and local officials for a "finger lickin' " home-made chicken dinner; the place cards are library cards. A summary of the annual report is at each place, and the County Library Director gives a brief report after a relaxed meal. A "Bacon, Books, and Ballots" breakfast meeting has been held in LeSueur, Minnesota, for librarians, legislators, and interested citizens as an opportunity to discuss mutual concerns on an informal basis.

Another way to get officials inside the library door en masse is to suggest that the regular meeting of the council or other agency be held at the library. Encourage browsing, prepare a display of specially selected materials, and serve coffee and refreshments. (If you have a circulating collection of framed pictures, for example, offer a choice for use in offices and municipal rooms; chances are the members are unaware of this service.)

A plan for regular written communication is next in order, but this should be more than routine forwarding of official information or copies of library publications or notices. A heap of mail arrives on the desks of legislators and officials daily; to assure that yours will get at least a brief glance, be selective in what you send, and personalize it with a short memo calling attention to one or more items or summarizing pertinent material. You are bound to be appreciated if you forward a list of new materials in the person's special field of personal interest or work from time to time. Include copies of newspaper clippings about the library, in the event that they may have been missed. Photocopy significant fan mail, letters of thanks or appreciation from patrons, and other favorable material. (A copy of one unsolicited and appealing letter, for example, is apt to have as much or more impact than the formal report of a survey that showed 78 percent of the people in the community

approve of the library.) Include a copy of any acknowledgment you have made of complimentary letters in which you have cited the support of the governing officials, by name or agency.

In some communities the number of elected and appointed officials with whom you would like to keep in contact would be too large for regular personal communication and mailings. In this case you might consider issuing a brief, informal VIP newsletter occasionally.

". . . give direct service . . ."

Providing good direct service is, of course, the best way to demonstrate the library's function and establish rapport. A few libraries have provided a special municipal information center for local government agencies, and many more would be well advised to do so. Experience has shown that selling the service takes considerable time and intensive individual cultivation, because government officials, like many others, overlook the library as a source of current and in-depth information that they may need for decision making. The long term payoff is well worth the diversion of staff time, for you are unlikely to "bite the hand that feeds you (information)."

Small community libraries can offer to store local government documents, both as a service to the public and as an aid to public officials. (The Wisconsin library that refused to do this at the request of the city council, citing lack of staff and space, was looked upon with disfavor at budget time.)

There are other ways to be of service and increase good will. Don't wait to be asked, but offer display space for information that officials want disseminated and for material on issues of concern to them.

Suggest the library as the scene for pre-election debates. The Iowa City Library has gone further; it has held semimonthly rap sessions for county legislators in an informal setting that gives them an opportunity to meet constituents. A reference librarian is on hand to supply material relevant to the questions or issues that are raised.

The Orlando Public Library cosponsored a series of programs for citizens and students entitled "Your Local Government," which gave elected officials an opportunity to describe their responsibilities and show how the community is governed at various levels, a useful service to both the legislators and the public, with a plus for the initiative of the library.

All such activities demonstrate, firsthand, the library's service role, and can go a long way in overcoming the too-common official view of the library only as a constant supplicant.

Legislators and other governmental agents want and actively seek as much publicity and exposure as possible, and you can and should turn this to your advantage. Let one or more officials have the limelight at programs or other events you sponsor. Inaugurate a new or expanded service with a news release that features an official receiving the first sample or cites the official's support in making it possible. If you have a literate or interested legislator, give him/her space in your newsletter to explain pending issues that may affect the library.

It is important to say "thank you" as often and in as many imaginative ways as possible, whether a simple, sincere letter or an open public affair with resolutions of appreciation and framed certificates of recognition.

Asking for actual involvement in or assistance with specific library activities is both constructive and flattering. Noting the importance of identification with populist rather than elitist groups in the community, K.R. Fielding suggests, in an article in *American Libraries,* November, 1976,

> Most local government officials are of the working or middle classes. To influence them, we should involve them directly in community projects—oral history, vocational advisory centers, branches or reading stations. . . . Such projects will benefit not only the target groups and their legislators but will win us strong political allies. And by using the legislators as advisors, by taking advantage of their community contacts, we improve chances of our project as well.

All politicians have a sensitive pressure point—that of local pride—and the library is in a good position to apply force there. The highly regarded sociologist, Edward L. Thorndike, often noted that a well-supported public library is a universal characteristic of an intelligent, progressive community. Few officials would deny a desire to build and maintain an intelligent, progressive community, and so a well-supported library is an

ipso facto argument, but one which must be stressed often, subtly and overtly. They may also need to be reminded that the public library can—and in many cases does—directly serve more people of every age and walk of life than almost any other single agency; a very broad if relatively silent constituency.

Your "Knows" for Business

All public libraries worthy of the name either have or have access to at least a basic collection of materials useful to the local business community. But surveys reveal what librarians know and are loath to admit—the vast majority of the "butchers, bakers, and candlestick makers" in the community are unaware of the resources available to them.

In a poll of businesspeople who were asked to rank local library service, most indicated that an improved collection was a first need and *an increased and improved public information program* was the second. (What also came through as a gut reaction was that businesspeople do not consider the library a very efficient operation, at least in terms of their needs. They are also accustomed to the fact that promotion is an intrinsic part of any organization's efforts, and the lack of it on the part of the library is reflected in the ho hum opinion.)

How far to go in building up a special collection, the how and what is needed, and the special services to be rendered are policy and administrative decisions. But the promotion of existing services and materials, at whatever level they exist, is a must. Even the smallest library has a wealth of pertinent material available through interlibrary loan and cooperative systems, and this should be brought to the attention of local merchants and businesspeople.

A promotional program must be ongoing to be effective; an occasional halfhearted gesture in the direction of Main Street or Commercial Avenue will do little or no good, and may actually turn off businesspeople who consider follow-up and follow-through with customers a necessary practice.

Standard promotional tools and activities can be used in a campaign addressed to business and industry—from printed materials, media publicity, in-house and outreach programs, to personal contact.

The Madison Public Library (WI) clearly identifies the area housing materials of special interest to business and industry.

Communicating information about the library's resources and services usually starts with printed brochures and bibliographies. (Unfortunately, it often stops there.) These are useful when and if they actually get into the hands of those who might use them, and are properly designed both in content and format. Businesspeople themselves indicate that direct mailings are the most effective way to get their attention and give them needed information, but this is true only if the mailing piece is specifically tailored to their interests and attractive in design.

You may have or can compile a mailing list of your own and you might occasionally ask to enclose pieces in mailings of the Chamber of Commerce, retail merchant's association, shopping center organizations, and others, to reach selected groups. Use the new business licenses list to keep your own up to date, and make direct mailings immediately to newcomers or new enterprises. In any case, do not depend on a handout from the circulation desk.

A secretary can be an invaluable ally in reaching the "Boss"; make contact with a direct reminder that the library has such useful material as handbooks, directories, and telephone reference for answers to questions. Enclose a special article directed to the attention of the boss.

Bibliographies should include, first and foremost, a list of periodicals. Others should be on subjects specifically tailored to the small businessperson or merchant, manufacturers, or professionals, according to the community composition. Make a list, too, of films, tapes and videocassettes of particular interest. Prepare material about available government documents. Stress the newest titles to help overcome the impression that the library is filled with outdated materials.

Foreign trade information was compiled by the Osterhout Free Library in Wilkes-Barre, Pennsylvania, as soon as the area was declared a Foreign Trade Zone, a good example of how a library can serve the community effectively by keeping abreast of and responding to new developments. In turn, the Chamber of Commerce cooperated by mailing copies of the Library's brochure to all firms in the area which had expressed interest in foreign trade. Listings included foreign telephone directories the Library acquired and numerous pamphlets and books for individual countries, as well as the more standard directories and handbooks.

Attention-getting brochures explaining the library's business services can take various forms, such as a *MEMO:*

From: The Yourtown Library

To: Yourtown Businesspeople

Subject: Your Information Needs

An elaborate facsimile of a stock certificate would make an eye-catching cover for a brochure, emphasizing the idea of the businessperson's potential investment in and with the library. A brochure might be captioned, "How to Succeed in Business with a Little Help from Your Library" (a title of a speech given by Walter Haber, Director of the Baldwin Public Library in New York).

Capitalize on any unsolicited endorsements you may have received, and use them in imaginative ways in your printed materials and publicity. For example, the newsletter of the Gilbert M. Simmons Library in Kenosha, Wisconsin, carried a note from the publisher of a newspaper, expressing appreciation for the response to a request for information concerning the four-day week. The Manitowoc (Wisconsin) Public Library received this commendation from the president of a large manufacturing firm, ". . . As a corporate manager, challenged each day by economic and social problems that affect personal responsibilities, I find the library an essential aid. . . ." Use such statements liberally as messages to help convince others.

Some libraries prepare regular newsletters for the business community. Recent acquisitions are usually listed, but other kinds of information can be included. The Iowa City Public Library bulletin carried notices of special programs of interest to businesspeople, both in the Library and elsewhere in the community, reminders about such resources as background information on political candidates, the up-to-date clipping file on legislative bills, and notices of relevant TV programs. Brief abstracts of magazine articles might also be included.

Other special handouts will help to increase awareness of the library, such as an adhesive sticker listing important telephone numbers, including the library's reference telephone service, prominently displayed; a fact book—your own or that of a cooperative enterprise—that takes the form of a directory of local public officials, officers of civic organizations, and media contacts; a list of basic office references with prices and purchase sources; or other factual compilations suitable to local interests and needs.

Your informational handout piece about the library need not be printed; a tape cassette is easy to produce and can be sent out (with a postage-paid return container if the budget does not stretch

Business Newsletter: Greenville County (SC) Library

to multiple copies); a soundsheet recording is relatively inexpensive in quantity orders and could be effective for larger libraries and cooperative systems in a direct-mail campaign. A videotape about the library can be circulated widely for presentation during management training programs, aired on cable or closed circuit TV, and used as part of an in-library program at other times. In Dallas, Texas, a large firm came to the library and made its own videotape of the resources and services of the library for staff showings.

The gift of an attractive mobile or poster relating to the library and presented during National Library Week or some other special occasion can make an impact. Many officials, executives, and media personnel would be willing to display it to impress clients or constituents with the fact that they are knowledgeable friends and supporters of the library. Other posters, notices, or bibliographies can be designed for display on company bulletin boards.

Personal contact with the business community on the part of the library director or a staff member is, of course, the most effective means of increasing awareness of and encouraging the use of the library. In addition to membership and attendance at meetings of business and professional organizations, a library representative can also set up a series of brief meetings with managers and executives of selected firms. Visitations are time consuming and should be carefully planned to reap the most reward for all concerned.

Research the interviewees so that you can relate the library's services directly to their operation in some way. Take something with you to leave after the interview (a basic premise of good salesmanship), and then try to involve them personally in some way by asking for their assistance, a subtle form of flattery. For example, offer a bibliography and ask that it be checked over for suggested additions or specific materials that could be useful additions to other businesspeople involved in similar activities.

You might conduct an informal survey of company presidents, either in person during a visit or as a mail follow-up, and ask each to name books that were read, found of interest personally or for business reasons, and could be recommended to others. Use these suggestions in the compilation of a list to mail out.

During the visit, offer in-library employee instruction in library usage at convenient times; ask for advice or assistance with library-sponsored program topics that would be of interest to other businesspeople. One library has a volunteer who calls businesses during the day and simply reminds them of telephone reference service and specific materials that might be useful to them.

A special project might serve as an excellent means of making contact with businesspeople and industrialists at the same time that it augments the library's collection in a significant way. Request cooperation in taping interviews to secure historical and biographical data about the business or industry as part of special local historical archives and to serve eventually as primary source material for research.

If qualified library staff personnel is available, offer aid in establishing a company library, or

make contact with the Special Libraries Association or a librarian in a similar type of library in the area. Explore the potential of a company library card for the convenience of employees.

Special exhibits and portable displays can be set up in the lobbies of office buildings, staff lounges of large firms, or on the occasion of organization meetings and conventions, with titles oriented to the company's field of interest, management aid books, and a few popular titles. Roving collections that are left for a period of time are not intended as a permanent company library, but only to encourage the use of the library as the first point of contact in a search for information. When such a collection is first set up, it could be combined with a drive for new card registrants. Newspaper coverage of a pilot event might lead to requests from other companies and firms.

Some large libraries maintain a permanent deposit collection of materials for both employers and employees at the place of business. Scattered reports of this practice indicate that it is a good public relations gesture and service, and that the collections often circulate well, but the use of the public library itself is not substantially increased.

A regional library literally took to the road in Leicestershire, England, to contact industrial firms in the area. A bookmobile was stocked with appropriate technical books and materials and a series of visits was set up in advance so that department and section heads, sales and purchasing personnel could visit "on the job."

One-to-one contact is time and energy consuming, and may be all but impossible in large communities. Then it becomes a question of how to lure busy executives into the library to sell your wares. Many librarians have gone the open-house route or have tried a specially scheduled "library tour," with varying degrees of success. It takes more than an invitation.

An outstanding example of a successful program won a John Cotton Dana Award for the Natchitoches Parish Library in Louisiana. A year-long project was designed in cooperation with the Chamber of Commerce with the stated objective of providing "an opportunity for businesspeople to learn about resources of the library and an opportunity for the library personnel to learn the interests and needs of the business community."

A joint committee designated a target business or group of businesses as the "Business of the Month." A coffee hour honoring the personnel of the particular business was set up each month, with a special display of books and materials and special booklists. The Chamber of Commerce sent out letters explaining the yearlong program of action. Individual invitations were issued by the Library for each monthly open house, and, in addition, all invitees were phoned a day or so before the event with a reminder. Extensive newspaper publicity preceded and followed each open house.

The financial community—officials and staff of the banks, savings and loan companies, credit and finance firms—was the first to be honored. This was followed by open houses for the members of the building and building supply industry, legal and professional services, food retailers and wholesalers, medical and related services, retail clothing and home furnishing businesses, etc.

There was an excellent turnout in all cases, and those attending learned firsthand about the range of materials at their disposal. In addition, the photocopy machine attracted many new customers, and the framed picture collection was discovered as useful for office wall display. The Chamber of Commerce, impressed with the competence and enthusiasm of the staff, asked the Library to host a reception for a state legislator. Good long-term planning, sustained publicity, and the snowball effect of a series all contributed to this significant contact with the business community.

The businesspeople of Youngstown, Ohio, were invited to a continental-style breakfast at the Library, and about 60 executives showed up. Some brought their secretaries to the breakfast to acquaint them with where and how to get information for the boss. It was reported that some businesspeople stayed away from the first affair because they thought it was a fund-raising gimmick, but when they discovered this was not the case, more were expected to attend the next get-acquainted breakfast.

The Mobile Public Library in Alabama sent out a flyer captioned, "When was the last time you let your secretary have the morning off? For some valuable training . . .", with information about a seminar for secretaries and urging employers to send their secretaries for this professional training in using sources of information.

The library's film collection can be a valuable resource to business for meetings and employee in-service training; a film preview of a few could serve as the focus for a meeting to demonstrate another facet of the library's resources.

Seminars and programs of various types on subjects of immediate concern to a selected group will draw many into the library. The Des Moines Public Library, for example, scheduled two films on burglary and pilferage for use with retail merchants, followed by a question-and-answer period conducted by a member of the Police Department; a short commercial by the head of the Library Reference Department closed the session. The Buffalo and Erie County Public Library conducted three workshops on how to manage your own business; feedback from questionnaires distributed at the conclusion revealed that many wanted to hear personal accounts (rather than textbook presentations) from those who had succeeded in establishing a small business. They wanted a step-by-step record of how they did it, what worked, the pitfalls, all preferences worth noting if you plan a similar presentation. The choice of appropriate topics related directly to local concerns and needs, and the timing of a program (e.g., tax and budget information, annual report preparation at the proper period of the year) will contribute to good attendance.

". . . make it worthwhile, timewise . . ."

Businesspeople put a high premium on their time and so you must convince them that the expenditure will be directly profitable to them, whether it is an open house, a tour, or a special program.

Other special events the library can sponsor include a business and industry fair, with a display of local products and special exhibits highlighting particular segments of the business community. This has the advantage of increasing businesspeople's awareness of the library (although not, necessarily, of its value to them) and increasing the awareness of the community at large of local industry. A display of the informational pieces of hometown businesses can be an exercise in getting-to-know-you.

Robert Alvarez, Director of the South San Francisco Public Library, reported an approach he used to dramatize reference services for businesspeople at a service club luncheon. He solicited questions from them as they arrived, and relayed them to the library. About 90 percent of the questions were researched, answered, and relayed back, all within the hour.

An unusual service is offered by the Madison Public Library in Wisconsin, which has compiled a list of successful businesspeople willing to be volunteer consultants and spend time talking to persons who want information about going into or running a small business. The referrals and one-to-one discussions are confidential, and the library simply serves as a go-between for those with knowledge and those seeking special information.

The small town of Sylacauga, Alabama, has encouraged local representatives of big business firms to use their microfilm reader-printer service free when they receive orders and technical data on microfilm. Local salespeople, engineers, and branch managers have taken advantage of this service. In Massapequa, New York, patrons of the Plainedge Public Library can plug into a minicomputer and get the stock market reports. The Westerly Public Library (Rhode Island) has loaned its library auditorium to business corporations for conference and personnel training.

Newspaper, radio, and television features related to the library's service should be used occasionally, if possible. However, the shotgun approach of the newspaper article, radio, or television time, all necessarily rather general, is not as effective as the use of local house organs or newsletters which pinpoint the audience. Establishing the contacts and preparing release materials tailored to special outlets requires a great deal of time and some expertise, but will be more valuable in the end. In talking with or preparing material for business people, avoid library jargon. Out-of-town telephone books and tax information are most often stated as the most-wanted items; publicize the availability of these constantly.

Your successful relations with the business world are based more on the staff attitude and desire to be of assistance than on the scope of a specialized collection. As one librarian stated, "You don't have to know how to make a widget to find a list of widgetmakers for the person who needs it." In order to initiate or upgrade your collection and services and to carry out a continuing information program, you might consider seeking special grants from the business community; a good selling point is the fact that it is cheaper and more efficient than for individuals to establish in-house libraries. Businesspeople are well aware of the advantages of cooperative buying and centralized professional administration, but may not have thought of their relationship to the library's operations in these terms.

Promoting Service to Rural Residents

What distinguishes a rural resident's need for library service from that of a city dweller? Very little. However, promotion of service to a group that is too often underserved is complicated by factors of distance and/or isolation, the potential patron's lack of familiarity with or information about library resources, and, to some extent, lack of knowledge on the part of a city-oriented librarian of the special interests and needs.

Bookmobiles, books-by-mail, and deposit collections are standard ways to extend service to outlying areas. In addition, urban libraries must make a concerted effort to encourage in-library use by rural residents, for these people are frequent visitors to the city for both business and pleasure.

The problem of reaching out to potential rural patrons is compounded by the image of the library as an institution for the educated, by the lingering distrust of "city slickers," the fear of fees and fines (even where these have been abolished), and general apathy due to lack of library access in the past. This all adds up to quite a job of public information!

What kinds of promotion, then, can be helpful in reaching this specific group? *Publicity,* of course, in many forms. News releases about library services and activities, both general and those of particular interest to rural residents, should go to all rural-oriented media regularly. These include weekly newspapers, shopping guides, farm bureau publications, newsletters of rural organizations, and radio and television stations with farm hours.

Robert Audretsch, Librarian at the Salem Public Library in Ohio, which has a successful rural library program, advises,

> Give rural media all releases sent to city organs. There are rural people interested in antiques, the latest best sellers, and rural people who need service to the handicapped. Visit the editor and let him or her know you are interested in serving the rural populace.

In addition, he has prepared news releases concerning the acquisition of a set of 80 tractor repair manuals (one of the best investments the Library ever made). The Library also acquired a Township Law Service, a complete guide for township trustees and clerks, and this was publicized with a photo of the librarian and local officials, under the headline "Library Aids Township Officials."

Publicity should also take the form of posters, flyers, and brochures on occasion. Distribution of these may present a challenge, but key individuals in various rural areas are often helpful in disseminating materials or posting them in well-frequented but often overlooked places. Make sure that the message, whatever form it takes, is simple, direct, and of specific interest to the rural resident. Hammer away at one theme if you know of any particular prejudice or misunderstanding about library service that must be cleared up, or play up one resource that may be little known (e.g., toll-free telephone reference service, continuing education opportunities, or even cassette tapes to "plow the fields by").

The Manhattan Public Library, system center for the North Central Kansas Library System, prepared an attractive brochure about their "Dial-a-Book Library"—a free telephone ordering service to rural residents, with a toll-free number. "You phone us—we send the books." The folder listed some of the subject areas which might be of interest.

Books-by-mail programs are generally publicized through mailings to all rural residents in selected areas, but even this direct contact often needs reinforcement through follow-up mailings and other publicity. Information about books-by-mail must be presented in an attention-getting way—it is not enough to send out an unadorned announcement or even a catalog, which may be overlooked, discarded, or misunderstood as a come-on for a service for which there will be a charge later. The service must be sold, and potential patrons motivated to use it—the outworn library "here-it-is-come-and-get-it" attitude is not enough.

Programs both of general interest and specific rural interest, held in the library or out in the community, are demonstrations of the library's interest in and resources for farmers and others. Imaginative planning and suitable publicity will encourage many to come in, feel welcome, and help to break down the library barrier.

One example of this was described in an issue of the *Alabama Librarian,* with a photo of a full parking lot outside the library. It answers the question, "What do you do when the corn crop fails?" If you are a farmer and you live in the Cross Trails Regional Library area, apparently you go to the public library to see what was wrong with last year's procedure and plan ahead for the coming year. The article describes farmers who arrived in pickup trucks, cattle trucks, Fords, and Cadillacs to attend an institute. Recommendations for the next year's crop were the order of the day, as 91 farmers listened to agricultural workers in a library that truly reached out to serve every patron's needs.

Special farm-and-town get-togethers can be programed to meet mutual interests (i.e., ecology, land use planning, collectibles, crafts, work-at-home possibilities, etc.) or to exchange viewpoints or "homegrown" expertise on various subjects. National Farm-City Week, in November, is a good time to plan a series of such programs, to sponsor special tours (of the library one way and of area farms and other rural operations the other way) or to arrange a farm-city youth exchange day. (You might hire a bus and provide shuttle service for such special exchange events or activities.) Farm-City Week might be concluded with a special Recognition Day for rural patrons—perhaps honoring the family with the most individual library cards, or the country dweller who makes the most use of library service. National Farm Safety Week in July, sponsored by the National Safety Council, and the U.S. Department of Agriculture, is another appropriate period for special programs or exhibits planned to appeal to rural residents. Take rural seasonal activities and routines into consideration when scheduling activities.

The library can cooperate with rural groups by presenting programs at their meetings—Homemakers, FFA, and 4-H, for example. Don't overlook the aid available from county agents, voc-tech schools, university extension departments, and rural government officials in setting up programs as well as acquiring materials that would be useful. You may be able to tap other agencies for assistance in underwriting programs and publications—farm equipment manufacturers, feed companies, power companies, etc. In South Dakota the Citizens State Bank contributes books to the Arlington City Library in fields of agriculture for use by area livestock raisers and feeders and grain farmers. The bank believes that the use of books from the library will increase the expertise of local people in the agriculture industry to make their businesses more efficient, and hence more profitable.

Personal contact by staff members is, as always, the best kind of promotion. Talks to rural schools, churches, grange members, etc., give the librarian a chance to describe library services and to get feedback on local concerns and attitudes. Get acquainted with leaders and key people in rural areas; in turn, they can give advice and, when needed, support for extended service.

How to Keep the Bookmobile More Visible

The bookmobile is a service vehicle and a self-contained mini-library, but it is also a great promotional tool—it is big, mobile, and difficult to overlook (or pass on the highway!). Use it as a traveling billboard; paint it in gay colors, attach posters to the side or back, give it a catchy name or slogan. Some examples: "Oz Mobile" (Ozaukee County, Wisconsin); "Follow the Pied Piper" (Daniel Boone Regional Library, Missouri); "Score with Books" (Peoria Public Library, Illinois); "Follow the Reader" (North Central Saskatchewan Regional Library, Canada); "Books by Bus" (Carnegie Library of Pittsburgh, Pennsylvania); "Page Coach" (Toledo-Lucas County Public Library, Ohio); "The Rambling Rack" (Boliver County Library, Mississippi); "The Loan Ranger" (Santa Cruz, California). Other names that have been used: "The Road Runner," "Wisdom Wagon," and "Soul Express." A third grader in Freeport, New York, won the name-the-bookmobile contest with the entry "Knower's Ark."

Slogans painted on the bookmobile are the world's largest bumper stickers. Samples: "You are Following 4,000 Books" (San Mateo County, California); "Check My Stops and Check Me Out"; "Wave If You Like the Library." Library posters or other signs can be mounted on the side of the bookmobile with magnetic holders. The Withers (Illinois) Library bookmobile carries simple homemade posters using tempera painted on grocery paper and then sprayed with clear plastic to withstand the elements for a time.

If your bookmobile needs a facelift, run a contest for a new design or arrange to have this done as a project by an art school or group. Students at the Milwaukee School of the Arts designed new graphics in bright shades of blue, green, and orange; the Bookfellows, the Library's Friends group, paid for the professionally applied white base coat, and library staff volunteers painted the design.

In a more temporary fun way, children at various schools in the area served by the Boonslick Regional Library (Missouri) were invited to paint anything they wanted on the bookmobile—with tempera paints. The designs were washed off each night for a fresh start the next day, but a photo was taken of each day's efforts, and displayed on a bulletin board.

". . . keep the bookmobile schedule legible and accessible . . ."

Promoting bookmobile service starts, of course, with wholesale dissemination of information about where it will be and when. A printed schedule is the first need, obviously. But most of them fail abysmally as publicity, or even as easily understood information; many closely resemble undecipherable airline or train timetables! Schedules or flyers should be made out for individual or very limited area stops, not as a roundup of every one from Podunk to Pumpkin Holler for the next month. They should be convenient to keep or easy to display, as a bookmark, for example, or as a piece that can be hung up at home or pasted down. Hand these out from the bookmobile itself, and give a generous supply to organizations, businesses, or other agencies to distribute.

Make the schedule available at township registration and polling places, at the post office. Some libraries have compiled a mailing list, updated regularly, and mail out information about scheduled stops and changes. Be sure the book-mobile schedule is included in every printed piece that the main library prepares, or, if the list is too long to reproduce with dates and time, name or map the stops with a phone number to call for further information. Ask rural churches and syna-gogues to include notice of the stop in their area in their bulletins, and be sure the schedule is promi-nently displayed in all schools. As a reminder to patrons, post a sign daily in the bookmobile that says, "We will be back on. . . ." The bookmobile schedule should also be sent to all newspapers and radio stations for daily or weekly listing.

Eye-catching notices can be posted in com-munity stores and centers. In Richmond, Virginia, the bookmobile received unexpected and wel-come publicity when a sign appeared under the marker for a local shopping center, "Bookmobile here Wednesdays, 2:30-5:00." The notice was put up at the suggestion of the manager after he had seen a flyer about the service. "The bookmobile brings us some business, so we'll try to help them out also," he explained. Perhaps community stores could even be persuaded to feature "Book-mobile Day Sales"! Permanent signs on the order of bus stop signs can be erected in many areas.

Announce your arrival in a community or neighborhood with a musical horn or over a loud-speaker, or raise a specially designed flag or banner.

The bookmobile of the Crow River Regional Library in Minnesota goes even further; when it circles Green Lake on a given day, it plays music from a loudspeaker, and can be waved down by a resident for a stop and a chance to browse. In short, be visible and audible.

Schedules and announcements will help the people who are likely to use a bookmobile, but the more difficult task is to let the less motivated know what you have for them and to persuade them to use the service. Just parking the bookmobile in a convenient spot is not sufficient, for many are timid about entering. Invite groups to visit together on a special date in different areas—Scouts, religious groups, senior citizens, women's and men's or-ganizations, town boards. When you inaugurate a new stop, invite a local VIP, one who has contact with many residents, on board for a tour and expla-nation of the service; this could be the postmaster, owner of the general store, gas station, or feed mill.

Demonstrate the bookmobile as often as pos-sible by taking it out to fairs, festivals, shopping

centers. You will have to be prepared to overcome the reluctance of many to enter the vehicle by planning a come-on: music, a giveaway, a film or demonstration of some sort. (If there is little ap-pearance of interesting activity, you may find your-self alone in a crowd. Have a dressed-up hawker arouse curiosity, and make sure there are people moving in and out, even if you have to fake it initially with staff and long-suffering friends who will troop through the doors.) Take the bookmobile to play areas and such unexpected places as farmer's or flea markets, summer church suppers, or community sports events, on a one-time show-and-tell basis. Visit a beach or a popular country picnic area unexpectedly. Join a parade. The St. Charles Parish Library in Louisiana, for example, used the bookmobile as a float in the Mardi Gras celebration. In keeping with tradition, staff mem-bers dressed as pirates and rode atop the book-mobile, throwing pieces of candy to the crowd with attached bookmarks and free fine coupons. Book-mobile schedules are frequently very tight, and such expenditures may be difficult to arrange; however, it is worth a try to loosen it up now and then, because the exposure is good for both the bookmobile and for the whole library system and service.

Arrange for feature stories in the newspapers and interviews on radio and television. A book-mobile librarian has a wealth of good anecdotes and human interest stories to tell, and both news-

Editors will frequently use a good photo of the book-mobile with a news or feature story.

papers and television stations are interested in angles that will appeal to the rural segment of their audiences. A picturesque shot of the bookmobile in slide form would make a good background for a TV spot announcement read by the station personnel. Newspaper publicity can be obtained by picturing the first registrant at a new bookmobile stop, or with a story marking the anniversary of the service or milestones in the distance traveled, such as when the first 100,000 or 200,000 miles have been covered.

The bookmobile, by virtue of its personal service and intimate one-to-one contact, can build up a strong cadre of supporters, as some Wisconsin county board members discovered when the service was about to be drummed out in an economy measure. A flood of letters soon convinced the supervisors that this was a monumental mistake as far as their constituents were concerned. Good contact with county and township officials, if only through the process of keeping them informed about the service in their area by individual letters and publicity, will help to avoid such possible head-on confrontations. Offer to take various officials out on the bookmobile run for some handshaking, or send them a schedule of bookmobile stops before elections, with the suggestion that it would be an opportunity to meet voters informally.

If direct involvement of community groups and residents is a key to good promotion and successful bookmobile service, then the Southwest Wisconsin Library System has one answer. Bookmobile stops are sponsored by an organized community group in an area where the service is desired. The group's responsibilities include arranging for a proper space, "informing the community of the bookmobile service through talks, announcements in newspapers, club bulletins and radio; posting the schedule; telling people by telephone and in person of the schedule." In addition, a member of the group serves as a host during the bookmobile visit, and aids in checking out books and helps with contacting patrons with overdue or lost books.

Bookmobile exhibit possibilities are somewhat limited by space but can be an effective way to interest potential patrons. In Brown County a different school class decorates the display area every two weeks; the Oshkosh bookmobile has a community bulletin board that includes advertisements of items for sale. Others have posted school

pictures on a rotating basis; clipped items of local interest; prepared regular "good supporter's profiles" about individual patrons; featured local authors; prepared displays of miniature crafts and handiwork; hung poster contest entries from the ceiling; and have even run a pet location service.

Some extracurricular bookmobile activities can have promotional value. Preparing a "bookmobile cookbook" of favorite rural or ethnic recipes of patrons can be both good advertising and a possible money-making project.

Handouts can call attention to the bookmobile—bookmarks, buttons, even lollipops with an attached message, "Lick your reading problems with the bookmobile!" A diagram of the bookmobile that can be cut out and colored will be popular with children, and is likely to be saved at home.

In South Carolina, the Southport-Brunswick County Library bookmobile has a portable TV on the vehicle so that patrons can get books without missing their soaps or other favorite programs, and a set of scales is available for weigh-ins for those on diets.

". . . special activities are possible . . ."

Many activities and programs can be conducted in, on, or outside the bookmobile with a little ingenuity and/or special equipment. Films can be shown, story hours or sing-alongs held, a celebrity can ride along to give autographs or have a brief chat with patrons. The Toledo-Lucas County Page Coach held an Easter egg hunt by hiding paper eggs in the pockets of books.

Attention was called to bookmobile service in Louisiana in a most unusual way. Several companies and individuals contributed to the restoration of a 1928 Chevrolet sedan, a replica of the state's first bookmobile. The car, accompanied by staffers in period dress, appeared during pregame ceremonies at football games, in parades, and at various other occasions.

Close to the ultimate in bookmobile promotion may have been achieved in New Mexico when the bookmobile librarians in the state were honored by the State Senate on a specially designated Bookmobile Librarians' Day.

This is a sample of the bookmobile sketch that several libraries have used as a cut-and-color diagram for children. This can be printed on heavy paper or cardboard and assembled as a model. It is also a good way to circulate the bookmobile schedule, if that is printed on the top!

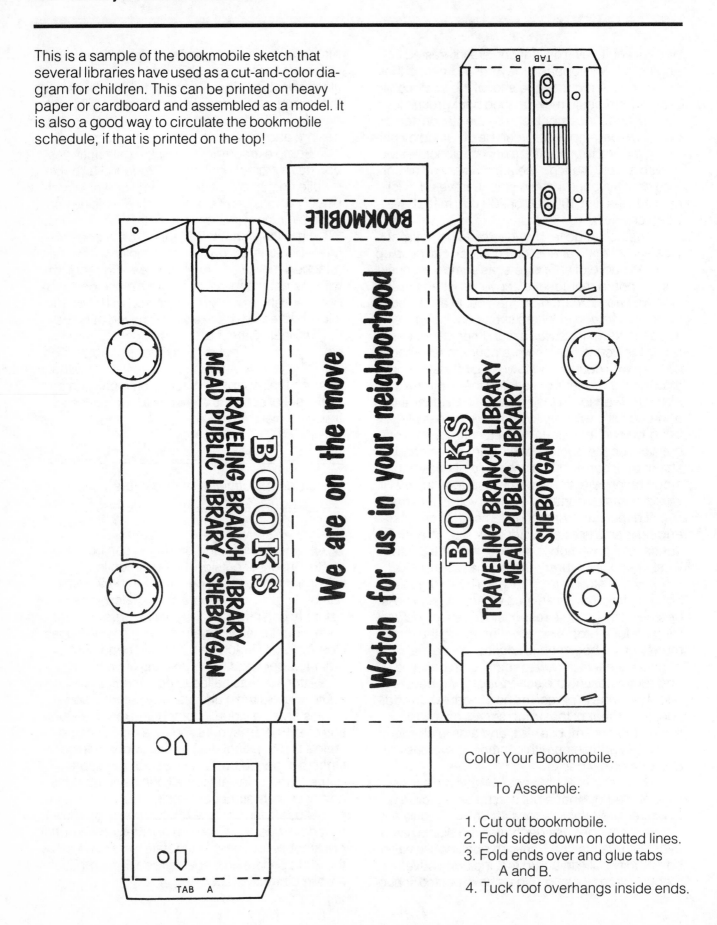

Color Your Bookmobile.

To Assemble:

1. Cut out bookmobile.
2. Fold sides down on dotted lines.
3. Fold ends over and glue tabs A and B.
4. Tuck roof overhangs inside ends.

Luring the Blue Collar Worker

Promoting library service to the blue collar class—a term rapidly becoming a misnomer—is one of the biggest challenges facing librarians. This group has been neglected for decades, despite the fact that it represents one of the library's largest potential constituencies.

The reasons for the neglect are many. Librarians and other workers often hold distorted images of each other. The uninviting attitude of "well, we're *here,* come and get it" is still prevalent among librarians. There is a marked and well-documented apathy toward libraries on the part of adult males in the nonprofessional, nonmanagerial group, and, in turn, the library has continued to have a middle class, WASP orientation. Local union officials may be disinterested or uncooperative in promoting library services to the union and its membership. Libraries have failed to offer materials and services that meet the needs of local unions, and librarians often have difficulty in identifying and relating to groups whose mores, needs, and definitions are undergoing change.

There are no easy solutions to these deep-seated and long-term problems. Obviously they can not be glossed over or remedied by a special poster, a display, a one-time contact, or the continuation of a routine activity that has borne little, if any, fruit in the past.

The problem must be faced, however, for in the words of one union official, "It is the responsibility of librarians to break down the resistance on the part of unions and labor because a library is a community service and as such, must serve all."

Promotion of library service to this large and basically disinterested segment of the public cannot begin until the full potential for a good, meaningful program has been developed; this may require a new attitude and understanding, plus development of a pertinent and expanded materials collection. Only then can the methods and means of promotion be considered.

Successful promotion may require new "packaging" procedures and will inevitably require the librarian to go outside the library building. No amount of drum-beating or flossy invitations will overcome the reluctance of many blue collar workers to enter the library, which may be viewed as the citadel of elitism. In addition, any promotional efforts must be undertaken with the understanding that they will be long-term, ongoing, and perhaps only modestly successful.

Assuming that there is a well-developed collection and a staff member eager and able to establish rapport, what can be done to encourage use of the resources and services?

General publicity can take all the usual forms—radio, TV, newspapers, bus cards, fliers, posters—but the message must be clear, specific, and designed for the special audience. Exhortation to "Get Ahead—Read" will fall on deaf ears, as will similar dictums or traditional appeals that smack of moral or intellectual snobbishness. Above all, library jargon must be avoided in publicity and conversation; straightforward terms are essential, not because the reader/listener won't understand, but because anything else sounds too much like a put-on, a status symbol, a talking down.

". . . work with and through union officials . . ."

After taking the first and essential step—solicitation of advice about materials, services, and special interests through face-to-face contact, surveys and questionnaires directed to local union officials and union members—you will have demonstrated a genuine desire to be of service. Gaining the confidence and cooperation of union officials is of the utmost importance, for it is through them that you can more readily reach the members. (The unionization of library staff members means that many are already in a position to "bore from within," a situation which should be used to full advantage.)

Make sure that union officers are fully aware of what the library has to offer and are kept informed of plans and new developments in service. Do this through personal contact, not form letters or printed handouts. Despite your past publicity efforts, it's a safe bet that in the course of your interviews you will hear, "I didn't know the library (had) (did) ___." (Fill in the blank yourself.) Be prepared for the possibility of a cool reception or a rebuff, but don't give up. Gaining entry through the front door is an important objective in your service promotion campaign.

While you are in the office or have a union official's ear, offer to assemble special materials for newly-elected officers that would be helpful to them in their new positions (how to conduct meetings, keep books, etc.).

Offer assistance in building up the union's own library or in pooling resources of several unions in an easily accessible collection at the library.

Suggest some library resources for union meetings—films, slide-tapes, speakers, music, and background material on controversial issues that are under discussion, formally or informally. Some union meetings are strictly business, with a full agenda, but union leaders, in common with officers of other organizations, must encourage regular attendance through varied programing; you can help with this.

Offer use of the library for a union meeting or for training sessions.

Propose the formation of a joint union-library committee to work out a program of activities and promotion.

Ask to be added to the union mailing list.

Ask for assistance in planning a library-sponsored forum, program, or seminar for the public on labor issues. Unions are struggling with a bad image problem, and many would welcome an opportunity to present their viewpoint to the community on neutral ground. Such discussions could be particularly timely in a pre- or post-strike period.

". . . back at the library . . ."

Meanwhile, back at the library, post the sign "Labor" in some area. If you have a Business and Science Division, change it to "Business, *Labor,* and Science," or designate a special section.

Educate your Board of Trustees to the needs of labor groups and the responsibility of the library in fulfilling them. Fill the next board vacancy with a union representative, if possible.

Prepare an imaginative exhibit of labor materials, activities, or history for the Labor Day period or other suitable time.

Declare a Labor Week or Labor Month and plan a series of in-house programs specifically for labor union membership on such topics as health care, money management, legal aids, preretirement, consumer information. Of course these subjects are of interest to the general public, but you may be able to attract a large union member audi-

ence by special promotion, cooperation of union officials, and participation in the program by union members (peers) rather than—or backed by—outside authorities. You might schedule a Union Family Night series.

Try to get union members into the library by emulating the Avon Township Public Library in Michigan, which sends out three school buses to blue collar residential areas on Saturday mornings to transport adults and children to the library. A special library tour can be part of the activity (and may all your books lose their bindings simultaneously if you use the term "orientation"!). You will need a good carrot or gimmick to make in-library programs successful; if it appears that few can or will be enticed through the front door, your only recourse then is to take the programs out to them.

Prepare special releases, announcements, and features for union publications. Make these lively, and prepare them in the style and format of the union newspaper, newsletter, or magazine. A "New Books" listing might be a regular contribution, but aim for more than that; discuss the possibilities with the editors.

". . . pool efforts with others . . ."

Get together with compatriots in school, special, academic, and (especially) voc-tech school libraries to discuss pooling your efforts and resources for providing service and attention to blue collar workers.

After due and careful consideration of indicated interests, prepare some attractive booklists on such subjects as the labor movement, job training and opportunities, a guide to library resources for labor leaders, trade manuals, as well as the more usual sports, crafts, and how-to-do-it listings. But resist the temptation to do this first! It should be well down on the list of your priorities, for it will have marginal impact. (And none at all if you do not make a special effort to get it directly into the hands of those concerned.) Attend union meetings, if possible. Give a short spiel, emphasizing telephone reference help and the library's information and referral service.

Send library program announcements, flyers, and brochures to the unions and companies for posting. Direct these by name to the responsible person. Take a tip from the Pickens County Library in South Carolina, which prepares a special monthly one-page newsletter which is sent out to plant managers for posting on bulletin boards.

Contact employee clubs or organizations and offer program and materials assistance in the area of interest.

Cultivate a cadre of enthusiastic supporters, in hopes of getting the best of all promotion, word-of-mouth.

Keep your eyes and ears open for unusual expertise (CB use, recreational vehicles, fly-tying, whatever) and solicit help for planning special programs or building up the library's collection in that subject area.

Take a books-and-media exhibit to plants, factories, and union meeting halls. For example, the Cumberland Public Library (Wisconsin) exhibited a collection of books and magazines at the local 3M plant; a staff member from the library was in attendance each day for a week during the shift change to check out materials to the plant workers. Remember the night shift, too. Schedule a well-promoted occasional or regular bookmobile stop, timed for shift changes; or deposit carefully selected loan collections at various outlets. Minimize the borrowing procedures and responsibility as much as possible, and change the collection frequently.

Explore the possibilities of "Books Sandwiched-In" during lunch breaks, or have an in-plant "Books and Beer Break" affair (a local brewery might supply the beer).

". . . long-term commitment is essential . . ."

Your labor relations program should be tailored to your local situation, based upon a careful assessment of needs and opportunities and a periodic review of your program. There must be a genuine and continuing commitment to service in terms of time and staff, and realistic goals must be set, with the realization that attainment may be slow and difficult to measure.

Local labor unions must also recognize (or be educated to) their responsibility for promoting the library's potential for educational and recreational services to union members. At the national level, organized labor has been a good friend of libraries and educational institutions, has supported funding requests, and lobbied for library interests. They may have good reason to issue their own "overdue notice" to libraries for more adequate return at the local level.

Speeding Over "Fifty-Fives" into the Library

Under the stimulation of various grants, studies, and governmental activities, libraries are recognizing their responsibility to that segment of the public called, variously, retirees, senior citizens, older Americans, or simply the elderly or aging. But recent studies reveal that libraries are serving only a small percentage of this rapidly growing segment of the population.

There are some excellent library service programs for the elderly in some areas of the country, but there are thousands of potential users who are unaware of even minimal library services available to them. Thus, in addition to designing suitable and expanded services, sustained publicity and promotion must be planned and carried out.

Too often librarians have failed to make a distinction between special services for the blind, handicapped, and homebound, and those for older Americans who are mentally alert, functionally active, and who have a large amount of leisure time. Those who did not develop the "library habit" in earlier years may be quite unaware of the variety of resources nearby. They need to be informed, to be actively sought out, and to have their interest piqued. Above all, they must be made to feel welcome and wanted in a predominantly younger milieu.

As with any age group, there is a great variety of interests, social and economic status, education, etc. Aging, per se, is not measured by birthdays, but is generally characterized by a narrowing of interests and a change of activities requiring less physical exertion. Studies show that the average person can expect to retain a high level of mental competence past the age of 80. The potential for active library use and program participation is far greater than is generally assumed.

The library's responsibility to this group includes:

> 1. Encouraging reading for those who are interested through the provision of suitable and selected materials, but with the knowledge that few if any nonreaders will be converted to readers at this stage. Instruction in and encouragement of the use of media other than print, such as records, cassettes, videotapes, and films—all less familiar to an older generation—is a corollary activity that may also help to bring the nonreader into the fold.
>
> 2. Offering an opportunity for both formal and informal education and creativity.
>
> 3. Serving as an information resource center and a "clearinghouse" for referrals.
>
> 4. Offering an opportunity for participation in individual and group activities, either passively or actively, in the role of volunteers, planners, or staff aides.
>
> 5. Serving as a catalyst for starting needed programs for the elderly in the community or assisting with and extending those that may be in existence.
>
> 6. Offering educational and informational aids to those who are living with, working with, or related to older people, a help often overlooked.

Word-of-mouth and face-to-face contact are, as always, the best way to spread information directly to those whom you wish to reach. For the librarian this may mean enlisting the aid of older patrons who can encourage their peers to use the library and join in activities there. A special each-one-bring-one campaign, conducted informally through flyers or bookmarks hand delivered by a patron to a friend, or run more formally through a contest to bring in new users, could almost double present usage by this age group.

Personal visits by the librarian to senior citizen centers and other places where older people gather offer a chance to answer individual questions and extend a meaningful invitation. Talks to groups on the subject of "What the Library Can Do for Your Elderly Parents and Friends" will encourage relatives and friends to urge library use.

Contact should be made with many agencies and persons who deal with older people. Those who belong to clubs and organizations are relatively easy to reach; the less gregarious, the loners, and the lonesome are more difficult. Flyers, posters, or notices can be posted in or distributed through such points of contact as the offices of doctors, dentists, optometrists, hearing aid companies, hospitals, post offices. Special announcements should be inserted in church bulletins and community group newsletters. Direct mailings might be made to a list of a labor union's retirees or a company's pensioners. A canvass can be made of special neighborhoods or apartment buildings with a high proportion of older people. Bus cards can carry a message to many.

Frequent newspaper articles, particularly those with a human interest angle, help to call the attention of the entire community to special services of the library for older people. A weekly or monthly newspaper column could be directed specifically to their interests. Some libraries issue newsletters especially for senior citizens; the publication may keep some informed, but it will not make others aware unless it is distributed directly to them.

Radio and TV spot announcements are important and should be aired as often as you can arrange with the stations. Suggest—in fact, beg for—the best time slot to reach this intended audience; consult the station manager or take a mini-poll of patrons if you are not familiar with local programing and the listening habits of older people. Cable television offers a golden opportunity for reaching senior citizens.

"... do's and don'ts to keep in mind ..."

Avoid stereotypes or unconscious condescension in terminology and graphics; "the little old lady in tennis shoes" doesn't picture herself that way, nor should you. Rocking chairs and shawls are out, but don't come on too strong with the elderly "swinger" angle. That ubiquitous insurance ad showing two happy people living on $200 a month isn't quite the image you want to use, either. The term "golden ager" may ring hollow, and the title used by one group, "The Happy Widows Club," is questionable. Try words on for size; would you want to be called that in a few years?

Less costly activities are important to those with reduced incomes; the fact that the library is free must be pointed out constantly as a selling point. The elimination of fines (if you are still caught up in that syndrome) for senior citizens would be an excellent goodwill gesture (surely you trust *them!*) and would solve a nagging problem for many who may be deterred from using the library by the fear of being unable to return materials on time.

Access to the library may be difficult for older people. Major or minor physical building changes may be necessary to encourage use. The availability of bus transportation should be considered; some libraries provide special bus service; others give free bus passes.

Some libraries are providing a full range of information resource services and telephone referrals, but even the smallest library has a listing of phone numbers and other basic "survival" information. Has a concerted effort been made to see that elderly persons in the community know that just one telephone number—that of the library—can help them? Has the number been printed in large type on a sticker and widely distributed? This could be the most important single service the library could render.

Consider a special area or nook that older people could call their own, perhaps with tables for games and cards.

Persistence and patience must be the keynotes of your efforts to reach many who are presently isolated from the mainstream, perhaps a bit fearful of new involvements and reluctant to make any change in habits.

Senior citizens represent a very large source of untapped talent, time, and energy. There may be good reason to say "ask not what you can do for them; ask what they can do for you!"

There are conflicting reports on the amount of interest shown by older patrons in various library-sponsored topics. For example, one librarian reports that "they did not feel they needed information on health care," whereas another reports great success with programs on Medicare, local health services, and nutrition. The Brooklyn Public

Library found that the people "who came to meetings were interested in the subjects which interest most people." This simply points up the pitfalls of attempting to categorize a diverse group. Very few studies are available for guidance and, in any case, selection of program subjects, events, and services must be tailored to local conditions. An advisory committee, composed of representatives of the age group, could and should be formed to aid in outlining programs; your from-behind-the-desk ideas may be all wrong!

The timing of programs and events (hour of the day, season of the year) will influence attendance. You may find that some programs will attract many older patrons because of the hour, even though not especially planned for them.

Many libraries schedule a special day, weekly or monthly, for the "Never Too Late," "Going Like Sixty," or "Live Long and Like It" groups, as they are called in Boston, Washington, D.C., and Cleveland. This may be an all-day affair (bring your own lunch), scheduled just for the morning, or an afternoon "Tea 'N' Things" as in Prince Albert, Canada. Speakers, films, various forms of entertainment, and demonstrations are usually featured.

The library can offer an opportunity for older Americans to interact with the younger generation. Some may be excellent story-tellers, both willing and eager to aid with story hours. The Island Trees Public Library in New York was the intermediary between senior citizens and high school students that resulted in an invitation to attend a holiday concert and luncheon at the school, and the selection of older people to serve as advisors in studies on a variety of subjects, such as the depression of the 1930s, immigration, and social adjustments. Developing a list of skills or special fields of knowledge of retirees would be valuable for referral, and in communities where this is not otherwise available it might also include listings of those interested in part-time or temporary work. The Medford Public Library (Massachusetts) created such a job bank, in cooperation with the Medford Council on Aging, and carried on vigorous campaigns to both encourage businesses to offer jobs to senior citizens and to encourage more seniors to apply.

The exemplary activities of two libraries, one small and one large, illustrate the wide range possible, each fulfilling a different need.

In Verona, Wisconsin, an average of 70 to 80 senior citizens meet at the Library each Wednesday morning for a variety of informational and recreational activities. Recently these included talks on "How the Sheriff's Department Works," the foster grandparent program, shopping on a fixed income, the Indians of northern Wisconsin, the conservation efforts to "save" a local river; illustrated travel talks by local residents; films; bus trips to a racetrack and to a baseball game; a guided tour to a nearby wildlife refuge; an egg decorating contest; and one regular "free" day monthly to play cards, dominoes, read newspapers, and select books. In December a booklet of the favorite holiday recipes of the women was compiled and distributed to the community.

In New York, The Queens Borough Public Library undertook a three-day Senior Citizens Convention at the Library:

> . . . to provide information and assistance to the senior citizens of Queens on a one-to-one basis, under one roof, eliminating the necessity of travel from agency to agency; to provide an opportunity for organized senior citizens groups to exchange ideas and discuss common needs; and to demonstrate how the library can be of daily assistance.

Over 500 attended the first year, and the convention has been repeated. Booths were constructed in an exhibit area for the participating agencies and old-time music was taped and played con-

---

Sampling of Program Topics and Activities

The following brief sampling of program topics and activities, from libraries around the country, may offer some ideas for future use:

- A talk by a 747 jet pilot on flying the big plane.

- The mayor discussing city plans and how they affect senior citizens.

- "The Metric Epidemic," explaining the switch in measuring systems, with "decimeter squares" and "lilting liter punch" for refreshments.

- A defensive driving course.

- The advantages and disadvantages of town house and condominium living.

- A preretirement workshop, with sessions on estates and wills, retirement health and activities, Social Security and insurance.

- Storytelling to youngsters by senior citizens.

- "Lost arts" and "old crafts" demonstrated by senior citizens.

- Sessions on part-time work and how to make money at home.

- Possibilities for volunteer work in the community.

- Joint programs for grandparents and children.

- Play reading and skits (use large-print scripts, if necessary).

- Exercise class for elderly.

- Sessions on using videotape equipment ("instant replay" is exciting to oldsters—or anyone, for that matter!).

- Nostalgia series, featuring old cars, railroads, ships, old radio programs, silent movies.

- Workshop sessions on adjusting to widowhood or living alone (coping with grief, money management, cooking for one, social readjustment).

- Creative writing and taping sessions to compile reminiscences.

tinuously. Signs invited senior citizens to test the telephone reference service; round table discussions were held for an exchange of ideas. The Library reported,

> . . . displays of flowers and house plants, hobby books, police memorabilia and safety devices gave the event a festive air. One gentleman even returned with his banjo. He played show tunes of the "good old days" just because he wanted to be part of the festivities.

In preparing printed material for this group, remember that anyone over 40 may have some difficulty reading small print. Use clear, good type always; fuzzy mimeographed material simply won't do! If you are not having type set so that you can specify at least 12 pt. or larger, use typewriter text, proportion the layout and page size, and then have it photographically enlarged to the page size of the final form. This is particularly important for newsletters and pamphlets explaining the library's services to older people. In preparing folders, include information about foreign language books and copying machines, items of potential interest that may be overlooked.

Opening the Door for the Blind, Handicapped, and Disadvantaged

Although libraries are making strides in initiating and expanding services to the blind and visually handicapped, a low percentage of those who might benefit is using them, and too many more are not even aware of them. This is as true for the well-stocked library with materials for direct use as for the smallest library whose function may only be one of referral. The valiant one-to-one efforts of the "outreach" librarian are not enough, and must be supplemented by promotion in other forms.

Many libraries now own or have access through interlibrary loan to a local stock of large-print books, materials in Braille, tapes, and records; some have a wide selection of reading aids (magnifiers, pillow speakers, prism glasses, ceiling projectors, etc.) either for loan or for demonstration, and a few provide such services as closed circuit TV systems that magnify print, Braille typewriters, special telephone recorded messages, special games and cards, a regular

radio reading service through FM receivers, and home delivery. And at the very least, all libraries can assist potential users by providing information about and referral to regional libraries for the blind and handicapped and other resources.

There are many ways to publicize the available services for this special group, and the difficulties of reaching the audience, even though a relatively small segment of the total population, can be overcome by both direct and indirect publicity. There's even an advantage in using broad spectrum publicity; although the message directly applies to only a few, it will gain public approval as a commendable use of tax dollars and enhance the image of the library as a concerned agency in the eyes of many more.

The first and foremost promotional effort should be in-house, through present library patrons. These users are already motivated, to some extent, and know something about the library's resources; many could be good ambassadors to others. A handout, a bookmark, and/or an in-li-

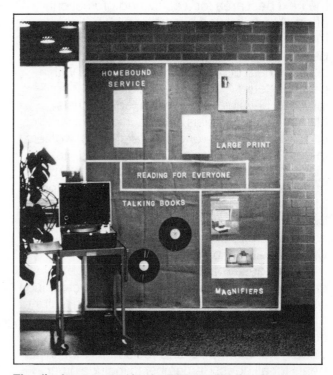

The display mounted by the Rodman Public Library, in Alliance (OH) "Reading for Everyone," is an example of an in-house exhibit publicizing such special services as homebound book delivery, large print book collection, optical aids, and talking books. This was designed to encourage mobile and normal sighted patrons to refer others who might need or use these services.

brary display about materials and services available to the blind and visually handicapped will increase your present patrons' awareness and knowledge and encourage them to tell others. A printed piece will be most effective because it can contain specifics and references that might otherwise be forgotten. Put this into books as they are checked out, or keep a good supply in a visible place. If you run out, reprint! It's not a one-time message, but an ongoing one. Post a notice in a prominent place in the library as well, but change or move it occasionally so that it doesn't fade into the wall.

Encourage staff members to ask, routinely, if the patron knows of anyone who would be interested in or eligible for this special service, and remind them to mention it at appropriate times in contacts outside the library as well. Include a reminder about the service in your newsletter at regular intervals.

There is a large group of people who may or may not be library users themselves, but who have direct contact with visually handicapped; this is the next best area for a concerted promotional effort. Again, printed pieces for distribution—to these people and for them to give to others—will be most effective. If the number is not too large, contact them in person, by telephone, or with a personal letter. The list of possibilities is long; it includes physicians, opticians, optometrists, clinics, school officials and teachers involved in special education work, ministers, social workers in both public and private agencies, hospital officials, and, specifically, hospital librarians, nursing and retirement home officials, and local chapters of appropriate national associations. In addition, local civic and service organizations may offer assistance and financial support, as well as help with the distribution of printed information.

Your descriptive handouts, whether brochures or flyers, should be brief and eye-catching. *Use large print.* In preparing the text, don't fall into the trap of thinking only of the elderly; there are children, young adults, and middle-aged who are visually handicapped, and you should plug in appeals for all ages. Remember to include other information about the library, such as telephone reference and material selection assistance.

You may want to make some special booklists available, either to indicate the scope of the collection or in areas of special interest. A compiled list of resources, local and national, would be helpful.

Promotional emphasis on the service to the blind is often only on home delivery, but there are many who may be willing and able to attend events at the library. An occasional or regular program will help to encourage wider use and serve to call attention to the service. Special story-telling, reading hours and music programs are possibilities, as well as games and contests. One library recently held a bridge tournament that mixed sighted and blind players, the latter using Brailled cards. The Loveland Public Library in Colorado has held special teas to demonstrate talking books to those interested for themselves or for relatives and friends. Arranging transportation through "Bring a Friend to the Library" promotion of the Trails Regional Library in Missouri has increased participation in both special and regular library programs of lectures, book talks, and discussions. Demonstrations of crafts and hobbies or performances of music by the blind have been sponsored. Special "touch and feel" exhibits are an enticement to come in. In Virginia, the Kings Park Branch of the Fairfax County Library goes further; a "Garden of the Senses" has been developed with planting areas connected by a railing so that patrons can enjoy the textures and fragrances of plants, with the aid of a cassette recording.

Less targeted publicity and promotion are also necessary to make sure that the word is spread far and wide.

Releases to the newspapers about special materials and services are in order, and an occasional feature spread is possible; editors will be receptive, because there is a built-in human interest angle. It may also be worthwhile to explore the possibilities of placing a large advertisement in the paper, perhaps on the occasion of a special week, such as "Save Your Vision Week" celebrated in March; the ad might be underwritten by local optometrists, firms, or Friends groups. The newsletters, bulletins, and house organs of various local agencies, civic groups, religious organizations, associations, and firms are valuable publicity outlets. These publications may be read more carefully than the newspaper, and assuming that many people know or are related to someone with visual problems, the information can thus be conveyed second-hand.

Radio and TV public service announcements will reach a large number of people. The following is an example from the American Foundation for the Blind:

> Many children can't read regular books, either because they are visually handicapped and can't see them, or because they are physically handicapped and can't hold the book or turn the pages. But blind and handicapped kids don't have to miss out on the adventures of Christopher Robin and Winnie-the-Pooh or the exciting legends of the Sioux Indians. They can find out why frogs are wet and how spiders are helpful—not by reading books but by listening to records and tapes called "Talking Books." For further information, call (Library).

A series of color slides, showing youngsters and adults using large print, talking books, and other aids, with a voice-over script for an announcer to read, is a simple way to put together a TV spot. You may also be able to use direct mail to local residents by arranging with banks or utility companies for an insertion in their monthly statement. Bus cards and posters placed around the community are other publicity methods; try the slogan "Heard a good book lately? Or felt one?"

Prepare a short canned talk, perhaps with appropriate slides, that you or other staff members can use with civic and social organizations. Assemble the components for a portable exhibit, and keep this on file for display in shopping malls, lobbies, etc.

The deaf and hearing-impaired comprise another group which requires a special promotional and informational effort. These people are often overlooked for they are not visibly handicapped or "different," and frequently they are not good readers, in part because of the difficulty of learning to read when spoken words cannot be heard. Although they are in the minority, there are ominous overtones to studies that show that the noise pollution level at present may seriously affect many of us in the near future, and the high volume music enjoyed by teenagers and others is already causing considerable loss.

The Prince George's County Memorial System in Maryland has an exceptional program of library services for the deaf and hearing-impaired, many features of which other libraries could adopt. Equally important, the service is unusually well-

This display, prepared by the Prince George's County Memorial Library Service (MD), called attention to the "communications-concept" kits prepared for circulation to deaf and hearing-impaired children. The kits contained a wide variety of materials, such as games, a toy rag doll with a hearing aid, "signed" picture books, annotated reading lists, and a parent's manual.

promoted and publicized. An attractive brochure, "Total Communication," describes the many services: information and referral by TTY (telephone-teletypewriter), library staff members who can use sign language, availability of silent and captioned films, special books, toys, and kits for hearing-impaired children, and in-library programs that are interpreted for the hearing-impaired. News releases to the media routinely repeat the phrase, "This program will be interpreted for the hearing-impaired," or "The entire program will be signed." In addition, special programs have been held, particularly for children and also for the parents of hearing-impaired children. (An interesting switch was pulled when a program of popular songs and dances, titled "I Can Sing a Rainbow," was put on by the Deaf Awareness Troupe of Gallaudet College, and the release read, "This program will be interpreted for the *hearing*.") Finger spelling and sign language classes have been held for staff, adults, and children. Numerous booklists have been made available, and special displays are prepared for such occasions as Deaf Awareness Week. Reminders about various aspects of this special service are included in all regular library publications, such as the newsletter, calendar of events, or other brochures. Publicity and promotion have been constant and widespread.

Informational and promotional activities of some other libraries are worth noting as suggestions for reaching out to this special group. The Needham Public Library in Massachusetts acquired the names of deaf residents of the community and held an open house for them, followed by a tour in groups of two, each accompanied by a staff member.

The Greenville County Library in South Carolina held a meeting for deaf persons to seek assistance in planning library activities for them. The first activity agreed upon was an historic tour of the community with an interpreter, and then a citizenship program based on an upcoming election.

In Indiana, the Lake County Public Library publishes a special newsletter for the deaf and hearing-impaired, with news items of interest, a schedule of special library programs, captioned film showings, and an annotated listing of books of particular or general interest.

Television has been used to good effect. The Spencer Public Library (Iowa) produced and aired a special 30-minute program, "Talking Fingers," in conjunction with Deaf Awareness Week; a book talk and children's story were both signed and spoken, and two deaf residents "talked" about their work, recreation, and the challenge of raising a hearing child. The Children's Librarian at the Bartholomew County Library in Indiana televises a regular story hour; she reads the story aloud, with the camera on her lips and shows the pictures while a 12-year-old signs the story at the same time.

Inasmuch as the hearing handicapped rely more heavily on their vision than most people, slides or captioned film spots are the most effective form of public service announcements.

Sign language is purported to be the third most prevalent "foreign language" in the United States, outranked only by Spanish and Italian, and

---

". . . encourage and promote more library usage by the hearing-impaired . . ."

---

many libraries have offered courses in this. Children pick this up quickly; the Neenah Public Library in Wisconsin capitalized on both their interest and ability by incorporating it into the Summer Library Program. After a time spent learning

the signs, a picnic was held with the young library patrons and a special group of deaf guests happily "conversing."

Identify the local deaf community through appropriate agencies, and enlist the aid of the hearing-impaired in reaching others.

Plan some special programs, which could include captioned films, interpreted activities, classes for parents of deaf children and for employers of deaf workers.

Hold a story hour in sign language, as an awareness activity.

"Sign" the library! Make sure that all directional signs are large and clearly point the way for those who are unable to ask or loath to do so (and this includes many more than hearing or speech handicapped!).

Train or hire one or more staff members who can communicate in sign language.

Keep paper and pencil handy so that inquiries can be written out by the deaf.

Offer meeting rooms for the use of organized groups of deaf or hearing-impaired persons.

Involve the community in expanding the service; suggest that a civic group or a service club raise funds for special materials or equipment.

There are other identifiable minority groups for whom the psychological and physical barriers to the library are formidable, often compounded by poor reading ability, physical handicaps, language difficulties, mobility, or cultural differences. These groups are usually invisible to the librarian behind the desk.

In recent years the removal of physical barriers has been mandated by law, and there has been considerable pressure or encouragement to establish special programs to meet special needs of the homebound, Spanish-speaking, or the so-called disadvantaged. Unfortunately, this often takes the form of a "project," and there may not be a long-term financial or moral commitment to such services. (Small wonder, given the difficulties of maintaining adequate service of any kind in the face of mounting costs and reduced funding!)

Most general publicity does not reach these small and often disinterested groups at all, and mass communication, in the usual sense, neither informs nor motivates. Thus, special forms of promotion are as essential as the initiation of or building up of a special materials collection or service—an integral part of the process, not an afterthought. Expenditures for the purchase of foreign language or low vocabulary materials, for the establishment of home delivery, etc., are useless without an equal expenditure for promotion. And as any good outreach librarian knows, it takes imagination, ingenuity, rapport, and empathy—which are not always in great supply—plus a great deal of plain hard footwork and personal contact, which most often is the key.

The following account from the report of the South Bronx Project of the New York Public Library is a graphic illustration of this. The project was designed to establish and demonstrate effective library service to ghetto neighborhoods, which were predominantly Spanish-speaking.

> Even when it was happening in front of the library, it was not easy to get people inside. A mother had come to watch her daughter help some 40 children and teenagers paint huge pieces of brown wrapping paper laid out on the sidewalk. When the little girl went inside, the mother refused to go in. 'No, thank you. You don't have anything for me.'
> 'We have books in Spanish.'
> 'Cookbooks?'

> The Puerto Rican staff member helped her fill out a borrower's card application after the mother found a cookbook in Spanish and a volume of poetry of Jose de Diego.

It is often necessary to work through the people and agencies more closely associated with particular groups to make the essential verbal or one-to-one contact; assurance, encouragement, and information are more readily accepted.

Members of these special groups are not apt to be print-oriented, but printed materials can be useful *if* they are designed specifically for the intended audience, and not according to the tenets of a sophisticated or middle-class graphics person. Flyers, brochures, or other handouts should have bright color, use a picture or cartoon approach, use simple words from street terms to foreign languages, and have a direct "gut" appeal.

Breaking down the barriers and selling library service to minorities with special needs or in special circumstances is a painstaking process, but it may be the ultimate test of the library's commitment to service to all.

Dewey or Don't We? Library Orientation

From Carnegie Library of Pittsburgh Brochure

Librarians constantly struggle with the library orientation problem and seek better means of aiding or teaching patrons to use the library's resources. They have used or experimented with library tours (conducted or self-guided), courses or classes in library usage, workshops, slides and videotapes, exhibits, brochures, closed circuit television, games, and other sundry methods of instructing library users. Despite these efforts, few have been truly successful, and as library resources expand in terms of volume, complexity, and form, the problem will, in fact, be ever more acute.

It is compounded by some fundamental difficulties. First, there is a widespread lack of understanding about *what* is available in the library (not where it is or how to get at it, but simply *what* is there), whether standard reference tools, vertical file materials, or specialized resources and services.

Secondly, the physical appearance, layout, and procedures of a library, standardized decades ago for the convenience of staff and ease of routine, are formidable and forbidding barriers to the nonuser and an obstacle course for the occasional or even regular patron.

There is no other institution or agency built on the idea of self-service which expects—even insists—that the user, client, or customer learn an arbitrary access sytem (Dewey method), paw through a less-than-satisfactory guide (the card catalog), and then search for wanted items in a "stock room" of eight-foot high book tiers, all in awesome and unfamiliar order. The merchandising principles adopted by other agencies and businesses have not been absorbed by libraries which are still locked into a format of their own making.

It is disheartening to know that the newest library buildings are seldom more than surface face-lifts on old standard patterns; that advice on revamping library layout and procedures for greater public accessibility, convenience, and acceptance is seldom sought from experts outside the library world; and that studies and surveys of public opinion and needs have not been addressed to these underlying reasons for public reluctance and disinterest in using the library.

In short, the real question is not how to orient library users, but how to reorient the library to the user. Until the problems of inadequate communication, antiquated layout, and outmoded self-help procedures are solved, any orientation will be less than satisfactory.

Signage

A dictionary definition of orientation refers first to physical adjustment to environment. Thus library orientation starts with the aids to understanding the physical arrangement and general layout of the building through the use of signs, labels, color, and directories, all based on a logical, inviting, and convenient progression.

If you have been answering the same questions about "where" over and over, perhaps you need to take a fresh look at your present signs. Put yourself in the position of one going into a strange supermarket. You can immediately identify the check-out counter, of course. And the specials are up front. But where are the paper towels, the salt, and the dairy products? In a well-run market, signs are posted overhead and on counter ends. Now what about your patron looking for the card catalog, the art collection, the vertical file? Take a fresh look through his/her eyes; perhaps your signs have faded into the wall, or worse, don't really say what is meant in layman's terms.

The terminology should be user-oriented, not libraryese: "Ask Here" not "information desk," "Check Out," not "circulation desk," for example.

Graphic directional communications should be clear, bold, and imaginative. Signage is an art, and some expertise in this area should be sought. At the Veterans Memorial Public Library in Bismarck, North Dakota, for example, a sign painter and an artist designed over 50 inexpensive hand-lettered Plexiglas signs, all color-keyed to a floor directory, that clearly identified areas and collection locations. The staff answered far fewer location questions and reported that patrons were a great deal more at ease in the building.

Large interesting banners have been hung from the ceiling in open areas of some buildings, adding both a space identification aid and a gay colorful note to an otherwise rather sterile interior. If the library is large enough to need a schematic diagram to show location of materials, this must not be so small and colorless that it is easily overlooked. It's worth the time and money to prepare a permanent, large, and illustrated diagram-display and to put it out front where it cannot be ignored. Not only will this save answering unnecessary questions, but it will also give the library user a chance to get his bearings before venturing into strange fields.

Personal Assistance

Most libraries of any size have a so-called "Reference Desk" or "Information Desk"; the function may be as much one of answering simple directional queries as that of offering actual reference assistance. A very large or imposing desk will impose a physical barrier, which many are hesitant to approach.

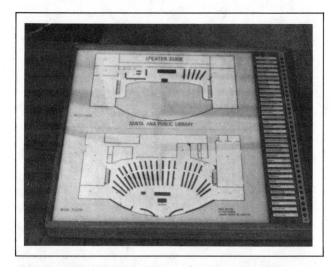

The Santa Ana Public Library (CA) constructed an illuminated location guide to aid patrons in finding various areas, collections, and services in the library. An alphabetical listing on one side of the panel has buttons, and when one is pushed, the location area lights up on the floor plan of the building. Thirty-four listings include catalogs, restrooms, reference service, telephone directories, typewriters, foreign language collection, science fiction, pamphlet file, etc. This simple but effective unit saves staff time and also serves to call attention to lesser known collections and aids.

The real key to helping patrons use the library is individual assistance, friendly, accessible, and even on occasion hustled, to overcome the reluctance of many to ask for help. Staff shortages may prohibit the use of sufficient personnel to staff the floor in numbers; but again, libraries can take a lesson from other self-help businesses where an intercom call for customer assistance brings an employee to the patron quickly. Others use lower-paid semiprofessional clerical help for the first patron contact, but this is backed up by a professional nearby, who is readily available. A few libraries have recognized the importance of personal assistance that is both visible and publicized. The Lawson McGhee Library in Knoxville, Tennessee, for example, hired a new staff member to be on duty every day from nine to five solely to aid library users in locating materials, and some have special posted hours when patrons can reserve time for individual help. Most librarians worthy of the name will assist users when asked, but therein lies the rub; a reluctance to admit ignorance on the part of the patron, coupled with the appearance of staff members busily involved in other tasks, deters a great number of people. Scheduling and publicizing particular days or daily times for special one-to-one aid could go a long way in allaying fears, and such a special assignment would back up the efforts of the reference librarian, already involved with a wide range of relatively simple queries.

How Much "Orientation"?

Orientation for the average public library user should be designed only to arouse awareness of resources and to introduce a few basic tools, and should not be considered a do-it-yourself course. Learning to use the library is a continuing process and user needs vary widely, even as an individual user's needs vary from time to time. Too often the basic question, "*What* does a patron need to know?" is overlooked in the rush to figure out *how* to teach what librarians think should be learned. Is memorizing the Dewey system really of any use, whether one is a third-grader, college student, or long-out-of-school homemaker? As Nancy Larrick wrote, "The Dewey system may be the orderly way to *keep* books, but to the reader it is often a barrier to browsing, borrowing, and complete reading en-

joyment" (*Catholic Library World,* February, 1976). As a matter of fact, why should anyone spend time trying to remember the various classifications of the Dewey system—or the even more incomprehensible LC system? It is enough for the user to know that there is a direct relation between the numbers on a catalog card, on the spine of a book, and the shelf area. There is no need to memorize the fact that the 500's are Science, 700's Fine Arts and Recreation, or 000 General Works. (It won't be recalled, anyway, unless the user is going to become a librarian.)

There is overwhelming evidence that library instruction is effective only at the time and in the terms of specific need. The hope of developing lifetime library user skills during the school years appears to be illusionary.

Printed and Other Self-Help Aids

Indirect assistance through the use of simple printed handouts is essential, but brochures, pamphlets, and handbooks on "How to Use Your Library" have been rolling off the press since Gutenberg invented it. Most of the handouts in current use by public libraries are stereotyped and/or deadly dull. They offer the average person very little if anything in the way of guidance in how to use the library; they proudly enumerate the services, coyly explain the Dewey Decimal System, or flatly list, by title only, the more common reference aids—which the patron doesn't know how to use in the first place. These same printed pieces are useless to the more serious reader or researcher, who is already familiar with the standard tools.

Some large libraries produce comprehensive and complicated library guides, both expensive and overwhelming in detail. The experience of many, however, has shown that single sheet handouts on a specific subject, whether a printed floor layout, information about a special collection, or a guide on how to locate information on a particular subject, are more effective, more easily updated, and less expensive to reproduce than comprehensive brochures. Compilation in printed form of the answers to the most frequently asked questions, frivolous or serious, will save staff time and make the newcomer a bit more comfortable in this strange new library territory. All such printed materials should be given to new card applicants (and

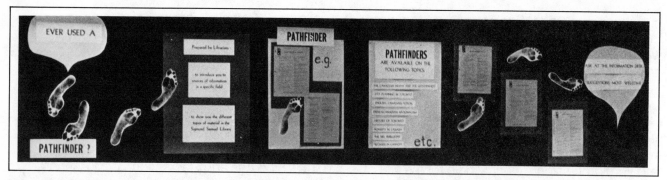

Patrons of the Sigmund Samuel Library, University of Toronto, Canada, are guided through the collection by a series of "Pathfinders" on various topics, and this display called attention to the concept and explained how it works.

renewals!) routinely and displayed prominently for handout.

It is difficult and all but useless to try to expose the average library user to the full and sometimes esoteric range of available materials with a general printed piece. A more practical method is to demonstrate through specific example by charting a course through the maze on a single subject. As in the example shown here, these are sometimes called "road maps." In addition to the listing of possible subject headings in the card catalog, indices, and periodicals, AV aids (films, cassettes, slides) could be listed.

Additional self-help orientation methods include the use of cassette tapes, which can also be part of a self-guided walking tour of the library. The Knoxville-Knox County Library in Tennessee produced one that quickly became one of the library's most popular features, a portion of which follows:

On behalf of the Library Director and the other '100 plus' staff members, welcome to the Knoxville-Knox County Public Library. Before we begin, make sure you understand how the tour works. You should have a map which indicates the location and sequence of the departments we will visit. After the tour of each

Sample Road Map used for studies in black-and-white still photography (front and back sides).

department, turn off the tape and wait to turn it back on until you have reached the next department. To stop, play and rewind the tape, punch the buttons indicated. If you have any problems, please stop the tape and ask the reference or fine arts librarians to help you. . . .

The Knoxville-Knox County Public Library System is composed of the central library, Lawson McGhee, 19 branches and one bookmobile. In 1973-74 we circulated 1,300,000 books, records and cassettes. That marks a 2.4% increase over the previous year. In fact, last year there were over 1,000 persons who came into Lawson McGhee Library each day. . . .

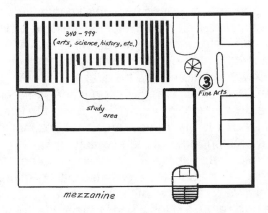

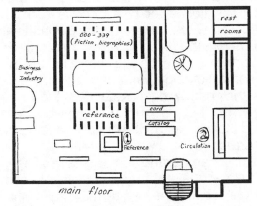

Library map used in conjunction with cassette tape library tour, Knoxville-Knox County Library.

The tour will begin here in the Reference Department. When it is completed, please return your tape to the reference desk.

Need a book and don't know how to locate it? Have a question that you can't answer? Then you need to ask for help at the Reference Department. Reference librarians are trained to look for information ranging from obscure investigation to simple fact-finding procedures.

The Reference Department is located in the center of the main floor of the Library and includes the large square reference desk and the Business and Industry section, just around the corner.

To help the staff answer your questions there are a number of aids, the most important of which, of course, is the card catalog. The card catalog baffles just about everyone a little, but isn't really that difficult to use. Just consider it as an index to the Library, where books are listed under author, title and subject, in alphabetical order. If you don't know the author or the title of the book you want, look under the subject—such as Volkswagen. If you don't find any listings there, go to a more inclusive subject, such as Automobile. If, after some searching you still don't find what you want, go to the Reference Desk and ask for help. . . .

Self-activated films, slides, or video presentations are also possible means of introducing the patron to the library's facilities, services, and resources. A small plastic hand-held filmstrip viewer was used by the Appalachian Adult Education Center in Kentucky; this intriguing gadget, cheap enough in quantity to give away, held a 22 frame captioned filmstrip.

Guided Tours

Guided tours are the usual form of direct library orientation for both students and the general public, but the value of this depends entirely on the skill in interpreting what the user really needs or wants to know. Lengthy dissertations at this time on how to conduct research are of very little long-term value, but the tour should be more than a peek at the physical facilities. It's nice to know where the *Reader's Guide* is kept, where the children's collection and the washrooms are, but this information does not unlock the treasure house. What the library patron needs to know is how to use the key—the library card—to get at all that treasure. Again, the best way is to *demonstrate* it.

One effective method is to pick a single subject of reasonably popular interest, and show how to pursue it all through the library, using every available resource, from card catalog, indexes, the vertical file, visual aids, to recordings. A lot could be done with such a subject as song birds, for example, or old cars, or dogs—from fiction, through fun and fact.

These sessions can be informal or programed, according to the need. The initial preparation and thought takes some time, but guided tours can become sufficiently routine so that they can be done on the spur of the moment.

The question of finding staff time for tours is always a knotty one. The Orlando Public Library solved this with special training for clerks, pages, and other staff members not on service desks, through a series of one-hour workshops.

The first session was devoted to who, what, when, why and how of tours, to the important public relations responsibility of tour guides, and to tours for children. The second session illustrated how to give tours for high school age students and included an example of how to research a paper, using the various types of materials available in the library, such as films, filmstrips, microfilm print-outs, periodicals, etc. The third workshop was devoted to conducting an adult tour.

Classes, Fun, and Games

A number of public libraries regularly hold workshops or classes for those library users who have recognized a need to learn more about the available resources and how to use them efficiently for business or personal reasons. It was a sad reflection of the lack of initiative on the part of the local libraries when a midwestern university extension department found it worthwhile to offer a short course for community residents, "Finding Facts Fast," and publicized it in these words:

> This course is for people who want to learn research techniques and sources for business reports, writing projects, papers or talks for clubs and organizations, classroom assignments, independent study, improving

teaching competency, or just to find out the facts. The library is an ideal first stop for information-seekers; unfortunately most people don't know the wealth of library resources ready for the tapping, don't know that libraries all across the country exchange books if borrowers ask, don't know how to locate specialized libraries inside businesses, foundations, and university departments, don't even know the most effective way to ask librarians for help.

(The course wasn't even conducted by librarians!)

Most workshops or skills exercises are pretty straightforward, but some highly imaginative instructors in a Madison, Wisconsin middle school equated "information retrieval" with survival (which may not be too far-fetched!) and designed a study unit which could be adapted by others for an unusual library usage "experience." Students were divided into groups of five, given the latitude and longitude of a remote area, and told that they were passengers in a plane which had just crashed there. Using all available resources, they were to learn about the area—its location, climate, terrain, vegetation, wildlife, and natives—to survive and return to New York. Upon arrival they were to be interviewed by a TV news team. The trek took six weeks from areas as disparate as the Gobi Desert, the Amazon Valley, and Baffin Bay. Each group arrived looking somewhat the worse for wear in clothing appropriate to their area to relate their harrowing experience to the TV audience. "The high percentage of survivors demonstrated the success of the project," according to the instructors.

Drills, games, and contests have all been designed to acquaint library users with reference resources so that they will be more self-sufficient, but an accessible and knowledgeable librarian is still the most important resource. There is no end in sight to the question, "Where's the card catalog?"

$$$—And Friends—For the Library

There is no library that cannot use additional dollars to augment tax monies received; fund-raising efforts on behalf of the library range from book sales, carnivals, encouragement of donations and memorials, to building fund drives and referendums. A volunteer Friends of the Library or similar group is usually in the forefront of these activities.

Therein lie two perils. First, when too much emphasis, publicity, and effort are centered on money-raising events, no matter how lofty the purpose, the library may become identified as a charity organization—the deserving but community "poor relation"—by a good many. Secondly, there is a tendency to regard Friends groups as primarily fund-raisers when, in fact, their actual or potential contributions are or can be far more than that. These two dangers must be kept in mind and a balance sought in terms of the library's total promotional and service program when considering fund-raising projects.

An understanding of the major reasons why people give money (or volunteer aid) to organizations and institutions will aid in determining the potential appeal and the focus of any fund-raising activity, whether a one-time affair, annual event, or a long-term campaign.

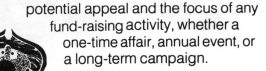

People contribute for the following reasons:

- They can see an immediate and pressing need close to home.

- They have been helped in the past, are familiar with the activities and know the value of the service firsthand.

- They are threatened by the loss or reduction of a service they value for themselves or for others.

- They have a good feeling about an agency, such as a happy memory from childhood.

- They are pressured by their peers, or it is an "in" thing to do.

- They feel a responsibility or a duty as good citizens.

- It gives them personal satisfaction as a measure of status.

- A contribution is tax deductible.

A direct appeal for funds or aid should be based on one or more of these factors if it is to be successful. Money can also be raised through projects or events that the public will enjoy or find educational, from carnivals to benefit programs, or that give people something tangible for their money, from used books, to crafts, cookies, or stationery; in these cases the agency itself is a secondary consideration, although the "worthy cause" aspect may also provide some motivation.

Voting "Yes" for Bond Issues and Referendums

Asking the public to vote for higher taxes is chancy at best, but the experience of many libraries is heartening. The "reservoir of good will" toward libraries has not been completely emptied, and on occasion the public has approved library bond issue proposals or increased tax levies even as other spending proposals are voted down. Projecting success or failure is about akin to gazing in a crystal ball unless you do a good, scientific sampling in advance, and post-election assessments are apt to be unreliable and prejudiced without a thorough and time-consuming analysis of the official ballot returns, which libraries seldom carry out.

Some of the factors that will influence the outcome may or may not be within the control of the library: the timing of the proposition, particularly in terms of other items on the ballot; the political climate, an intangible which may defy prognostication; the number of voters who will turn out; and the complexity and clarity of the wording of the proposition on the ballot.

The groundwork for success at the polls must be laid long before a specific campaign is undertaken. The foundation is good service and a good communication program that has built a base of supporters and has developed community awareness. Those are the essentials. The rest is very hard work and an aggressive publicity campaign.

The first step in campaign strategy and planning is analysis of what people know and what they need to be informed about. This can be determined through some opinion research—a formal survey if time and funds permit, or informal listening to patrons, opinion leaders, and citizens at large.

Then it must be determined whether the issue is "saleable" or not. Can the issue or the need be defined in terms that will be understood and supported by a sufficient number of people? For example, it is easier to sell the request for a new building which is tangible and appeals more easily to civic pride than to secure money for the intangibles of service and staff. Can you make a case for the latter that will be valid and that will strike home to individual voters?

You must face up to the fact that many people see no need for improved or even existing library

Sample campaign material taken from a brochure by the Toledo-Lucas (OH) County Public Library.

service either for themselves or for others; they will vote "no" and no effort should be expended to reach them. The "yes" voters must be identified, and their potential support reinforced. Someplace in between lies a mass of undecided or apathetic voters whom you must try to motivate to vote "yes."

Set up the campaign organization and time-table early. Give the responsibility to one person, form as many committees as may be necessary, and recruit volunteers. It will take many helping hands, since, as all electioneering experts have discovered, the amount of personal contact at the neighborhood level is crucial to success. Prepare a calendar that states who does what and when.

Establish the total communication program and schedule. Use mass communication methods initially and then concentrate on personal approaches as much as possible in the final days of the campaign.

Secure sufficient funds for the campaign. Determine needs and costs first and then get the money. Don't, repeat *don't,* try to design a cam-

". . . $ $ $ . . ."

paign to fit an arbitrary sum plucked out of the blue. At this point in your planning there is a complication. Libraries, by virtue of their tax-exempt status and other regulations, cannot spend tax funds or solicit money for campaign purposes. It is imperative that an active citizens group, Friends, and/or staff association undertake the important task of securing sufficient dollars and pledges for the campaign expenses.

The reasons for success or failure of a specific campaign are not easily spelled out, but the article "Winners vs Losers—What Makes the Difference?" by William J. Banach in the *Journal of Educational Communication,* Spring, 1977, Vol. 2, No. 3, discusses the results of a large number of school elections in the previous year, and concludes, "The overwhelming difference between winning and losing was diligence—carefully planned strategies, commitment to a plan, and dogged attention to detail." The author's listing of the winning "characteristics" has considerable application for libraries, and should be noted in planning similar campaigns:

The winners spent as much time planning their campaigns as they did implementing them. Most spent more time planning than communicating.

The winners studied previous elections in their districts before planning the campaign.

The winners relied on face-to-face communication (block visitations and coffees) to build support for their ballot issues and reinforce the positive attitudes held by yes voters.

The winners augmented their face-to-face communications with printed material. Rarely did printed material carry the full communication load.

The winners took steps to identify target audiences. . . .

Campaign literature in winning districts centered on . . . programs rather than finances.

The winners were more committed to year-round . . . communication than the losers.

The winners typically placed responsibility for the campaign in the hands of one person. . . .

One form or another of citizen involvement characterized the campaigns of winners.

The winners began their campaigns by informing all voters of the ballot issue and its implications for the educational program.

The winners made special efforts to communicate with . . . supporters.

Most winning campaigns were organized by elementary attendance areas, and the elementary principals had key communication responsibilities. [For libraries, this would mean branch libraries and service outlet areas.]

Most winners had a history of working with the news media on a year-round basis. No winner relied solely on the media for campaign communication.

The winners didn't threaten voters with cuts in program, but they did clearly explain what would happen in the event of financial defeat. Most often the winners provided this information as "locally" as possible, i.e., general explanations of what defeat would mean were provided by central office; more specific information was provided . . . by the building principals.

Bumper stickers, lawn signs and posters were noticeably absent in winning campaigns.

Citizens in winning . . . districts seemed to know well ahead of the election that funds were needed. The announcement of the election wasn't a surprise.

Staff communication was considered a priority in winning districts. Staff members were first to know the need for the election and the ingredients of the campaigns. Simply put, winners considered staff involvement an essential campaign consideration.

Winning districts carefully timed their communications and campaign activities. Care was taken to get the right information to the right place at the right time.

Winning districts followed the rule of "into/out-to." They stressed the year-round importance of getting citizens into schools for various programs and activities . . . and they made sure they went out to the public before and during the financial campaign.

Winners had provisions for obtaining grassroots feedback, and they used the information they obtained to improve their communications.

Winners invited—sought out!—citizen questions about the financial issue. And they provided believable answers to questions asked.

Winners telephoned . . . supporters the evening before the day of the election with a reminder to vote.

These are some of the things that contributed to election success.

The following four more-or-less verbatim case history reports from libraries in small, medium, and large communities are examples of successful campaigns, all of which incorporated many of the "winning characteristics" just listed.

The first is a report of a campaign conducted in the town of Shelton, Connecticut, population 27,000, excerpted from an article "How to Campaign for a Library Bond Issue in Your Spare Time—and Win!," by Jerri Lynn in *Connecticut Libraries,* Vol. 18, No. 1. The title is misleading, for no successful campaign is run on "spare time," but the article points up the value of a strong, determined group of Friends and the part they can play in a small community. The Plumb Memorial Library, built in 1896, was described as "hopelessly, indescribably, unimaginably overcrowded." An earlier appeal to the Board of Aldermen for an addition had failed, and later a referendum was defeated. A Friends of the Library was formed, and while waiting for another referendum to be announced, they

. . . kept this standing army busy presenting programs of cultural and semi-cultural interest to the community at large. For three years the Friends sponsored programs on architecture, art, gourmet cooking, candlemaking, wine tasting, as well as book discussions and storyhours in conjunction with the Junior Woman's Club. For three years they worked at

establishing good public relations while subtly pointing out the serious physical shortcomings of the Plumb. When the referendum was announced, the Friends were ready. . . .

These are the steps they took to sell the idea of a present-day library to the voters:

1. They wrote to organizations and community leaders urging them to spread the word about conditions at the Plumb.

2. They worked with the local League of Women Voters on the LWV's pro and con fact sheet distributed to all residents. The Friends furnished them with the "pro" and let the League research the "con"—on their own, of course!

3. They held an essay contest for school children on "Why We Need an Addition to the Library."

4. The Friends held a poster contest in all the public schools, with the sanction and approval of the Board of Education, on the subject of "My Library." Students were allowed to choose one of the three themes: the practical ("How Do I Use the Library?"), the humorous ("Inside a Crowded Library"), or the ideal ("What I Think a Library Should Be"). Over 300 youngsters entered these contests, and each one received a yellow happy face button with the message "Happiness is a Library Addition." Prizes were awarded the winners, and those canny Friends used the best posters in store windows all over town for additional publicity.

5. They formed a Speakers Bureau, and, in conjunction with the library board, spoke to any community group that would have them—Rotary, Kiwanis, PTA, and League of Women Voters among them.

6. They held a meeting with the influential Shelton Taxpayers' Association, including a tour of the library. Shortly after, the Association came out in favor of the addition.

7. They also paid for and distributed book covers to all juvenile borrowers (Be a Friend—Plumb Memorial Library).

8. They used the local newspaper to report Friends meetings and for discussion of the library's needs. Many "Letters to the Editor" were submitted. Paid ads were considered, but not used.

9. Friends composed and sponsored a brochure which was well-researched, very professional in appearance, and convincing. This was mailed to all registered voters in Shelton, timed to arrive one week prior to the vote.

10. They followed up these brochures with telephone calls to active library borrowers, urging them to go to the polls and vote "yes."

11. They put up wooden signs provided by STAND, a community agency for young adults, stating "Vote Yes"—on the front lawn of the library and the Huntington Village Green.

Their campaign took money, of course, which was garnered from dues, used book sales, and gifts from the library board, Kiwanis, and the Connecticut National Bank. . . . Their methods were not particularly innovative or unusual—just many areas of attack, pursued diligently.

In Bloomington, Illinois, voters authorized the sale of bonds for the construction of a new library building by 2,608 yes votes and 1,964 no votes. The report of the campaign included some interesting—and possibly applicable—information. The vote was to be held in November, but an effort to recruit volunteers in the summer was not too successful because it was held too early. Committees were subsequently organized in September.

At the outset, a four page Fact Sheet was put together that was to be used as a training tool for volunteers. However, the Board felt it was the kind of publication that would speak frankly and knowledgeably to voters so a mailing campaign was launched. Using lists for the City's 33 precincts, volunteers matched library card holders with registered voters and came up with some astounding statistics: there were 18,000 registered voters and 11,000 adult card holders but only 4,100 who were both! By the time this was discovered, it was too late to effect a full-scale registration drive. Thus, the first mailing went to a select list of library card holders eligible to vote. This was followed with a telephone call to determine if the voter-patron had read the fact sheet, had any questions and comments and had decided on how to vote. Approximately 2,000 of the 4,100 could be contacted, with 72.9% in favor, 21.2% undecided and 5.9% indicating opposition. Calling was accomplished by resident volunteers in 25 precincts with the remaining eight precincts contacted by a team of Junior Chamber of Commerce and League of Women Voters members and General Telephone Company and citizen volunteers who worked four nights on 12 telephones made available in the General Telephone Company Offices. [See Appendix IV for copies of the forms used for the telephone calls and the campaign timetable.]

In October, 37 coffees were held, and at these and other meetings a statement supporting the referendum was passed around for those present to sign. The day of the referendum the "Citizens for a New Public Library" called all those people who had signed the supportive statement at the coffees and those listed as favorable on the voter list but who had not voted by noon.

The local newspaper did a series of articles supporting the referendum as did the radio station. TV stations in the area interviewed the director a few days before voting day. The last week before the voting day a brochure was mailed out using the water billing addresses.

In this community many of the businesses and stores are moving to the shopping centers away from downtown. Since the new library location was in the downtown area there was much support from the downtown businessmen. Some of the stores put displays in their window. We also had a large display in the main shopping mall the weekend before the vote. On voting day one of the banks put a reminder to vote on their message sign.

Pastors were also asked for their support, and one clergyman and his wife wrote and mailed at their own expense 260 supportive letters to Bloomington residents who were members of the church.

The emphasis in this relatively low-key campaign on the identification of known supporters and the use of many volunteers for personal contact were important elements in the success.

The use of an outside "coordinator" and heavy media saturation were key points in the successful campaign for voter approval of a 30 percent increase in the library levy in Bismarck, North Dakota, population 40,000. The final count in an election which set a record for the number voting was 67 percent in favor of the issue. At the same time, the voters reduced the state sales tax. Thomas T. Jones, Director of the Veteran's Memorial Library, reported:

A number of factors contributed to the success of the campaign: a very highly visible reference service at the library, which includes a successful information and referral center; a department which routinely programs for children and adults, providing summer children's programs at locations within the community, and which coordinates service to shut-ins and the elderly; a staff which works closely with many organizations and groups in the community—providing help in the form of programming, information assistance, and ordinary good neighborly concern and involvement; a Board of Trustees in tune with the community and deeply concerned about and committed to the long-range development of the Library—as well as realistic in its appraisal of the funding situation; a campaign which was highly effective in its orchestrated "sell" of the Library's financial need, and in clearly conveying the importance of the Library and its value to the community at large.

The steps taken to initiate the campaign were deliberate and effectively timed. The first announcement came with the publicity release of the Fiscal '77 budget in June, 1976. However, for several months prior, the library administrator had used every available opportunity in speeches and public appearances to underscore the Library's financial plight; i.e. the lack of funds for materials.

Soon after the June announcement of the pending November levy, final arrangements were made to present the request to put the issue on the ballot to the Bismarck City Commission. Careful advance planning and a full Library Board appearance at the City Commission meeting assured that approval was given—without a petition being necessary. This was an excellent opportunity for newspaper and television coverage—without cost—and the appropriate facts were printed and distributed and the Campaign Coordinator announced.

Choosing the Coordinator was probably the most critical decision which the Library Board undertook once it moved to seek the mill increase. The Board sought out an individual willing and able to spend sufficient time to handle the task effectively, and with the ability to motivate others to act. Such a coordinator was found . . . and agreed to accept the challenge. She acted immediately to assemble a steering committee called the "Citizens for a Better Library." Effective leaders from the professional and business community and several concerned citizens, as well as some members of the Library Board, made up this committee of 21 persons. At its first meeting on September 10, the committee appointed a Treasurer and proceeded to hammer out the details of a fund-drive to support needed campaign expenditures originally estimated at roughly $2,000. A timetable was presented by the Coordinator, and the committee agreed on the major publicity theme for the campaign:

'BUY BOOKS FOR BISMARCK.'

It was decided this would appear on yard signs, four car-top signs, posters to be placed in public places and store windows, printed flyers to be distributed throughout the city,

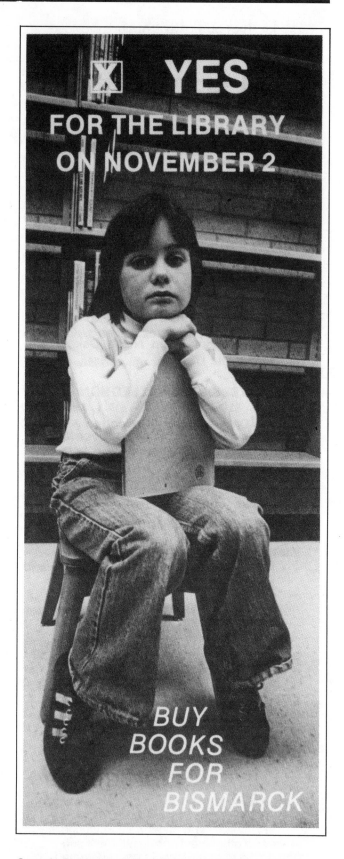

Sample Campaign Material: Bismarck (ND)

and in all newspaper advertising. At this meeting each member of the committee was asked to take at least sixteen businesses from a master list (broken down on index cards) and contact them for donations. It was also announced at this time that contributions were not tax deductible because the campaign was not legally recognized as a charitable group or a political organization. By the October 4 meeting of the committee, donations were more than half completed (in the end more than $1,400 was raised), and the budget was adjusted. The sub-committee on radio spots was already hard at work. Additional sub-committees were formed for newspaper advertising, distribution of flyers (which were designed by the staff, the Coordinator, and a local photographer), distribution of yard signs (which were prepared on donated materials by staff volunteers), and for arrangements for store and professional building window displays.

In the meantime, the Library distributed bookmarks printed with the publicity theme. Fact sheets were prepared, giving book costs and answering basic questions. Library activities were reported in the daily newspaper and the other media as much as possible. The impending levy was mentioned at Library programs; however, for the most part, the staff did not involve themselves in the campaign. The Director and the President of the Board did make a number of appearances to key groups and organizations, and these presentations were carefully thought out and presented.

In the final two weeks the campaign increased its crescendo. Radio spots produced by children, senior adults and members of the committee were carried twice daily—during the morning rush hour and in late afternoon. There were television appearances by the Coordinator, the Board President, the Library Director, and staff members on the daily talk shows. Signs appeared in many store windows downtown and at other shopping areas. One dry-cleaning establishment pasted levy signs (which were stenciled on fluorescent green posterboard) on three sides of its three panel trucks which transversed the city daily. Letters were sent asking for support to over 200 organizations in the city, including all churches and major institutions. Endorsements received were used in the daily advertisements appearing in the *Bismarck Tribune*. One of the car-top signs was placed on a stationwagon loaned by the local Chevrolet dealer and parked in prominent locations throughout the city on a seven-day-week schedule, including a large church parking lot the last two Sundays. Walking sandwich board signs were utilized at a mall on heavy

shopping days and in the downtown area on Saturdays. The Chamber of Commerce endorsement was almost unprecedented in the city, and certainly had an impact on the business community.

With all of the 15,000 flyers distributed in areas of the city where it was thought additional impact was needed, with about 80 yard signs on lawns and prominent along heavily traveled streets, with radio and television and newspaper coverage as thorough as was manageable—the campaign climaxed the day prior to the election. From the earliest returns, the winning margin was evident. North Dakota law requires a 60% approval for a library levy increase; the margin was always safely above the necessary 60%; the final tally was 67%.

The Toledo-Lucas County Public Library (T-LCPL) in Ohio, serving a population of more than 480,000, conducted a levy campaign which garnered 2½ million dollars a year for a five-year period.

The following account, taken from various reports issued by T-LCPL, is a blueprint for success, and illustrates, particularly, the importance of long and careful planning to set the stage, the involvement of many people, and the use of a skilled coordinator. (See Appendix IV for timetable.)

As summed up by a trustee who served on the steering committee,

> It was a great community effort participated in by more than 2,000 individuals and many organizations. There was enthusiastic and dedicated participation and at times it seemed more of a crusade than an election campaign.
>
> The results are all the more impressive when we reflect that in 1974 two library levies were defeated by large margins. I think the difference was the enthusiastic participation of so many individuals and an effective communication to voters of the financial plight of the library.

In 1977, the Library faced a projected budget deficit of $300,000; the financial plight of the Library was demonstrated by the proposed closing of three branches. Public protest at this action received notice from the news media, and a public awareness of the Library's real financial need seemed to be established.

The first step toward a solution was the organization of a Citizens Task Force by the board.

The Task Force was made up of citizens representing all geographic areas of Lucas County, various organizations, the Republican and Democratic parties, governmental units, and boards of education.

The charges to the Task Force were to study and evaluate the library service program in Lucas County and its financial requirements; to recommend means to achieve adequate funding for the proposed service program. The Task Force divided into four subcommittees and probed every phase of the Library's operation and analyzed its fiscal situation. The result was that the Task Force as a whole strongly recommended that the Library place a levy on the November ballot.

For several months prior to the trustees' final decision to place a levy on the ballot there was an accelerated thrust to keep the public informed and involved in Library affairs.

Two flyers, "The Grim Facts" and "Q's and A's," which told the Library's financial story simply and concisely, were distributed widely.

The Friends of the Library launched an all-out membership drive with the theme "It Isn't Easy Being Public (as in public library). People Take You for Granted. But It's Easy Being a Friend of the Library." Over 100,000 membership flyers were distributed in bank statements. Banks, savings and loans, stores, and schools, displayed posters advertising the membership drive and placed the membership flyers at tellers' windows and service desks. Ninety posters with the same theme were installed in public transportation buses. A contest was held for persons selling the most memberships and for the branch Friends chapter with the largest increase in members. Seven additional chapters of Friends of the Library were formed to bring the total to 14. (There are 17 branches and Main Library in the Toledo-Lucas County Library System.) The drive was a success; 1,280 joined the ranks, making a total of 2,205 members. This activity produced a ready reservoir of potential volunteers and a satisfactory amount of publicity.

The Friends and Library staff joined forces to sponsor a variety of events and programs which involved community businesses, agencies, and the public in general, focused on Library resources and the need to maintain services. All provided opportunities to point up the Library's financial plight through person-to-person contacts, and also generated positive news coverage.

Branch Library chapters of Friends sponsored sidewalk festivals, arts and crafts shows, and meet-the-author parties. At the Lucas County Fair, staff and Friends staffed a booth where an eye-catching sign at the entrance proclaimed, "Ouch, Everyone Feels the Pinch"; Library literature was distributed; the Library situation was explained, and a large chart displayed the woes of inflation.

Levy campaign action began in August with the formation of the campaign committee, "Concerned Citizens for the Library." Prominent citizens from all areas of community life served on the committee.

A public-relations consultant was hired, and a coordinator appointed, the latter a former Republican Chairperson for Lucas County and a former member of the Lucas County Board of Elections, who was an expert in the political process.

"Yes for the Library" was adopted as the campaign slogan, and the color theme of all publicity was the same as that used in the Friends of the Library membership drive.

Historically, in Lucas County no issue on the ballot except statewide issues had been numbered. Research was undertaken which brought to light the fact that local boards of elections have the option to number issues if they choose to do so. Consequently, a request was made to the Lucas County Board of Elections to number countywide issues. After contact with individual Board members and its Director, the Board voted to number these issues on the ballot, and the Library was assigned Number 7. Stickers saying "Vote for Issue No. 7" were placed on large banners and "Vote for Issue No. 7" was added to brochures and other publicity. It was felt that this would clarify the Library issue for the voting public, which is often confused by ballot language.

The grand opening of campaign headquarters with full media coverage was September 19. The high point was the presentation of a $10,000 check from The Friends of the Library to the campaign chairperson. This, plus a subsequent donation of $1,000 from the Staff Association, assured success in obtaining $25,000 needed for campaign costs. The remainder was raised by the United Toledo Committee, a unique, select group of community business leaders who solicit contributions to aid community agencies in approved levy campaigns. The entire county was saturated with the Library's message.

There was comprehensive distribution of "Yes for the Library" flyers, brochures, and buttons. Posters were distributed for use in home windows, storefronts, and as yard signs. Large banners were placed on most libraries and in a few strategic outdoor spots.

Endorsements of the levy were sought from all types of organizations, clubs, unions, churches, synagogues, political parties, office holders, and school boards. One-hundred twenty-seven of these responded with endorsements. This list was used in paid newspaper ads and on posters in every branch library. Important support was gained when WSPD-TV (the only TV station whose policy allows endorsement of issues) gave the library levy its editorial support, and when the *Toledo Blade* gave wholehearted editorial support. Contacts with these two news sources were made by the Director and President of the Trustees of the Library. Both political parties endorsed the library levy on their sample ballots.

Friends of the Library, staff members, and other citizens volunteered to conduct a month-long phone-a-thon, calling as many registered library borrowers as possible; 19,000 calls were completed.

A door-to-door distribution of literature was held on the second Sunday before election. The county was divided into areas served by each branch. A map of a four or five block area to be covered by each volunteer was placed on a 3 × 5 card for assistance. Volunteers met at the branches at 1:30 P.M. for refreshments provided by the Friends and assignment of territory. Over 900 people participated in this effort. Two young women actually distributed literature on horseback, which naturally generated TV coverage.

A rally-on-the-lawn with entertainment and refreshments was sponsored by the Friends to generate enthusiasm and publicity.

The day before election, staff members spent their lunch hours distributing literature on downtown street corners, some wearing sandwich boards.

On election day, polling places in selected areas were staffed by volunteers distributing "Yes for the Library" flyers.

The campaign momentum never let up from beginning to end. The dedicated cooperation of trustees, administration, staff, Friends, patrons, and general public—more than 2,000 active participants—created an indomitable spirit, which made its mark in a resounding two-to-one approval.

". . . more hints—and hard work . . ."

Useful hints and the reiteration of important campaign principles appear in the accounts of other successful elections. The Public Library of Youngstown and Mahoning County, also in Ohio, won a levy with a strong campaign that included an active Citizens Committee, a "Salute to Libraries Week" sponsored by the Jaycees, and an eight-page newspaper tabloid section as the major piece of campaign literature. This was marked "Paid advertisement. Not paid for with public funds. Prepared by the Citizens' Committee for the Library Levy." The front page carried a large heading, "If the Library Loses EVERYBODY Loses! Vote for the Library Levy." Inside were numerous pictures of the library in action, lists of books, a crossword puzzle, word quiz, and explanation of the need. The back page carried a full page spread of scissors slicing through a book, "Don't Cut Library Services."

T-LCPL staff members carry the message on sandwich boards at the "Rally Round the Library," a pre-election campaign event.

In a report of the fight for funding for the Port-land-Multnomah County Library (*American Libraries,* November, 1977), part of the success of a "landslide victory" was attributed to the fact that there was recognition that "professional expertise in journalism and communications was required and quickly recruited. The coordinator's office operated semi-autonomously and without the division of the coordinator's attention between fund-raising and the actual conduct of the campaign." Over $41,000 was raised for publicity.

The Public Library of Columbus and Franklin County (Ohio) won a property tax levy increase by first raising $20,000 for campaign expenses through wine and cheese parties, bake and book sales, and auctions (they even auctioned off the campaign treasurer!). In addition to many other more standard activities, voter registration was held at every branch and bookmobile, and 20,000 new voters were signed up in three months. Campaign brochures were included in the pay envelopes of two of the county's largest employers, and in many areas the literature was delivered door-to-door. Although local politicians predicted a less than 40 percent chance of the levy passing, voters approved it by a margin of 2 to 1.

In Atlanta, Georgia, the expenditure of $23,000 for an unprecedented advertising blitz, much of it in full-page, hard-hitting newspaper ads ("Today our problem is decaying books, tomorrow it may be decaying minds"; "Does the world's next great city deserve the South's dingiest library?"), was cited as a major reason for the success of a bond issue campaign for a new building.

The experience of the Cleveland Public Library holds hope for those who have met defeat in the past. In a letter to all the helpers in a successful campaign, the chairman of the citizen's committee wrote,

> The lessons we learned last year stood us in good stead. We remembered that despite some organized opposition our narrow defeat revealed the strong base we had, and this year we all built on that base. . . . In Cleveland politics it is customary to talk about one's base—the ethnic base, the Black base, the women's vote, the senior citizen's vote, etc. Our base was the 36 branches, the Main Library, and all the various outreach agencies. This formed an unbeatable combination, and all these branches and services were outposts in our battle. . . .

Bricks in the Drive for Building Funds

Building a new library is usually a once-in-a-lifetime experience for most librarians, but securing the funds, whether by bond issue or through a public solicitation, is based on the same principles of planning and promotion that have been discussed.

The fund drive must be based on a demonstrable need, and any possible controversy about site, size, or design anticipated and settled in advance "behind the scenes" as much as possible. The city fathers or other legislative bodies should be well informed and should thoroughly understand the need, and their tacit or open approval should be secured. Their cooperation—or at the very least, noninterference—is essential.

The campaign should be carefully conceived and scheduled, should involve many individuals and community agencies, and should be executed with as much flair and imagination as possible, stressing both civic pride and the "reasons for giving" listed at the beginning of this chapter.

The procedure followed by the Vigo County Public Library in Indiana is an excellent example of how to fend off any potential controversy about a new building, make the community aware of the need, and involve the citizens in all phases of the planning. Project "Help Plan the New Library" was initiated during the preparation of the building program statement and carried on during every step in the planning process; residents were asked to submit comments or opinions on any aspect of the new building through forms available at every Library service area, through service clubs, through a limited direct mailing, and on a coupon published in the media. Opinions were also solicited during public appearances of the architect and Library staff. Criticism, ideas, and comments were all accepted and considered, and a full report to the community was made. The sale of municipal bonds to build the Library was successfully negotiated with no objection by the taxpayers (who had been prone to file objections in the past) and a great deal of goodwill was generated by going directly to the people.

In Sun Prairie, Wisconsin, an 18-month fund drive for expansion of the existing Library building was undertaken by the Jaycees and Jaycettes, an example of how a community group can spear-head this activity. Funds for expansion of the Library had been set aside by the City Council, but they were insufficient and the project had a low priority; therefore, donations were sought to make the plans a reality. The Jaycees started with a "Library Awareness Week," designed to bring people into the Library so that they could see the need for expanded facilities. Each day was designated for a special group and concluded with a Saturday evening appearance of a noted author. Subsequent fund-raising activities included a massive phone-a-thon when every person with a telephone number was called for a donation to a buy-a-brick sale.

Although a variety of fund-raising activities, such as those detailed in the next section, are used in drives for new buildings, the "buy-a-brick" or a "two-by-four" is popular and often very successful. The bricks or boards are "sold" individually, for 10¢ up to $1 or more—or in carload lots!—with the result that the donor has a feeling of making a very tangible contribution and of personal ownership.

Public interest in a building fund drive can be heightened in many small ways. A scale model of the building can be prepared by students or secured from the architect and displayed in various areas throughout the community. A thermometer or similar device can be posted to show the progress of the drive. At the outset of the drive a contest can be conducted for the best slogan. A rubber stamp design with a suitable message can be imprinted on every piece of outgoing material, up to and including circulation slips. A continuous automatic slide presentation can be set up in areas where it will attract attention. As part of a building fund campaign, for example, the Tombigee Regional Library in Mississippi had a program running continuously in one of the local banks, showing all of the bad features of the old Carnegie building compared to modern well-designed libraries.

Ways-and-Means: Fund-Raising Projects

Name any kind of fund-raising project, and somewhere, sometime, it has been undertaken in the name of the library. The type of activity or

project is often determined by the interests and energies of the sponsoring or lay group, but there are also a few other considerations.

A goal must be set in terms of a specific number of dollars, whether for a single project or part of a long-term campaign, which is reasonable and cost effective. The specific purpose for which the money is to be raised should be clearly stated and understood by all volunteers and workers. These questions need to be answered as well: Is "seed money" for the event or project available to carry out all of the details, or will there be an undue burden on the library staff? Is the fund-raising activity one that the community is likely to support because it has been successful in the past; is it sufficiently novel to attract a large public? Or will it

". . . seasoned fund-raisers offer these tips . . ."

appeal to a generous select group? A good knowledge of the spending habits and life-style of the area residents is an important guide.

In choosing a time or date for the activity avoid any possible conflicts with other similar community events. Seasonal holiday weekends are poor choices, but the weekend after or immediately preceding a holiday may be a good time.

Seasoned fund-raisers offer these tips. Keep all expenses at a minimum, and get as much as possible donated. Consider discounts for students or senior citizens, or other groups if appropriate to the event. More money may be raised if a contribution is requested instead of a fixed charge. Offer something "free" such as coffee or a giveaway to make people feel that they are getting something extra for their donation or admission fee.

Book sales are far and away the most popular money-raising activity for libraries, and there are a number of good references on the subject (see Bibliography). Both library discards and donated books can be included. A clever title will often help in the publicity, such as "Duplicates, Disasters, and Discards," "Twice Told Tales," or "Secondhand Prose."

Libraries have enlivened interest in the book sale in various ways. The Friends of Ann Arbor Public Library called theirs a "Dutch Auction

Booksale"; hardback book prices started at $1 on Friday, and were progressively reduced to 10¢ on the last of four days. The Manhasset Public Library in New York sold books for 20¢ a pound, and elsewhere they have been sold by the yard on the final day. In Hennepin County, Minnesota, books were sold sight unseen for $2 for a 40 pound box containing a selection of 40 books, and on the final day of the sale at Taylor Memorial Public Library in Cuyahoga Falls, Ohio a browser could take all that could be carried for $1. Favorite books of well-known people were signed and donated to the sale held in the Mayville Library, New York.

Many libraries display items that are for sale by Friends groups—stationery, book bags, postcards, T-shirts, and cookbooks, for example. There is also a growing trend toward establishing a year-around bookstore in the library itself, carrying both new and used books, and staffed by volunteers; a project that may be particularly appropriate in an area where there are no other retail bookstores.

Outdoor library fairs and festivals are often good money-raisers, and they may include book sales, flea markets, auctions, and games of chance and skill. The success and attendant publicity of walk-a-thons and bike-a-thons has encouraged some libraries to sponsor similar events, and the idea has been extended, perhaps more appropriately, to "read-a-thons," whereby students or others solicit sponsors for so many minutes or hours of uninterrupted reading. The Chatfield Public Library in Minnesota, for example, stayed open for 32 hours straight while a read-a-thon was held. Readers were sponsored by the book, page, or hour, and free coffee and cookies were given to all who stopped in.

Benefits for the library are occasionally sponsored by other organizations, and these have ranged from donkey basketball games to a "Grab for Goodies—Great Grocery Race," which have little relevance to the library but are harmless and can be more or less lucrative, according to the fund-raising skill of the sponsors. Beware, however, of lending the library's good name to questionable commercial charity schemes; often the percentage of the profits that actually goes to the library is less than 10 percent.

Auctions of unneeded library equipment or donated items and services have netted many dollars, as have raffles and drawings for cars or

trips. In Putnam, New York, the library solicited donations of items of value, issued tax deductible credits to the donor, and then sold the items to buyers. In one case the library accepted the equipment and furnishings of a small movie theater, had them appraised, gave a tax credit deduction to the donor, advertised, and then sold the equipment to a theater owner in another community. Laws and restrictions on these activities vary, so be sure to check the legality of your activity.

Purely social events, such as dinners, dances, and picnics, or special programs such as theater parties, fashion shows, and home tours have all been held for the sake of the library.

Many fund-raising activities have a value beyond the number of dollars raised that can be measured in terms of extensive publicity and the involvement of many people, both as workers and as participants, and, in sum, the success is likely to be determined by the initiative, imagination, and enthusiasm of the volunteers or sponsors.

Seeking Donations, Gifts and Memorials

Outright gifts of money in the form of bequests and memorials can be an important source of additional income. These may occasionally come from unexpected sources, but they are more often the result of direct encouragement, purposely planned as an important phase of the total promotional program. Unfortunately, libraries have been less than aggressive in seeking such funds and publicity or reminders are often so low-keyed or discreet that they have been all but lost among the appeals from universities, churches, and well-organized charitable groups.

An attractive brochure or pamphlet, citing the advantages of donations to the library and suggesting the ways they can be accomplished, is the starting point, followed by well-planned distribution. The format can be a simple folder with an attached form, or a more elaborate version. A piece prepared by the Oshkosh Public Library (Wisconsin) lists the purposes for which a $5 million endowment fund is sought and explains how—through bequests, trusts, insurance, and gifts of money or property—and is accompanied by a sheet with four suggested legal forms for a bequest to be adapted to specific cases by counsel. The Milwaukee Public Library folder is entitled "Book Memorials, a meaningful way to remember a person, a group, an occasion, a milestone." A facsimile of the gift plate is illustrated inside, with a simple form to fill out, and this explanatory text:

> For thoughtful people who wish to add an appropriate "personalized" touch to their giving—as an individual or as a group—the library has an answer.
> A gift to the Milwaukee Public Library's collection is one of the most satisfying ways of insuring that your gift will live, will be cared for, and will continue to be used. It can reflect the taste of the giver or, in the case of memorials, of the individual in whose memory it is given. Moreover, it provides an excellent way for an organization to help the community with books or materials in the field in which it is especially interested.
> For example, a history-minded person might increase the library's holdings in the field of local history, biographies, maps and pictures. A nationality group might provide for the purchase of language records or the literature of their native land. (If you do not wish to designate a specific subject, you can make your contribution in general for the purchase of books for the people of Milwaukee.)
> A book gift to the library need not necessarily be in memoriam. It can be—and has been—given to commemorate an occasion, a birthday, an anniversary, or other milestone.
> A minimum memorial (because the price of books and processing has been going up) is $10. The donor has the option of naming the subject area in which the book(s) should be purchased.
> Acknowledgement goes to the donor and to the person, or the family of the person being honored, and a bookplate is placed in the gift book.

The Kent County Library System in Michigan prepared a pamphlet entitled "The Cost of Giving is Going Down" which detailed information about income tax deductions for library donations. As a result of the distribution through member libraries, over $1,300 in cash was received in the first few weeks.

In Orlando, Florida, a book endowment fund drive was initiated with a specific request for a gift of $150, stating, "Each book endowment is $150; it provides each year in perpetuity a worthwhile book for any unit of the Orlando-Orange-Osceola Library System designated by the donor. . . ." An

Memorial Book Drive Brochure Cover, Greenville County (SC)

Memorial Books Iowa City Public Library

"If we work upon marble it will perish. If we work upon brass, time will efface it. If we rear temples they will crumble to dust. But if we work upon men's minds, if we imbue them with high principles, with the just fear of God and love of their fellow men, we engrave on those tablets something which no time can efface, and which will brighten and brighten to all eternity..."

Daniel Webster

Memorial Book Drive Brochure Cover, Iowa City (IA)

Ohio library made a very direct pitch with the heading, "Would YOU Like to Be Immortal?" The Racine Public Library in Wisconsin went directly to the public with a boxed newspaper advertisement, "YOUR GIFTS TO THE PUBLIC LIBRARY will be lasting memorials bringing pleasure, knowledge, enlightenment and service to the community. . . ."

Acknowledgement of gifts should be made promptly, and publicized in newsletters and newspapers. If the bequest or endowment is large, it will rate both space and interest, as this example from a Minnesota newspaper:

LIBRARY PATRON SAYS "THANKS" IN WILL

He wasn't one of our weekly borrwers, but he always came to us when he had a specific need. He was always very appreciative of our help.
Ms. M. Dewey, Director of the Cityville Public Library, was describing the late John Smith.
Smith's gratitude for the Library's help has been shown in a big way through a donation of $___. . . .

An important endowment received in the past should be acknowledged annually through a letter to the family (who may give more later!) explaining how the money was used, and in a local news release, in this simple form:

Nine new volumes on gardening available at the Cityville Public Library have been made possible from the interest provided by the Jane Smith Library Endowment Fund. The endowment was established in 1977 by family and friends of Mrs. Jones, who was noted for her prize-winning flowers.
Books on flower gardening are in great demand at the Library," Ms. Dewey, Director, said. These new volumes are a fitting memorial to Mrs. Smith. . . .

A static list of donors will receive scant attention, but an indication of the purposes for which the money was used or the subject matter of titles purchased will arouse more interest.

Publicity about gifts received on less than usual occasions may stimulate other presentations. A photo accompanied a release about the donations given by the Junior Women's Club of Warrier Run, Pennsylvania, when they voted to donate a book to the Library for each infant born to a club member. In Pine River, Minnesota, a newspaper account told of the presentation of a film projector to the Library by the children of parents celebrating their 50th wedding anniversary. It read, "The gift, which will benefit the community for years to come, is especially appropriate since their parents were active in the campaign to establish library services in the county, and have been faithful library users. . . ."

Memorial or other gift books can also be displayed on occasion, either in the library or in a public area, as a nice way to honor those involved and to encourage other contributions. As proof that this works, the Jefferson Public Library in Iowa received memorials from 19 donors after a display of such books.

Gifts of used books, book collections, and new books of questionable interest or content are a recurring headache for all libraries. The problem can be short-circuited by an explicit policy adopted by the Board of Trustees and clearly stated in writing. In Illinois, the Bloomington Public Library included this tactful list of considerations for donors in a small folder suggesting gifts to the library:

Considerations for Donors:

1. As a first step, consult the library director to determine the library needs and the suitability of your proposed gift.
2. Please, don't attach unnecessary "strings" that may restrict the usefulness or hamper the effectiveness of your gift.
3. The library is not a museum. Please keep in mind that sculpture and other works of art are rarely suitable for a public library.
4. Help in meeting the basic purposes of the library (Information, Education, Recreation) is most suitable. Your gift will work best and will be most valuable if it purchases furniture or equipment or provides library materials such as books, records, films, etc.
5. The library will retain unconditional ownership of the gift, will make the final decision regarding its own use or other disposition of the gift, and the library reserves the right to decide the conditions of the display, housing, and access to the gift.
6. A book plate will be placed in all books accepted by the library. This plate will contain the donor's name, and words or phrases of the donor's choice. Gifts other than books, when possible, will also be identified in a like manner.

Posting or publicizing a specific "want list" of either equipment or book titles, with prices, is a good way to suggest and channel contributions.

". . . when you go begging . . ."

Local merchants and businesspeople receive a tremendous number of requests for money or contributions in-kind for community "worthy causes," with the result that an approach by anyone representing the library may meet reactions ranging from cool to outrage. Nevertheless, a good case can be made, but the way should be paved by a prior demonstration of service (an appropriate booklist, a program of specific interest, a mailing); too often the sole contact that is made with many is on the occasion of a plea for funds or materials. Many civic-minded agencies, particularly banks and savings and loan companies, will be receptive to well-conceived projects or activities when the resulting publicity reflects credit to them. Others have standards or regulations they apply to various appeals, and these should be "researched" in advance.

A specific request may meet with more success than a generalized appeal. For example, the Port Ewen Free Library in New York canvassed businesspeople and solicited money for subscriptions to magazines from a prepared list. Of the 32 people approached, 31 responded. The donors of the periodicals were suitably identified both in the library and in the business establishments.

Making Friends with a Capital "F"

It is apparent from this discussion that a Friends of the Library or similar lay group is essential for fund-raising activities.

The care and feeding of Friends and volunteers has been well-documented, but some important points should be kept in mind.

There is a distinction between "Friends" and the cadre of volunteers who help out in many libraries. Friends are, indeed, volunteers, and many assist with in-library clerical work and outreach activities, but groups are organized on a dues-

Let's be friends - -

Everybody needs one - even libraries!

Please join the FRIENDS of SCRANTON PUBLIC LIBRARY.

Promotional Literature: Friends Group

paying membership basis for the purpose of promoting and supporting the library. Volunteers, on the other hand, generally work directly under the supervision of a library staff member or a volunteer coordinator, performing tasks more directly related to the library's routine operations.

The More We Get Together...

...The More We Can Accomplish!

JOIN THE FRIENDS OF ROCHESTER PUBLIC LIBRARY!

Sample Friends Brochure: Rochester (MN)

The structure and program of Friends groups vary widely, reflecting the needs of the library and community, and the interests and abilities of the members. Although fund-raising has traditionally been a major function, often in creative and imaginative ways, such activities as lobbying for support at the local, regional, and national levels, promoting and publicizing library services, and sponsoring or assisting with special library programs have been equally important. They are an important pipeline to the public and are library "promoters" par excellence.

State-level Friends organizations primarily serve to encourage and assist with the formation of local groups. In addition, they aid in the exchange of information and ideas between local organizations, sponsor or participate in statewide activities such as National Library Week, and often serve as citizen liaisons with state library agencies and committees.

The formation of a "Friends of the Library" can be initiated by the library director or staff member, by one or more trustees, by a "friendly" community organization such as the League of Women Voters, or simply by interested citizens. The impetus most frequently comes with the need for a new building or expansion of desired services, but a successful library-oriented activity that has involved many persons in the community often produces the nucleus of a group that will go on to organize formally.

Friends groups are most successful when they have strong and interested support from the library director and staff, and develop an on-going program; either a series of short-term projects or

"... failing friends?"

regularly scheduled activities and responsibilities. Failures are most often due to lack of leadership, misunderstandings of the role of the Friends and their relationship to the library and library board, and the lack of significant projects. Friends groups occasionally falter after a good start. A lethargic or inactive membership may be due to the lack of short- and long-term objectives; specific projects related to the objectives and within a time frame will engender a needed sense of accomplishment. Without good direction, the high level of enthusiasm maintained during a building drive, for example, may ebb when the goal is obtained and a transitional period occurs. Dependable and imaginative leadership is always necessary, and too much dependence on staff for guidance and assistance is a warning sign that this is missing and an infusion of new blood is needed. With good leaders and good liaison and rapport with the library administration, Friends can be a joy; without it they can be a headache. Their function and relationship must be clearly understood so as to avoid any infringement on the role of the trustees.

Friends are often the unsung heroes in a library's struggle to meet community needs and maintain a high level of service, and their efforts should be recognized and rewarded regularly.

Promotional Potpourri

Speaking Up

Giving a talk or making a speech is an excellent opportunity to promote the library; one that is either welcomed or dreaded, according to the nature or experience of the person asked to do it. Some speakers seem so at home behind a podium, so at ease and so glib that they appear to be born showpeople, but behind the ease and glibness lies well-rehearsed practice and preparation. Thus, whether a talk is for a group of ten club members or a speech for hundreds, advance preparation is the key.

Self-confidence, either actual or assumed, is an important ingredient in a successful talk. This is based on familiarity with your subject matter—in this case, the library. This assurance will offset any tendency toward trembling knees and a dry mouth. When you must rise to the occasion, remind yourself that you know more about the subject than anyone in the audience; that's why you were asked to speak in the first place!

There are numerous good references on the techniques of speech-making which will help to develop an individual style, or at least aid in making a passable presentation. A few basic principles and hints are worth reiterating.

Gear the talk to the group, both in content and style. Know the interests and the age range of those likely to be in the audience. Get their attention right in the beginning with a quip, an anecdote, or a local reference; never start with the hackneyed phrases, "It's a privilege to be here"; "Today I'm going to talk about . . ."; "To begin with, let's start off with. . . ."

Should you read your speech, use outline notes, or talk "off the cuff"? Despite the usual advice, it all depends upon the individual. If you are the type who is apt to forget your own name when you look at a sea of upturned faces, you may need to get launched into the water with an outright reading of your opening. Once underway, a few sentences and notations may be all you need

---

". . . to read it or wing it?"

---

to carry on. You run the risk of falling into a singsong cadence, absorbed in what's coming next rather than what you are saying, if you attempt to memorize your talk word for word. A speech that is read from beginning to end can be deadly, but if you find that necessary, you can still hold the audience if your talk is well-rehearsed, sounds conversational rather than read, and you make frequent eye contact with listeners. Your speech is not likely to be a technical paper intended for publication, and so avoid a pedantic tone.

Practice your talk with a tape recorder so that you can hear your own inflections, locate dull passages, and time yourself. Keep your talk short. Anything over 20 minutes is dangerous, and it takes a real pro to hold many spellbound for a longer period. You also run the risk of telling listeners more than they want to know. You can communicate a great deal of information in a short time if you edit your material carefully. Don't be dismayed if the program chairperson tells you that you have an been alloted 45 or 60 minutes; s/he has misjudged the audience's listening capacity or is desperately filling out the program.

Use the extra time for a question and answer period, discussion with members of the audience, or a show-and-tell period with sample materials or visual aids.

Make your material as lively as possible; you know the library is not dull—so prove it. For example, choose human interest anecdotes about patrons, named or unnamed, to illustrate the type and abundance of services and materials available.

Be yourself, both in the content and delivery of your talk, but don't let "self" blot out your message. Avoid distracting gestures, unusual attire, or eye-riveting jewelry and accessories.

Visual aids in the form of charts, pictures, and other materials can be helpful if properly used. When employing them, avoid the pitfalls of staring at them too long, talking into an easel or chart, or exposing them too soon. If you have handouts, distribute them at the end of your talk, and never circulate one or more during your speech. (A talk is not a workshop session.)

". . . finish with a flourish . . ."

Wind up with a good closing—a startling statement or conclusion, a good, relevant story, a call to action, or a quotation.

If you have stirred your audience in any way, there are bound to be some questions directed to you. When none are forthcoming, you have either exhausted the subject or your audience. If a question-and-answer period is scheduled, prepare for this by planting a few questions with members of the audience in advance to avoid a slow start. Or throw out a question yourself. On the other hand, you may be placed in a defensive position by some aggressive persons, who wish to get their own ideas across by disguising them as questions ("Don't you think that . . . ?") and expounding at length. A good meeting chairperson can help to control this, and you, as the speaker, can recognize the questioner's concern, appear to agree, and offer another opinion on some aspect of the

question. The questioners who try to put you down or seek a platform for their own ideas will probably receive short shrift from fellow listeners unless you have purposely or inadvertently touched a sore spot with the audience. This is not likely to be the proper time or place for a debate.

It may happen that the library's designated public information officer is not good at giving talks or is not the best possible spokesperson for the library in some situations. The person's responsibility, then, will be one of giving aid and comfort to the library director, board members, willing staff personnel, or volunteers. Writing a speech for someone else is difficult, because it should be tailored to the style and personality of the speaker. The material can be organized and written out, but then it should be adjusted by the individual and carefully rehearsed; only then will it become an oral presentation rather than a written message.

One or more "canned" talks in reserve that can be given on short notice by various staff members or other volunteers are well worth the effort of preparation, but the speaker should take time to become completely familiar with the material and to add his/her own comments and phraseology. If you type up a script for someone else, use wide margins, type lines in a series of natural phrases rather than as run-on sentences, and never continue a line from one page to another that requires turning the sheet in the middle of a sentence.

It may be possible or advisable to set up an informal speaker's bureau, and enlist staff and others with special interests or expertise. Seek assistance from a qualified speech teacher or a member of the Toastmasters' Club for one or more initial training sessions to help prepare the corps. There may be built-in motivation for volunteers and staff at the time of a building drive or referendum, but other incentives should be offered when such a bureau or pool of speakers is part of a total promotional program.

Publicity to ensure speaking engagements is essential, and can take the form of direct mail or handouts to organizations and clubs, press releases about the speaker's bureau, media releases, or reports when a speaker is engaged. If the performance is good, word-of-mouth advertising will also generate some requests. A listing of the names of the speakers, the date, place, and subject should be carried in newsletters and reports to the board, as well.

Now Picture This . . .

Slide showings have become an increasingly popular method of presenting information about the library to groups of people. They are easier and far cheaper to produce than films, can be changed in length and content to suit various audiences, and are readily updated.

The fact that the narrator becomes a disembodied voice in a darkened room is a disadvantage and audience contact is easily lost, whether the material is read in person from a script or heard on a tape. This can be overcome to some extent if the speaker stands in the front of the room, in a dimly lit area, and changes the slides by remote control; some eye contact can be maintained and the tempo adjusted as necessary. If the oral portion is taped and automatically keyed to the slide changes, either by an audible or inaudible beep, no on-the-spot timing changes can be made, and it is a horrendous job to make changes or adjustments after the taping is completed. This disadvantage is outweighed, to some extent, by the fact that a tape recording offers the opportunity to use a musical background, special sound effects, and professionally trained voices.

Producing a slide show appears deceptively easy, and eager amateurs are prone to forge ahead on the basis of a heterogeneous collection of slides. The usual result is a strained script with little continuity or, worse, an uninspired visual catalog of library materials and services.

". . . make your point visually . . ."

As usual, considerable preplanning is necessary. The audience for which the showing is intended must be identified and a statement of the purpose developed if it is to be an effective communication rather than entertainment. Next a theme or story line is outlined and a tentative "story board" drawn up. Laying out the story board is roughly comparable to designing the pages of a picture book, each of which carries an illustration and complementary text, from one-liners to short sentences. The visuals can be roughed in, and then the photographs or drawings made specifically for this purpose. "A good picture may be worth a thousand words," but it is worthless if it doesn't say something relevant. If an undue amount of verbiage is necessary to make a transition between slides or to explain what is on the screen, you will know that the picture is not suitable or is in the wrong place. A slide show should last no more than 20 minutes, with a maximum of 140 slides.

A high degree of sophistication can be achieved with multi-screens and other techniques, but this is not a shoestring operation and it requires professional know-how. The audiovisual specialist in a local school or college may be a good source of assistance, or a firm or free-lancer specializing in such productions can be hired. Local radio stations are often willing and able to aid with tape recordings.

A slide show worthy of numerous showings is not easy to produce and so, once in hand, do not let it collect dust. Hold a preview showing for a selected group or groups to help publicize it, and prepare the usual press releases and other notifications. The message you have written into your program can also be reinforced if a few of the best pictures are reproduced with captions or short text in a handout to distribute as a come-on or at the conclusion of the showing.

Libraries are also experimenting with videotape as a relatively inexpensive medium for small group programs. This can be effective in terms of immediacy and intimacy if some minimum technical standards are maintained. A fast-paced, 20-minute production of the Rock County Library System (Wisconsin) is a good example of a simple but graphic presentation that emphasizes the wide range of interests of Library patrons and the variety of services offered by the Library to meet their needs. Local people were interviewed and taped at the Library, and each gave a brief, spontaneous response to the question, "Why did you come to the Library today?" The tape concludes with one man responding, "I work here," followed by an explanation of his work as the reference librarian.

Miscellaneous Promotional Ideas and Gimmicks

There are no new promotional ideas in the world, only new applications and different settings. What is "old hat" in one community may be new and worth trying elsewhere.

Involving people in the organization's activities, whether by asking for opinions or aid, is a method of increasing awareness and establishing rapport.

Many libraries mount a suggestion box in a prominent location and seek comments from patrons. A printed form is helpful, either with blank space or with one or more leading questions (i.e., "Did you find what you wanted?"). Replies may be provocative, disheartening, facetious, sincere, or thoughtful. However, this is a dead-end gesture unless there is some follow-up to all but the crank messages in the form of a response, either posted publicly or made directly to individuals.

Answering telephone reference questions is a valuable public contact. An extra dividend for rendering the service can be acquired when the question is answered satisfactorily by adding, "We're always glad to help by answering your questions. Would you help us by telling your friends and business associates about this service?"

Ask vacationers and travelers in the community to remember the library as they wend their way about the state, nation, or overseas by bringing back maps, brochures, slides, and guidebooks to add to the collection. The Cocoa Public Library in Florida provided patrons with a colorful plastic bag for this purpose, and the project was publicized by a map of the world with pins showing where people had been.

Ask patrons to submit pictures of themselves, with a brief biographical notation, and pick some "winners" as illustrations in a brochure with the theme, "People like YOU use the Cityville Library. . . ."

Initiate some book and materials advisory committees, and involve groups of people with special interests or knowledge by asking them to assess parts of the collection in their fields of interest and to suggest additional titles. Participants could include businesspeople, hobbyists, travelers, professional people, farmers, or ethnic groups.

Try some nontraditional ways of getting a message across.

In Amherst, New York, supermarket shoppers hear public announcements about the library over the store's intercom.

Supply a printed "reading menu" to accompany the food menu in cooperative restaurants or fast-service outlets, or distribute paper placemats.

Pique curiosity. A special message about the library was put on a jigsaw puzzle and the Frank L. Weyenburg Library in Mequon, Wisconsin, challenged patrons to put a piece or two into the puzzle so that the notice could be deciphered.

Piggy-back on the printed materials of other agencies. The Mead Public Library in Sheboygan, Wisconsin, got space for information about hours and locations on the back of a wallet-sized calendar that was given away by a local bank. The milk cartons in Racine, Wisconsin carried a special publicity panel for the library. Bus passes, real estate brochures, store bills, or payroll receipt computer printouts have all carried piggy-backed messages.

Place a display ad in the yellow pages of the telephone directory giving hours and listing services and special numbers. Get a listing under "Information Bureaus" and other suitable headings. Make sure that any and all possible variations of the library name appear in the white pages.

*   *   *   *

Involvement is invaluable promotion.

*   *   *   *

Some libraries have found it worthwhile and within the scope of their service policy to loan nontraditional materials, to set up "exchanges" or to make special equipment available for public use. Examples: tools; soil testing kits; admission or organization membership cards to museums, historic sites, etc.; garden plots; self-teaching machines; "birthday boxes" of party games, songs, decorations, films, and balloons; computer terminals; specialized sewing equipment; "Mother's helper kit" for children confined to home by illness containing paperbacks, filmstrips, cassettes, games; puppets and portable theater; tape recorders; engravers; telescopes; cameras;

microscopes; binoculars; guitars; craft equipment; weather instruments; umbrellas; live pets; opaque projectors; laminating machine; mimeograph machine; darkroom and photo lab; piano, or organ for practice.

* * * *

Try something way out. An image was demolished when the Perry County District Library in Ohio sponsored an entry—and the only female—in a demolition derby. And home runs have been scored for the library by sponsoring Little League teams.

* * * *

Grab a little publicity by stopping motorists and issuing "citations" for driving without a library card and a "summons" to report to the library. (The mayor was one of the first caught when this was tried in the Pacific Northwest.)

* * * *

Try some unusual giveaways. Offer a drawing for an all-day, all-expense-paid trip to the library, with six hours of personal assistance from a reference librarian, and unlimited photocopying. Join the annual auction of the local educational TV station by "donating" a year's free loan of a revolving rack of paperbacks, a story hour, puppet show, or film showing for a home party.

* * * *

Take the time and spend the money for postage to win new friends by clipping out newspaper notices of weddings, birth announcements, anniversaries, honors, election to office, or retirements, and forward them to the person with the message, "We saw your name in the paper . . ." and a congratulatory note, plus a word or two about the services the library would like to offer them. (Imagine the astonishment in discovering that the library knew about them—and cared!)

* * * *

Trustees, who should be valuable allies in the library's promotional activities, deserve more public recognition than they get. Identify them frequently in news releases and at public functions because this helps to establish their credibility as spokespeople. In New York, the Onondaga Library System creates an occasion for calling in the press for a story and picture by staging an impressive ceremony, complete to a judge giving an oath of office, when new trustees are welcomed to the board.

Quips, Phrases, and Slogans

These notable (or reproachable, according to your likes) lines can liven up a poster, brochure, or newsletter. At the very least, they may spark some better twists of your own:

- Here are FREE reasons to use your library.

- Don't reinvent the wheel . . . find out how someone else did it first—at the library.

- Information retrievers are a new breed of dog.

- You have a right to know; the library has the right know-how.

- You are not only WELCOME at the library—It was DESIGNED for you.

- JACK AND JILL WENT UP THE HILL,
  TO FETCH AN ARM OF BOOKS.
  JACK FELL DOWN,
  AND BROKE HIS CROWN.
  AND JILL WENT AHEAD,
  CHECKED OUT FOUR MYSTERIES,
  TWO COWBOY STORIES,
  AND A BOOK OF WORD GAMES
  TO HELP JACK PASS THE TIME
  IN THE HOSPITAL. . . .

- Computers can never replace human errors.

- These books have a lethal amount of DDT—Darn Daring Thoughts.

- Reading is a know-know.

- Using the library just for a book is like using Babe Ruth just for a bunt.

- You have __ more days in 1980 to catch up on your reading.

- Books of a feather flock together.

- When words fail, try a record, a film, an art print—from the library.

- We have things you didn't even know you wanted.

- Selective service still operates in the library.

- Save trees—recycle books and magazines at the library.

- We're not all that smart—we just have our ignorance organized.

- Books that didn't quite make the Big Time:

DAVID IRONFIELD

JACK AND THE GRAPEVINE

CATCH 21

TALE OF THREE CITIES

THE BOBBSEY TRIPLETS

THE FLIMSY REPORT

COLD FINGER

THE COUNT OF MONTE CARLO

MOBY RICHARD

For Further Reading: A Chapter-by-Chapter Bibliography

The Library "Image" and Imagery

Angoff, Allan, ed. *Public Relations for Libraries; Essays in Communication Techniques*. Westport, CT: Greenwood Publishing Corp., 1973.
One of the few books which considers the public relations needs of school, academic, and special libraries as well as those of various types of public libraries and systems.

Bernays, Edward L. *Public Relations*. Norman, OK: University of Oklahoma, 1970.
A basic text in the field. Traces the development of public relations, analyzes case histories to illustrate principles in action. Stresses the need to understand individuals, institutions, social groups, and their inter-relationships.

Cutlip, Scott M., and Center, Allen H. *Effective Public Relations*. 5th ed. Englewood Cliffs, NJ: Prentice-Hall, 1978.
Textbook classic.

Kies, Cosette. *Problems in Library Public Relations*. New York: Bowker, 1974.
In analyzing case studies, the author argues that the public relations function must be an integral part of the total library service program. Illustrates the application of basic public relations principles to real situations.

Lesly, Phillip, ed. *Lesly's Public Relations Handbook*. Englewood Cliffs, NJ: Prentice-Hall, 1978.
Articles by experts on both the theory and techniques of public relations. Although aimed at business, selective use will provide valuable information for libraries. Extensive bibliography and glossary.

Norton, Alice. *Public Information Sources*. Detroit: Gale, 1971.
Includes many book and article references on PR, organizations, and resources. Somewhat dated.

Rice, Betty. *Public Relations for Public Libraries: Creative Problem Solving*. New York: H.W. Wilson, 1972.
Discusses public relations as an aspect of service and meeting community needs. Suggests channels of communication other than the mass media. Includes chapters on the PR role of Friends groups, and the importance of PR in budget and bond issues.

Richman, Saul. *Public Information Handbook for Foundations*. New York: Council on Foundations, Inc., 1973.
Another handbook for nonprofit groups that has good advice for libraries too. Recommended for chapters on the annual reports and distribution.

Steinberg, Charles S. *The Creation of Consent; Public Relations in Practice*. New York: Hastings House, 1975.
A good general text. Discusses the philosophy of PR as it relates to media communication, with examples from many nonprofit organizations; principles relevant to libraries.

Getting Started

American Society for Hospital Public Relations. *Hospital Public Relations Management Development Program*. Chicago: American Hospital Association.
Excellent model for planning and assessing status of public relations and promotional program.

Bittner, John R. *Mass Communication*. Englewood Cliffs, NJ: Prentice-Hall, 1977.
Detailed consideration of the techniques, methods, resources, and problems of mass communication, particularly as related to special audiences.

Dillman, Don A. *Mail and Telephone Surveys*. New York: John Wiley and Sons, 1977.

Very comprehensive text on developing and conducting surveys.

Fontaine, Sue. *PR Tick Click*. Chicago: American Library Association, 1976.
A lively 30-minute slide tape production about library public relations; interviews with library administrators and PR specialists. Designed as an audiovisual learning tool.

Koestler, Frances E. *Planning and Setting Objectives*. Norton, Alice. *Measuring Potential and Evaluating Results*. In series, *Managing Your Public Relations: Guidelines for Nonprofit Organizations*. New York: Public Relations Society of America, 1978.
Two excellent small booklets.

Kotler, Philip. *Marketing for Nonprofit Organizations*. Englewood Cliffs, NJ: Prentice-Hall, 1975.
Marketing strategy, concepts, and tools interpreted for noncommercial organizations.

Oaks, Robert. *Communication by Objective: How Non-Profit Organizations Can Build Better Internal and Public Relations*. South Plainfield, NJ: Groupwork Today, Inc., 1977.
Stresses theme that key to PR is planning and setting objectives in designing promotional programs.

Vance, John E. *Information Communications Handbook: Policies for Working with the Media for Public Officials, Citizens, Business, and Community Groups*. St. Paul, MN: John E. Vance, 1973.
Philosophic approach to public relations, based on long experience in a public agency. Stresses definition of goals and audience, and determination of best and most economical means of reaching them. Good reference for large libraries and library systems.

Weiss, Carol H. *Evaluation Research: Methods of Assessing Program Effectiveness*. Englewood Cliffs, NJ: Prentice-Hall, 1972.
In-depth discussion of the problem of evaluation.

Periodicals of Interest to Public Information Officers

Editor's Newsletter. Box 243, Lenox Hill Station, New York, NY 10021. Monthly.

Journal of Educational Communication. Box 657, Camp Hill, PA 17011. Monthly.

Library Public Relations News. P.O. Box 687, Bloomfield, NJ 07003. Bimonthly.

PR Aids' Party Line. 221 Park Ave. South, New York, NY 10003. Weekly.

Practical Public Relations. Box 3861, Rochester, NY 14610. Twice Monthly.

Public Relations Journal. Public Relations Society of America, 845 Third Ave., New York, NY 10022. Monthly.

Public Relations News. 127 E. 80th St., New York, NY 10021. Weekly.

Public Relations Quarterly. 44 W. Market St., Rhinebeck, NY 12572. Quarterly.

Public Relations Review. College of Journalism, University of Maryland, College Park, MD. Quarterly.
Winter, 1977, Vol. 3, No. 4 particularly recommended for readings in evaluation and measurement of PR and publicity; from corporate viewpoint but offers insight in problems and methods.

Publicist. 221 Park Ave. South, NYC 10003. Bimonthly.

The Ragan Report. Lawrence Ragan Communications, Inc., 407 S. Dearborn St., Chicago, IL 60605. Weekly.

Using the Media for Publicity

Associated Press. *Broadcast News Style Book*. New York: Associated Press, 1976.
Excellent how-to tips for writing radio copy.

Biegel, Len, and Lubin, Aileen. *Mediability: A Guide for Nonprofits*. Washington, DC: Taft Products, Inc., 1975.
Radio and television stressed, with chapters on cable TV and telethons.

Bloomenthal, Howard. *Promoting Your Cause*. New York: Funk and Wagnalls, 1971.
Practical suggestions for using the media and other channels of communication as publicity tools. Contains excellent chapters on the principles of communication, on the choice and coordination of communication channels.

Flesch, Rudolph. *The Art of Readable Writing*. New York: Harper and Row, 1974.
The author dispenses with the formal rules learned in English class and provides information culled from research in linguistics, psychology, and communication. To develop an effective style, he suggests that you write the way you talk, and relearn informal, colloquial English.

Fowler, H.W. *A Dictionary of Modern English Usage.* New York: Oxford University Press, 1965.

Klein, Ted, and Danzig, Fred. *How to Be Heard; Making the Media Work for You.* New York: Macmillan, 1974.
Strategies and techniques for using the media and how to prepare an effective campaign. Also includes advice on campaigning for a cause, running seminars, surveys. Useful information that can be applied by libraries in planning promotion.

Leidung, Oscar. *A Layman's Guide to Successful Publicity.* New York: Ayer Press, 1976.
Guide to all elements of good news writing.

Library Publicity Clippings. Box 742, Santa Ana, CA 92702. 10 issues annually.
Includes "canned" newspaper and radio releases of varying lengths.

Martin, Dick. *The Executive's Guide to Handling a Press Interview.* New York: Pilot Books, 1977.
Advice and techniques for getting the message across, even in the face of hostility.

National Association of Broadcasters. *So You're Going on TV* and *If You Want Air Time, a Handbook for Publicity Chairmen.* Washington, DC: Public Relations Department.
Two brief pamphlets.

Schmidt, Frances. *Using Publicity to Best Advantage.* Chicago: Public Relations Society of America, 1978.
Another booklet in the PRSA series, *Managing Your Public Relations: Guidelines for Non-Profit Organizations.*

Skillen, Marjorie E., and Gay, Robert M. *Words into Type.* Englewood, NJ: Prentice-Hall, 1974.
Combination style book, word usage guide, and grammar book; an aid for better prose writing.

Strunk, William, Jr., and White, E.B., *The Elements of Style.* New York: Macmillan, 1959.
A classic.

Tilden, Scott A. *Communicating Via Radio: 101 How-To Ideas.* Fanwood, NJ: Scott Tilden, 1975.

Weiner, Richard. *Professional's Guide to Publicity.* New York: Richard Weiner, Inc., 1976.
Pragmatic advice for preparing material for the media, with an appendix of examples. Written for the generalist but applicable to library publicity.

University of Chicago Press. *A Manual of Style.* 12th rev. ed. Chicago: University of Chicago Press, 1969.
This is a widely-accepted style reference.

University of Wisconsin, Programs in Journalism/Mass Communications. *Monographs.* Madison, WI: Journalism-Communication, UW-Extension.
A series of monographs that includes a variety of subject headings. (Ex: "Hints on the Nature and Use of Publicity," "News Value Scale," "Publicity Copy Check-List.")

The Library's Printed Materials and Publications

Art Direction Book Company. *The Art Director's Library.* New York: Art Direction Book Company.
Comprehensive free catalog of books, new and in-print, available on order from this firm.

Brigham, Nancy. *How to Do Leaflets, Newsletters and Newspapers.* Somerville, MA: New England Free Press, 1977.
Basic information with helpful illustrations.

Burke, Clifford. *Printing It: A Guide to Graphic Techniques for the Impecunious.* New York: Ballantine Books, 1972.
A concise but thorough introduction to the process of offset printing, and instructions for preparing the materials to be reproduced. Discusses paste-up, camera-ready copy, paper and ink, and talking to the printer.

Cabibi, John F.J. *Copy Preparation for Printing.* New York: McGraw-Hill, 1973.
Emphasis is on typography, though chapters on layout fundamentals and paste-up are included. Most useful as a sequel to a more general work such as Burke's *Printing It.*

Craig, James. *Production for the Graphic Designer.* New York: Watson-Guptill, 1974.
Good reference with clear explanations and illustrations.

Darrow, Ralph. *House Journal Editing.* Danville, IL: Interstate Printers, 1975.

Editor's Newsletter. *How to Conduct a Readership Survey.*
A guide to conducting readership surveys of internal publications.

Federal Library Committee, Task Force on Public Relations. *Guidelines for Library Handbooks.* 0-496-682. Washington, DC: Superintendent of Documents, GPO, 1972.
A concise checklist to consult when preparing printed materials intended to convey to the library user the scope, resources, and services of the library.

Fochs, Arnold. *The Very Idea; a Collection of Novel Retail Advertising Ideas.* Duluth, MN: A.J. Publishing Co., 1971.

Glaser, Milton. *Graphic Design.* New York: Overlook Press, 1973.

Graphic Arts Monthly. *Practical Handbook of Effective Illustration.* Chicago: Graphic Arts Monthly.
How to mark, crop, size, and edit illustrations.

Graphic Arts Monthly. *Printing Layout and Design.* Chicago: Graphic Arts Monthly.
Should serve the needs of anyone requiring a sound, basic background in the layout and design of printing. Presents both good and poor examples of design.

Gross, Edmund J. *101 Ways to Save Money on All Your Printing.* North Hollywood, CA: Halls of Ivy Press, 1971.
Money-saving tips on the entire process of preparing printed material—writing copy, creating a layout, choosing the correct art medium, handling photography, selecting type, etc.

Hodgson, Richard S. *Direct Mail and Mail Order Handbook.* Chicago: Dartnell Corp., 1974.
A 3-inch-thick monster book that will tell you everything you could possibly want to know (and more) about direct mail, lists, formats, campaigns.

Kodak Co. *Photo Reports Make It Happen.* Pub. #AT-5. Rochester, NY: Consumer Markets Division, Kodak Co., 1970.
How to use photographs to add impact to a report.

Koestler, Frances A. *Creative Annual Reports.* New York: National Communication Council for Human Services, Inc., 1969.
Excellent booklet with step by step procedures for preparing annual reports for public consumption.

Mills, Vernon. *Making Posters.* New York: Watson-Guptill, 1976.

National School Public Relations Association. *Putting Words and Pictures about Schools into Print: A How-To Guide to Better School System Newsletters, Annual Reports, and Special Purpose Materials.* Washington, DC: National School Public Relations Association.
Equally useful for libraries.

Nelson, Roy Paul. *Publication Design.* Dubuque, IA: Wm. C. Brown, 1972.

Wales, LaRae H. *Practical Guide to Newsletter Editing and Design.* Ames, IA: Iowa State University Press, 1976.

Good down-to-earth guide for both novices and experienced editors.

White, Jan V. *Editing by Design.* New York: Bowker, 1974.
This well-written, well-illustrated book will show you how to improve the layout of your annual report and other library publications so that form and content work together to communicate your message.

Graphic Arts Periodicals

Graphic Arts Monthly. 222 S. Riverside Plaza, Chicago, IL 60606.

Graphic Arts Buyer. Advertising Trade Publications, Inc., 19 W. 44th St., New York, NY 10036.

Picturescope. Special Libraries Association.
Quarterly newsletter of the Picture Division of SLA that describes holdings of libraries, museums, commercial agencies.

Print. 19 W. 44th St., New York, NY 10036.

U & LC. International Typeface Corp., 216 E. 45th St., New York, NY 10017.
Free periodical describing creative things to do with letters of the alphabet.

Sources of Illustrations and Copyright-Free Art

Advertising Arts and Sciences Co. of America, Valdes Associates, Inc., Westbury, NY 11590.
The Encyclopedia of Borders, Noodles, Doodles, and Nuggets is an oversize collection of "clip" art.

Council for the Advancement and Support of Education. *Creative Communications: 202 Sources of Free and Inexpensive Pictures and Illustrations.* Guide to sources of art for publications.

Dick Sutphen Studio, Inc., Box 628, Scottsdale, AZ 85252.
A number of copyright free books from this firm (e.g., *Old Engravings and Illustrations*) are useful, especially if you have a sense of humor.

Dover Publications, Inc., 180 Varick St., New York, NY 10014.
The Dover Pictorial Archive Series and Dover Coloring Books are an inexpensive source of cuts and illustrations. (e.g., *Picture Sourcebook for Collage and Decoupage; Quaint Cuts in the Chapbook Style.*)

Dynamics Graphics, Inc., 6707 N. Sheridan Rd., Peoria, IL 61614.

A monthly "Clipper Creative Art Service" on a subscription basis, plus various packages of camera-ready art, including camera-ready color separations for full color illustrations.

Harry A. Volk Art Studio, Stock Art Booklets, Box 4098, Rockford, IL 61110.

Idea Art, 750 Broadway, New York, NY 10003; National Creative Sales, Inc., 435 North Ave., New Rochelle, NY 10802.
Preprinted announcement sheets, clip art.

Library Educational Institute, Inc. *Library of Clip Art.* LEI, Inc., P.O. Box 687, Bloomfield, NJ 07003, 1978.

McDarrah, Fred W. *Photography Market Place.* R.R. Bowker. Annual.
Comprehensive listing of picture sources, organizations, equipment sources, and technical services.

Novotny, Ann, ed. *Pictures Sources 3: Collections of Prints and Photogaphs in the U.S. and Canada.* Special Libraries Association, 1975.

Parrot Graphics, Inc., P.O. Box 687, Bloomfield, NJ 07003.
The Library Border Book, a collection of camera-ready borders and headings for brochures, flyers and booklists.

Tompkins Graphics, Inc., RD 1, New Hope, PA 18938.
Clip art source.

The Library on Display

Ask, Guvnor, and Ask, Harriet. *Simple Paper Craft.* Newton Centre, MA: Charles T. Branford Co., 1971.
Directions for making 3-dimensional figures, animals, flowers, and many objects out of paper. Most are suitable for use on bulletin boards, or in display. Especially useful for holiday or seasonal themes.

Barber, Bruce T. *Upson's Designer's Dictionary; a Handbook of Design Ideas for Retail Display.* Lockport, NY: Upson Co., 1974.
Excellent resource for unusual display and exhibit ideas easily adapted to libraries.

Bowers, Melvyn K. *Easy Bulletin Boards for the School Library.* Rev. ed. Metuchen, NJ: Scarecrow Press, 1974.
Sketches of bulletin boards for holidays, for introducing new books, and for special subjects and reference. The quality of the design and art work is better than in most books of this sort.

Coplan, Kate. *How to Prepare and Promote Good Displays.* Dobbs Ferry, NY: Oceana, 1974.
Comprehensive reference that has gone through numerous printings; full-page illustrations of displays.

Coplan, Kate, and Rosenthal, Constance. *Guide to Better Bulletin Boards, Time and Labor Saving Ideas for Teachers and Librarians.* Dobbs Ferry, NY: Oceana, 1970.
The best of the many books which illustrate displays and give instructions for copying them. Designed mainly for classroom use, but adaptable to the library. Includes a section of line drawings to be traced or enlarged.

Creative Signs and Displays. 37 West 39th St., New York, NY 10018. Bimonthly.
Display ideas, information about materials to use in creating displays and signs, sources of supply for graphic arts materials. Annual illustrated guide issue is good listing of sources for materials.

Ezell, Mancil. *Making Nonprojected Visuals and Displays.* New York: Boardman Press, 1975.
A small pamphlet with some simple principles for the novice to follow in making inexpensive posters. Few illustrations but clear instructions.

Garvey, Mona. *Library Displays: Their Purpose, Construction, Use.* H.W. Wilson, 1969.
An introduction to the principles and techniques of visual communication. Discusses types of messages, forms for presenting them, design elements, and sources of ideas. Helpful illustrations.

Kaspar, Karl, ed. *International Window Display.* New York: Frederick A. Praegar, 1966.
Ideas that could be adapted to library or community area window displays, using realia and mannequins.

Wallick, Clair. *Looking for Ideas: A Display Manual for Libraries and Bookstores.* Metuchen, NJ: Scarecrow Press, Inc., 1970.
Photographs of window displays are critiqued to illustrate the elements contributing to effective displays. Imaginative, inexpensive, and easy to construct, these are all good examples.

Warren, Jefferson T. *Exhibit Methods: How to Design, Construct, and Decorate Exhibits for School Displays, Science Fairs, Shop Windows, Museums, Trade Fairs and Conventions.* New York: Sterling Publishing Co., 1972.
Good information on design and construction of three-dimensional exhibits.

Wood, Louise, and Wood, Orvelo. *Make It with Paper.* New York: David McKay Co., 1970.
Directions for making three-dimensional animals, masks, flowers, etc. Also chapters on techniques and materials that will help to devise original creations. Useful for displays, bulletin boards, mobiles.

Library Programs and Special Events

American Library Association. *Seven ALA Criteria for Book Fairs*. Chicago: ALA, 1972.
Presents criteria for a purposeful fair, plus checklist of procedures for planners.

Baker, D. Phillip. *School and Public Library Media Programs for Children and Young Adults*. Syracuse, NY: Gaylord Professional Publications,1976.

Duran, Dorothy B., and Duran, Clement A., *The New Encyclopedia of Successful Program Ideas*. New York: Association, 1967.
Over 5,000 program ideas, most of them adaptable to libraries, plus sources for free or inexpensive resources, films, speakers (slightly dated).

Golden, Hal, and Hanson, Kitty. *How to Plan, Produce, and Publicize Special Events*. Dobbs Ferry, NY: Oceana, 1960.
Helpful hints for producing special library events. Should also stimulate imaginative ideas for serving as a resource for community groups that are planning special events.

Leibert, Edwin R., and Sheldon, Bernice E. *Handbook of Special Events for Nonprofit Organizations: Tested Ideas for Fund Raising and Public Relations*. New York: Association, 1972.
Covers basic planning for all types of special events, and discusses public relations and cultural events as well as those designed to raise funds. Includes case studies.

Robotham, John S., and LaFleur, Lydia. *Library Programs, How to Select, Plan and Produce Them*. Metuchen, NJ: Scarecrow Press, 1976.

This, Leslie. *Small Meeting Planner*. Houston: Gulf Publishing Co., 1972.
The information in the chapters on meeting dynamics, audiovisual aids, and discussion techniques could be applied to special events programming, and to in-house workshops.

Warnicke, Ruth. *Planning Library Workshops and Institutes*. Chicago: ALA, 1976.
Valuable "how-to" reference to aid those responsible for planning in-service training for librarians and library-sponsored workshops.

$$$ and Friends for the Library

Department for Board and Service Volunteers. *Fund-Raising: A Crucial Role for Board Members*.

Federation of Protestant Welfare Agencies, 281 Park Ave. South, New York, NY 10010.

Friends of California Libraries. *California Extention Kit*. Friends of California Libraries, P.O. Box 455, Sierra Madre, CA 91024.

Friends of the Free Library of Philadelphia. *Find Out Who Your Friends Are*. Friends of the Free Library of Philadelphia, Logan Square, Philadelphia, PA 19103.

Friends of the San Francisco Public Library. *A Book Sale Manual*. Friends, SFPL, Civic Center, CA 94102.

Friends of Wisconsin Libraries. *Planning to Be Friends*. FOWL, Mrs. Denise Wenger, W244 N. 4840 Highway J., Pewaukee, WI 53702.

Grantsmanship Center News. *I Hate Charities: The Views of a Corporate Charity Administrator*. Grantsmanship News, 1015 West Olympic Blvd., Los Angeles, CA 90015.
A reprint, with a checklist of how corporate officials view request for donations.

Knowles, Helen K. *How to Succeed in Fund-Raising Today*. Bond Wheelwright Co., Freeport, ME.

Library Administration and Management Association. *Friends of the Library National Notebook*. American Library Association, 50 E. Huron St., Chicago, IL 60611.

Musselman, Virginia. *Money Raising Activities for Community Groups*. New York: Association, 1969.

National Catholic Development Conference. *Bibliography of Fund Raising and Philanthropy*. National Catholic Development Conference, 130 E. 40th St., New York, NY 10016.
Eighty-four page listing of related books, periodicals, etc.

Seymour, Harold J. *Design for Fund Raising: Principles, Patterns, Techniques*. New York: McGraw-Hill, 1966.

Sheridan, Philip G. *Fund Raising for the Small Organizations*. New York: M. Evans Co., 1968.

Taylor, Bernard. *Guide to Successful Fund Raising*. South Plainfield, NJ: Groupwork Today, Inc., 1970.

Warner, Irving R. *The Art of Fund Raising*. New York: Harper & Row, 1975.

Promotional Potpourri

Eastman Kodak. *Planning and Producing Slide Programs* and *Slides with a Purpose.* Eastman Kodak, 343 State St., Rochester, NY 14650.
Two excellent booklets with how-to advice.

Quick, John. *I Hate to Make Speeches—Help for People Who Must.* New York: Grosset and Dunlap, 1973.
A witty book on the subject of public speaking which may help in preparing for book talks, a speech before a community group, or the introduction of a library program.

Starr, Douglas P. *How to Handle Speechwriting Assignments.* Pilot Books, 1978.
Guide for writing speeches for someone else.

Miscellaneous Sources of Promotional Materials

American Library Association, 50 E. Huron St., Chicago, IL 60611.
Posters, bookmarks, publicity items for National Library Week; other special publicity materials occasionally.

Antioch Bookplate Co., Yellow Springs, OH 45387.
Bookmarks.

Channing L. Bete Co., Inc., Greenfield, MA 01301.
Library-related pamphlets for purchase in quantity as handouts for patrons.

Children's Book Council, 175 Fifth Ave., New York, NY 10010.
Children's Book Week and Summer Reading Program materials.

Fordham Equipment and Publishing Co., 2377 Hoffman St., Bronx, NY 10458.
Bookmarks, Children's Summer Reading Program materials.

Haddon Wood Ivins, P.O. Box 922, New Providence, NJ 07974.
Posters, bookmarks, library postcards.

Kimoto Ideas, P.O. Box 24508, Dallas, TX 75224.
Miniature bookmarks, posters, design books.

M.G. Associates, 251 Peachtree Way, N.E., Atlanta, GA 30305.
"Display 6 Pack," a kit containing booklet and components for preparing bulletin boards and posters.

Michael M. Murphy, P.O. Box 1108, St. Cloud, MN 56301.
Bookmarks, posters, reading club aids.

Sturgis Library Products, Sturgis, MI 49091.
Bookmarks, posters, reading club aids.

Upstart Library Promotionals, Box 976, Hagerstown, MD 21740.
Posters, bookmarks, radio tapes, and other library promotional items for National Library Week and throughout the year.

Calendars and Almanacs

Chases' Calendar of Annual Events, Flint, MI: Appletree Press.
Issued annually in late fall. Recommended.

Gregory, Ruth. *Anniversaries and Holidays.* 3rd ed. Chicago: ALA, 1975.
Revised standard reference.

Kane, Joseph N. *Famous First Facts.* 3rd ed. New York: Wilson, 1964.
Use the chronological section to track down "firsts" that might lend themselves to unusual library promtions or displays.

Krythe, Maymie R. *All about the Months.* New York: Harper, 1966.

Millgate, Linda. *Almanac of Dates: Events of the Past for Every Day of the Year.* New York: Harcourt, 1977.

Mirken, Stanford M. *What Happened When.* New York: Washburn, 1966.

Murphy's Lists. *Historical Anniversaries of Notable People* and *Bibliography of 200 Articles on Anniversaries and How They Were Celebrated.* Murphy's Lists, 60 E. 42nd St., New York, NY 10017.

Myers, Robert J. *Celebrations: The Complete Book of American Holidays.* New York: Doubleday, 1972.

National Research Bureau. *What's Happening . . . When . . . in . . .* 424 North Third St., Burlington, IA 52601.
Similar to *Chase's Calendar.* Extensive listing of sources for free promotional materials related to special observances.

Spinrad, L., and Spinrad, T. *Instant Almanac of Events, Anniversaries, Observances, Quotations, & Birthdays for Every Day of the Year.* Englewood Cliffs, NJ: Prentice-Hall, 1972.

Appendix I: List of Selected Major and Minor Calendar Dates

January

Specially Designated Observances for the Month
March of Dimes Month

Weeks
Save the Pun Week
Joke Revival Week
Jaycee Week
Thrift Week

Birthdays
Jan.   1: Paul Revere, 1735
      3: David Griffith, film director, 1875
      4: Sir Isaac Newton, 1642
      6: Carl Sandburg, 1878
      7: Millard Fillmore, 1800
      8: Wilkie Collins, 1824
    11: Philipp von Ferrary (famous philatelist)
    12: Charles Perrault, 1628
    13: Horatio Alger, 1834
    14: Albert Schweitzer, 1875
    15: Martin Luther King, 1929
    17: Benjamin Franklin, 1706
    18: A.A. Milne, 1882
    19: Robert E. Lee, 1807
    22: Lord Byron, 1788
    25: Robert Burns, 1759
    27: Lewis Carroll, 1832
    30: Walter Johannes Damrosch, 1862
    31: Franz Schubert, 1797

Events
Jan.   1: New Years Day
     5: First woman governor of a state sworn in, 1924; Mrs. Nellie Taylor Ross, Wyoming
     5: George Washington Carver Day
     6: Twelfth Night
     6: Jet propulsion invented, 1944
     7: First election for a President of the United States, 1789
   10: Second woman governor sworn in, Mrs. "Ma" Ferguson, Texas, 1925
   13: Stephan Foster Memorial Day
   14: Henry Ford inaugurates the first "assembly line," 1914
   16: Prohibition came in force in 1920
   17: U.S. buys the Virgin Islands from Denmark, 1917
   20: Inauguration Day
   22: First American novel published, 1789 (*Power of Sympathy,* by Mrs. Sarah Wentworth Morton)
   23: First M.D. awarded to a woman, Dr. Elizabeth Blackwell, 1849
   24: Cape Horn first rounded, 1616
   24: Gold discovered in California, 1848
   27: First demonstration of television by John Logie Baird, 1926
   28: First commercial telephone switchboard opens with 21 subscribers, New Haven, CT, 1878. Calls were answered by crying out "Ahoy-ahoy" rather than "hello."

February

Specially Designated Observances for the Month
Heart Month
American History Month
American Music Month

Weeks
Boy Scout Week
Crime Prevention Week
Future Farmers of American Week
Brotherhood Week
Catholic Book Week

Birthdays
Feb.　1:　Victor Herbert, 1859
　　　2:　James Joyce, 1882
　　　3:　Felix Mendelssohn, 1809
　　　4:　Charles A. Lindbergh, 1902
　　　7:　Charles Dickens, 1812
　　　8:　Jules Verne, 1828
　　　9:　William Henry Harrison, 1773
　　10:　Boris Pasternak, 1890
　　11:　Thomas Alva Edison, 1847
　　12:　Abraham Lincoln, 1808
　　13:　Grant Wood, artist, 1892
　　14:　Anna Howard Shaw
　　15:　Susan B. Anthony, 1820
　　16:　Giambattista Bodoni, printer, 1740
　　17:　Marian Anderson, 1902
　　19:　Nicolaus Copernicus, 1473
　　22:　George Washington, 1732
　　25:　Pierre Auguste Renoir, 1841
　　27:　Henry Wadsworth Longfellow, 1807
　　28:　Vaslav Nijinsky, dancer, 1890

Events
Feb.　1:　First session of the U.S. Supreme Court held 1790, N.Y.
　　　2:　Groundhog Day
　　　9:　United States Weather Service established, 1870
　　12:　Alexander Selkirk, the prototype for Robinson Crusoe, was taken off his island in 1709
　　14:　Valentine's Day
　　16:　First Esperanto Club organized, Boston, 1905
　　17:　Armory Show in NYC, opened 1913; officially introduced modern art to America
　　18:　Planet Pluto discovered, 1930
　　19:　Edison's phonograph patented, 1878
　　20:　Lt. Col. John Glenn, Jr. became the first American to orbit Earth, 1962
　　22:　Woolworth opens first five-and-ten-cent store, 1879
　　25:　First Federal Income Tax became law, 1913
　　29:　Leap Year Day

March

Specially Designated Observances for the Month
Red Cross Month
Youth Art Month
National Peanut Month

Weeks
Save Your Vision Week
National Poison Prevention Week
National Wildlife Week
Girl Scout Week
Camp Fire Girls Week
U.S. Constitution Week
Return the Borrowed Book Week
American Forestry Week
Hobby Week

Birthdays
Mar. 2: Sholem Aleichem, 1859
3: Alexander Graham Bell, 1847
5: Gerard Mercator, map maker, 1512
6: Elizabeth Barrett Browning, 1806
7: Luther Burbank, 1849
8: Kenneth Graham, 1842
9: Mickey Spillane, 1918
12: Edward Albee, 1928
14: Albert Einstein, 1879
15: Andrew Jackson, 1767
18: Nikolai Rimsky-Korsakov, 1844
20: Henrik Ibsen, 1828
21: Johann Sebastian Bach, 1685
26: Robert Frost, 1875
27: Edward Steichen, 1879
31: Joseph Haydn, 1732

Events
Mar. 1: Peace Corps established, 1961
3: "Star Spangled Banner" designated by act of Congress as "the national anthem of the U.S."
4: First woman to serve in Congress takes seat, 1917 (Jeanette Rankin, R., MT)
10: First paper money of the U.S. government issued, 1862
12: United States Post Office established, 1789
17: St. Patrick's Day
25: National Agriculture Day
29: Niagara Falls stopped flowing, 1848 (30 hrs. later an ice jam upstream broke, and the cascade resumed)
30: General anesthesia used for an operation for the first time, 1842
31: Daylight savings time first tried, 1918

April

Specially Designated Observances for the Month
American Lawn and Garden Month
National Home Improvement Month

Weeks
National Library Week
National Garden Week
National Artichoke Week
National Coin Week
Secretaries Week
Bike Safety Week
Earth Week
National Volunteer Week
Canada-U.S. Goodwill Week
Pan-American Week
National YWCA Week
Consumer Credit Week

Birthdays
Apr. 2: Hans Christian Anderson, 1805
      3: Washington Irving, 1783
      5: Booker T. Washington, 1856
      6: Harry Houdini, 1874
      7: William Wordsworth, 1770
      9: Clare Booth Luce
    10: Joseph Pulitzer, 1847
    13: Thomas Jefferson, 1743
    14: A.J. Toynbee, 1889
    15: Leonardo da Vinci, 1452
    16: Anatole France, 1844
    17: Thornton Wilder, 1897

21: John Muir, 1838
21: Charlotte Bronte, 1816
22: Lenin, 1870
23: William Shakespeare, 1564
26: John James Audubon, 1785
27: Ulysses S. Grant, 1822
29: Duke Ellington, 1899

Events
Apr. 1: All Fool's Day
     2: First moving picture theater opened,1902
     6: Student Government Day
     6: Robert E. Peary discovered the North Pole, 1909
     8: Ponce de Leon lands in Florida, 1513
   12: First man orbited the earth, Yuri Gagarin,1961
   14: Dictionary Day (Webster's Dictionary first published, 1828)
   15: S.S. Titanic sunk, 1912
   16: Distribution of first Book-of-the-Month-Club selection, 1926
   17: First permanent North American Newspaper established, 1704, *Boston News Letter*
   18: Paul Revere's historic ride, 1775
   19: Israeli Independence Day
   21: Founding of Rome, 753 B.C.
   24: Congress votes to create a Library of Congress, 1800
   25: St. Lawrence Seaway opened, 1959
   27: Arbor Day
   30: Walpurgis Night (Witches' Sabbath)
   30: NBC introduced television as a regular service, 1939

May

Specially Designated Observances for the Month
International Air Travel Month
Hearing and Speech Month
Mental Health Month
Radio Month
Senior Citizen's Month

Weeks
National Be Kind to Animals Week
National Music Week
Police Week
Nursing Home Week
Let's Go Fishing Week
Drug Abuse Prevention Week
World Trade Week
International Pickle Week
National Peace Corps Week

Birthdays
May 2: Bing Crosby, 1904
    3: Niccolo Machiavelli, 1469
    4: Horace Mann, 1796
    5: Karl Marx, 1818
    6: Orson Welles, 1915
    7: Robert Browning, 1812
    8: Harry S. Truman, 1884
    9: James M. Barrie, 1860
  11: Irving Berlin, 1888
  12: Florence Nightingale, 1820
  15: Katherine Ann Porter, 1894
  18: Bertrand Russell, 1872
20: John Stuart Mill, English philosopher and economist, 1806
25: Ralph Waldo Emerson, 1803
27: Julia Ward Howe, 1819
28: Jean Louis Agassiz, 1807
29: John F. Kennedy, 1917
31: Walt Whitman, 1819

Events
May 1: May Day
    1: Law Day
    6: First postage stamp issued, 1840
    6: First university library building opened, S.C., 1840
    8: Hernando de Soto and Spanish explorers discover the Mississippi River, 1541
    9: Christopher Columbus sets out on 4th and last voyage, 1502
  10: First transcontinental railway completed, 1869
  13: Jamestown, VA, settled, 1607, first permanent New World settlement
  14: Lewis and Clark Expedition sets out for Pacific Coast, 1802
  16: First "Oscars" awarded by Academy of Motion Picture Arts and Sciences, 1929
  21: Lindbergh's historic trans-Atlantic solo flight, 1927
  28: Two monkeys, Able and Baker, make 300-mile trip into space in nose of rocket, from Cape Canaveral, 1959
  29: Top of Mt. Everest reached, 1953
  30: Joan of Arc burned at stake, 1431

June

Specially Designated Observances for the Month

National Rose Month
Dairy Month
Italian Heritage Month
Cat & Kitten Month

Weeks

Girl Watching Week
Little League Baseball Week
National Flag Week
Country Music Days Week

Birthdays

Jun. 1: John Masefield, 1878
    3: Allen Ginsburg, 1926
    6: Nathan Hale, 1755
    7: Beau Brummel, 1778
    9: Cole Porter, 1892
  13: William Butler Yeats, 1865
  14: Harriet Beecher Stowe, 1811
  19: Blaise Pascal, 1623
  21: Jean Paul Sartre, 1905
  27: Hellen Keller, 1880
  29: Peter Paul Rubens, 1577

Events

Jun. 1: "Don't give up the ship" becomes Navy slogan during battle with British frigate, 1813
    2: Congress confers citizenship on all American Indians, 1924
    5: First meeting of the Baker Street Irregulars, 1934
    6: First drive-in theater opens, 1933
    7: Freedom of the Press Day
    7: Daniel Boone starts exploration of Kentucky, 1769
  14: Flag Day, Stars and Stripes becomes national flag by resolution of Continental Congress, 1777
  14: First commercial electronic computer demonstrated and dedicated, 1951
  15: Magna Carta signed, 1215
  16: First woman space traveler, Lt. Valentine Tereshkova, launched into orbit, 1963
  19: First baseball game between organized teams, 1846
  20: Purchase of Alaska, 1867
  23: Midsummer Eve
  24: First report of "flying saucers" 1947, from Boise, Idaho
  25: Battle of Little Bighorn, 1876
  26: Pied Piper of Hamelin lures 130 children out of town, 1284
  27: First John Newbery Medal awarded, 1922 (Van Loon, *Story of Mankind*)

July

Specially Designated Observances for the Month

Barbecue Month
Hitchhiking Month
National Hot Dog Month

Weeks

Joke Exchange Week
Safe Boating Week
National Farm Safety Week
Let's Play Tennis Week

Birthdays

Jul. 3: George M. Cohan, 1878
  4: Louis Armstrong, 1900
  5: P.T. Barnum, 1810
  6: John Paul Jones, 1747
  11: John Quincy Adams, 1767
  12: Henry David Thoreau, 1817
  15: Rembrandt, 1606
  19: Edgar Degas, 1834
  20: Sir Edmund Hillary, 1919
  21: Ernest Hemingway, 1899
  22: Stephan Vincent Benet, 1898
  26: George Bernard Shaw, 1856
  29: Booth Tarkington, 1869
  30: Emily Bronte, 1818

Events

Jul. 1: Dominion Day, Canada, 1867
  3: First savings bank in America opened, 1819
  4: Independence Day
  5: Stone-Skipping Day
  7: Hawaiian Islands annexed by U.S., 1898
  13: U.S. Northwest Territory established, 1787
  15: St. Swithin's Day
  16: First test of an atomic bomb, New Mexico, 1945
  19: First Women's Rights Convention, 1848
  20: Moon Day, anniversary of man's first landing on the moon, 1969
  21: World Law Day
  23: Ice cream cone invented, 1904
  28: U.S. Senate ratifies the Charter of the United Nations, 1945
  30: The U.S. Motto, "In God We Trust," authorized, 1956

August

Specially Designated Observances for the Month
Sandwich Month

Weeks
Hobby Cartoonists' Week
National Smile Week
National Aviation Week

Birthdays
Aug.　3:　Rupert Brooke, poet, 1887
　　　4:　Percy Bysshe Shelley, 1792
　　　5:　Guy de Maupassant, 1850
　　　6:　Alfred Lord Tennyson, 1809
　　　9:　Izaak Walton, 1593
　　13:　William Caxton, first English printer, 1422
　　14:　John Galsworthy, 1867
　　15:　Sir Walter Scott, 1771
　　17:　Davy Crockett, 1786
　　18:　Virginia Dare, 1587, first American-born child of English colonist
　　19:　Orville Wright, 1871
　　22:　Claude Debussy, 1862
　　27:　Confucius, 550 B.C.

Events
Aug.　1:　First U.S. census begun, 1790
　　　4:　Coast Guard Day
　　10:　Smithsonian Institution established, 1846
　　14:　Social Security Act passed by Congress, 1935
　　14:　V-J Day
　　14:　First books printed in color, Germany, 1457
　　15:　Traditional beginning of hay fever season
　　22:　International Red Cross founded, 1864
　　25:　National Park Service authorized, 1916
　　26:　Women's Liberation Day

September

Specially Designated Observance for the Month
Fall Clean-Up Time

Weeks
National Dog Week
Back-to-Work Week
Heritage Week
Constitution Week
National Microfilm Week
National Hispanic Heritage Week

Birthdays
Sep. 2: Eugene Field, 1850
      4: F. Scott Fitzgerald, 1896
      6: Jane Addams, 1860
     11: D.H. Lawrence, 1885
     15: James Fennimore Cooper, 1789
     18: Samuel Johnson, 1709
     25: William Faulkner, 1897
     26: "Johnny Appleseed" John Chapman, 1774
     28: Kate Douglas Wiggin, 1856

Events
Sep. 2: Great fire of London begins, 1666
      3: First professional football game, 1895
      4: Eastman patented Kodak, first roll-film camera, 1888
     14: "Star Spangled Banner" written, 1814
     17: Citizenship Day
     19: First appearance of Mickey Mouse, 1928
     25: Balboa discovers the Pacific, 1513

October

Specially Designated Observances for the Month

National Cranberry Harvest Month
National Indoor Games Month
National Wine Festival Month
Lets Go Hunting Month
National Hobby Month
Country Music Month
Gourmet Adventures Month

Weeks

Fire Prevention Week
Unicorn Hunting Season
American Education Week
International Letter Writing Week
National 4-H Week
National Business Women's Week
National Employ the Handicapped Week
Drug Abuse Prevention Week
National Newspaper Week
International Whale Watching Week

Birthdays

Oct. 2: Graham Greene, 1904
      3: Thomas Wolfe, 1900
      6: Jenny Lind, 1820
     11: Eleanor Roosevelt, 1884
     14: Dwight D. Eisenhower, 1890
     16: Noah Webster, 1758
     21: Alfred Nobel, 1833
     25: Pablo Picasso, 1881
     27: Dylan Thomas, 1914
     27: Theodore Roosevelt, 1858
     29: James Boswell, 1740
     30: John Adams, 1735

Events

Oct. 1: First World Series baseball game, Boston, 1903
      3: First Woman Senator appointed, Georgia, 1922
      6: First talking picture, 1927 ("The Jazz Singer," with Al Jolson)
      6: Pilgrims set out in Mayflower, 1620
      9: Leif Erikson Day
     21: Thomas Jefferson's personal library purchased by the government to replace Library of Congress burned, 1814
     27: Good Bear Day
     28: Statue of Liberty dedicated, 1886
     29: Stock market crash, 1929
     30: Orson Welles' "War of the Worlds" radio program panics audience, 1938
     31: National Magic Day—anniversary of death of Harry Houdini, 1926

November

Specially Designated Observances for the Month
Jewish Book Month

Weeks
Children's Book Week
Latin America Week
National Bible Week
National Farm-City Week
National Stamp Collecting Week
Cat Week

Birthdays
Nov. 1: Stephen Crane, 1871
     2: Daniel Boone, 1734
     3: Karl Baedeker, guidebook publisher, 1801
     4: Will Rogers, 1879
     5: Ida Tarbell, 1857
     6: John Phillip Sousa, 1854
     7: Albert Camus, 1913
  10: Muhammed, 570
  11: Fyodor Dostoyevsky, 1821
  12: Elizabeth Cady Stanton, 1815
  12: Auguste Rodin, 1840
  13: Robert Louis Stevenson, 1850
  14: Robert Fulton, 1765
  18: Louis Daguerre, 1789, pioneer photographer, 1789

20: Selma Lagerlof, 1858 (Swedish writer, first woman to win Nobel Prize for Literature), 1909
24: Baruch Spinoza, 1632
25: Andrew Carnegie, 1835
28: William Blake, 1757
29: Louisa Mae Alcott, 1832
30: Samuel L. Clemens (Mark Twain), 1835
30: Jonathan Swift, 1667

Events
Nov. 1: National Author's Day
  10: Marine Corps established, 1775
  14: Nellie Bly starts first tour of world by a woman alone, 1889
  17: Suez Canal opened, 1869
  19: Lincoln's Gettysburg Address delivered, 1863

December

Weeks
Human Rights Week

Birthdays
Dec. 1: Rex Stout, 1886
3: Joseph Conrad, 1857
5: Walt Disney, 1901
6: Ira Gershwin, 1896
7: Willa Cather, 1873
8: Jan Sibelius, 1865
9: John Milton, 1608
10: Melvin Dewey, 1851
12: Gustave Flaubert, 1821
13: Heinrich Heine, 1797
14: Nostradamus, 1503
16: Ludwig van Beethoven, 1770
17: John Greenleaf Whittier, 1807
19: Ty Cobb, 1886
21: Benjamin Disraeli, 1804
24: Kit Carson, 1809
25: Sir Isaac Newton, 1642
26: Mao Tse-tung, 1893
27: Louis Pasteur, 1822
28: Woodrow Wilson, 1856
30: Stephan Leacock, 1869
30: Rudyard Kipling, 1865

Events
Dec. 2: World Community Day
2: First nuclear reaction, 1942
7: Pearl harbor attacked by Japanese, 1941
10: Human Rights Day
10: Nobel Prizes awarded (anniversary of Alfred Nobel's death in 1896)
11: UNICEF founded, 1946
15: Bill of Rights Day
16: Boston Tea Party, 1773
18: First giant panda arrived in San Francisco, 1936
21: Pilgrims landed, 1620
24: Franz Gruber composed "Silent Night," 1818
26: Boxing Day

Appendix II: Sample Library Quizzes

These two quizzes, informational handouts about the library, are intended to call attention to various services. They can be adapted to local situations. The first, under the heading, "YOUR LIBRARY—A PLACE FOR ALL REASONS," comes from Saskatchewan, Canada.

"WHAT HAS YOUR LIBRARY DONE FOR YOU LATELY?"

SCORING

Give yourself one point for each "yes," and think about your "no" answers.

Did you use an atlas or get maps and travel information before you went on vacation? ___ And did you get a Spanish phrase book or language cassettes so that you could enjoy Spain more? ___

Did you borrow a repair manual when your snowmobile developed peculiar noises? ___ Or a pet care book when junior came home with hamsters? ___ Or pictures to help present your history report? ___

Did you request enough books for everyone in your upholstery class? ___ Or to help you with your 4-H project? ___

Did you borrow films for the program at your school's ecology club meeting? ___ Or records and cassettes for the fifties record hop? ___

Did you ask your librarian to find the rest of the poem, when you only knew the first line? ___ Or a recipe for a casserole that was in a magazine last year? ___ Or did you get the statistics you needed for the computer printout for your Government Department? ___

Do your children go to story-time? ___ Did you enjoy the film evening at the library? ___ Or hearing a poet read from his works? ___

Did you borrow books with large print for someone with failing eyesight? ___ Or talking books? ___

Did you read a novel in German? ___ Or poetry in French? ___ Or history in Ukrainian? ___

*   *   *   *

SCORING

0 - 5   Are you taking advantage of either a community or school service that was designed with you in mind?

5 - 10   You know your library exists, but look at the other services it offers.

10 - 15 Your tax money helps to support your library; are you getting your money's worth?

15 - 20 Your librarian loves you!

REMEMBER:
When you need to know what, how, when, where, why, who or whatever . . . check at your library. A public, regional, school or special library can answer all your questions.

And this, in a light-hearted vein, has been used with variations in several areas:

How's Your Library IQ?

1. Your wife tells you that she is on a waiting list for *The Eagle Has Landed*. This means your wife is:

    a) For the birds

    b) Seeing an ornithologist

    c) Keeping up with the best sellers at the library

2. You love to read but squinting at small print gives you a headache. You can:

    a) Hire a freelance reader

    b) Purchase a high-powered magnifying glass

    c) Take two aspirins before reading

    d) Check out books from your library's large-print collection

3. Your dear Great Aunt Tillie is coming to spend a few weeks with you. She's on a very restricted diet so you:

    a) Float a small loan and hire a dietician for a few weeks

    b) Float a larger loan and eat out every day

    c) Ask your librarian about cookbooks for people with dietary problems

4. Your boss has strongly suggested that you read a series of magazine articles which appeared two years ago. You can:

    a) Keep making doctor appointments until you find one who has the magazines in his waiting room

    b) Place a personal ad in the newspaper

    c) Look for another job

    d) Request the magazines at your library

5. Your child likes to be read to but you don't always have the time to read to him. You can:

    a) Pretend you lost your voice

    b) Get him interested in television soap operas

    c) Take him to the story time offered at the library

6. It is important that you reach your old college roommate in Portland. You've lost his address so you:

    a) Drive to Portland and rent a sound truck

    b) Clean the attic and find your old college scrapbooks and hope the address is there

    c) Go into hypnosis. Maybe the address will come back to you

    d) Look up his address in the Portland telephone directory at the Library

7. There's one particular book you absolutely must have to finish your school paper, and it's available only at the Springville Library. You live in Provo, so you:

    a) Move to Springville

    b) Hire a driver to go steal the book for you

    c) Pick another topic for your school paper

    d) Ask your librarian to get the book for you through interlibrary loan

8. You lost that important telephone number from the classified ads in last Sunday's newspaper. You can:

    a) Call random numbers in the phone book until you get it

    b) Try to find the newspaper in the trash

    c) Check the local newspapers at your library

How's Your Library IQ? (continued)

9.   Your high school history teacher wants you to read a book about women's rights, but right off hand you can't think of any. You:

   a) Place a collect call to Gloria Steinem

   b) Go into meditation and hope for a vision

   c) Ask for the "All About Women" booklists, available at Provo Library

10.   Your kindergartner just informed you that she's invited her whole class to her birthday party tomorrow. You:

   a) Pretend you never saw the kid before

   b) Disguise yourself and leave town on the next plane out

   c) Burst into tears screaming: "Why does everything happen to me?"

   d) Borrow a good children's movie from your library

11.   You're tired of botany, biology, history, and math; you want something different to read so you:

   a) Ask your Mom to buy YUMMY TUMMY cereal so you can read the box

   b) Stand on the street corner and read license plates

   c) Ask your librarian to recommend some good books for teens

12.   A tune from a movie you saw last year keeps running through your head but you can't remember what it's called and who sang it. You:

   a) Hum it to the policeman on the corner

   b) Wait until the movie is on the late show

   c) Go to Greece where the movie is currently playing

   d) Ask your librarian to look it up in the Audio-Visual Department

13.   You would like to be more meaningfully involved with your public library. You can:

   a) Take out a library card

   b) Take out a librarian

   c) Take out books, records, films, pictures, paperbacks or cassettes

   d) Take advantage of your library's programs

   e) All of the above

THE ANSWERS TO THESE AND LOTS OF OTHER QUESTIONS CAN BE FOUND AT YOUR PUBLIC LIBRARY

Appendix III: Sample Trivia Contest

Following are the questions used in the first annual adult trivia contest held at the Oshkosh Public Library in Wisconsin. The answers, in parentheses, are those supplied by and accepted as correct by the library:

1. How many electoral votes could a U.S. presidential candidate possibly receive? (538)

2. What university has the world's largest drum? (Texas University. Disneyland has the largest)

3. What is the last great battle between the giants and gods in Norse mythology called? (Regnarob or Gotterdammerung)

4. On the top of which mountain was Moses given the Ten Commandments? (Mt. Sinai)

5. A chukker is a period in what game? (Polo)

6. Who was the first man to set foot on the moon? (Neil Armstrong)

7. Who shot and killed Billy the Kid? (Sheriff Pat Garret)

8. How many U.S. presidents have been assassinated? (Four)

9. Who is the leading consumer protection advocate? (Ralph Nader)

10. Who was the most famous stripper of all time? (Gypsy Rose Lee or Sally Rand)

11. Who invented the cotton gin? (Eli Whitney)

12. What do you call the appetizer made of the roe of a sturgeon? (Caviar)

13. When is Bunker Hill Day? (June 17)

14. What is the gadget you hold when using a Ouija board? (Planchette or Ouija)

15. What was the name of the first giant killed by Jack the Giant Killer? (Cormoran)

16. What was the original rate per ounce for air mail in 1918? (24¢)

17. What mayor of New York read comic strips to children over the radio? (Fiorello LaGuardia)

18. Who said "A woman is only a woman, but a good cigar is a smoke"? (Rudyard Kipling)

19. What was Bing Crosby's real first name? (Harry)

20. What was the name of the battleship on which the Japanese surrendered to end World War II? (Missouri)

21. What was the name of the Aztec god represented by a feathered serpent? (Quetzalcoatl)

22. What is the name of the "Happy Hooker"? (Xaviera Hollander)

23. What U.S. president served longest in that office? (F.D. Roosevelt)

24. Who played the tin man in the "Wizard of Oz"? (Jack Haley)

25. Who narrated the TV show "The Untouchables"? (Walter Winchell)

26. Who was called "Man of a Thousand Faces"? (Lon Chaney)

27. In what nation was the first steam engine invented? (Greece or Egypt)

28. A bolide is another name for what object? (Meteor)

29. In what year was the Buddha presumably born? (563 B.C. Several other years also accepted.)

30. Who said "I never met a man I didn't like"? (Will Rogers)

31. When is Wisconsin's Admission Day celebrated? (May 29)

32. What group did Grace Slick sing with before Jefferson Airplane? (Great Society)

33. Who was "Little Miss Sure Shot" in Buffalo Bill's Wild West Show? (Annie Oakley)

34. What newspaper did Clark Kent (Superman) work for? (Daily Planet)

35. Baggataway was the original name of what American Indian sport? (LaCrosse)

36. On October 30th, 1938 the most famous radio broadcast of all time took place. What was it? (War of the Worlds—Attack from Mars)

37. In what year did the famous San Francisco earthquake take place? (1906)

38. What mythical monster did Theseus slay? (Minotaur)

39. What is the Emerald Isle? (Ireland)

40. The opening bars of what symphony were widely used as a call sign on allied radio in World War II? (Beethoven's Fifth)

41. When Edward VIII abdicated, he became the Duke of Windsor. What was his title before he became King? (Prince of Wales)

42. What giant airship crashed and burned in New Jersey on May 6, 1937? (Hindenburg)

43. What vegetable is a member of the thistle family? (Artichoke. Question was poorly phrased so many answers were accepted.)

44. What nation put the first woman into orbit? (USSR)

45. What kind of insects keep cattle and slaves, and make war on each other? (Ants)

46. Where did Robin Hood live? (Sherwood Forest)

47. Which of the great cats cannot retract their claws? (Cheetahs)

48. What two comedians starred in the famous "Road" pictures? (Bob Hope and Bing Crosby)

49. What is the minimum number of victories over enemy aircraft needed to become an ace? (5)

50. Where is the Circus World Museum located? (Baraboo, Wisconsin)

51. What is the name of the exotic dancer associated with Wilbur Mills in the tidal basin? (Fanne Foxe)

52. Which presidents' faces are carved into Mt. Rushmore? (Washington, Jefferson, Lincoln, T. Roosevelt)

53. What was the name of the angel who announced to Mary that she was "with child"? (Gabriel)

54. By what geometrical term is a five pointed star known? (Pentagram or decagon)

55. Name the heaviest metal in the world. (Irridium or osmium)

56. What was Rutherford B. Hayes' middle name? (Birchard)

57. How many knights are there in a game of chess? (4)

58. What famous overalls are manufactured in Oshkosh? (Oshkosh B'Gosh)

59. What is the longest river in the world? (Nile or Amazon)

60. Name an article of clothing named after a British leader in the Crimean War. (Cardigan sweater or Raglan sleeves)

61. What baseball player was called the Iron Horse? (Lou Gehrig)

62. What piece of clothing had a reet pleat, a rough cuff, and peg pants? (Zoot suit)

63. What country has the greatest number of daily newspapers? (USA or USSR)

64. Conviction on what charge finally ended Al Capone's career? (Income tax evasion)

65. When was Oshkosh incorporated as a city? (1853)

66. What three letter word in the English language does not contain an A, E, I, O, U, or Y and means a cirque? (CWM or KWM)

67. The first successful manned space flight was launched by what country? (USSR)

68. What was the first name of Dr. Watson in the Sherlock Holmes series? (John)

69. What was the name of the book in which Darwin first expounded his theory of evolution? (Origin of the Species)

70. For whom was America named? (Amerigo Vespucci)

71. Who are the mythological characters to which the letters of Captain Marvel's SHAZAM refer? (Solomon, Hercules, Atlas, Zeus, Achilles, Mercury)

72. What general was called "Old Blood and Guts"? (Patton)

73. What radio show opened with the sound of a creaking door? (Inner Sanctum)

74. What 15th century artist designed early versions of the airplane, the machine gun, and the submarine? (Leonardo da Vinci)

75. For what accomplishment did Dr. Frederick Grant Banting receive the Nobel Prize? (Discovery of Insulin)

76. What is the second most expensive property in the game of Monopoly? (Park Place)

77. According to Luke, what were the names of the three women who went to Jesus' tomb on Easter? (Mary Magdalene, Joanna, Mary—the mother of James)

78. Who directed the 1934 version of "Cleopatra" and also "The Ten Commandments"? (Cecil B. DeMille)

79. Who was the Boston strangler? (Albert De Salvo)

80. What were the five Indian Nations of the Iroquois Confederacy? (Mohawk, Oneida, Cayuga, Seneca, Onondaga)

81. What was the original name of "The Ed Sullivan Show"? (Toast of the Town)

82. What mythical animal native to Wisconsin eats only white bulldogs, and those only on Sunday? (Hodag)

83. What is the name of the magic island where King Arthur sleeps? (Avalon)

84. What was the flagship of Admiral Yamamoto at the Battle of Midway? (Battleship Yamato)

85. In the Broadway version of "My Fair Lady," who played Eliza Doolittle? (Julie Andrews)

86. What is the better known name for acetylsalicylic acid? (Aspirin)

87. Some months have 30 days, some 31—how many have 28 days? (All twelve)

88. What was the baptismal name of Christine Jorgensen? (George Jorgensen)

89. What element can weaken or even kill Superman? (Kryptonite)

90. Who were the first seven astronauts? (Walter Schirra, John Glenn, Alan Shepard, Virgil Grissom, Donald Slayton, Scott Carpenter, Gordon Cooper)

91. Whom did Sherlock Holmes describe as the "Second Most Dangerous Man in London"? (Colonel Sebastian Moran)

92. What were Cords, Daimlers, Dusenbergs, Panhards, and Hispano Suizas? (Automobiles)

93. What is carved into the stone above the entrance to the south side branch library? (Library and/or 1911)

94. What was the name of the plane in which Charles Lindbergh flew across the Atlantic? (Spirit of St. Louis)

95. What Ford automobile introduced in 1957 was an utter disaster? (Edsel)

96. What was the name of the Lord High Executioner in the "Mikado"? (Koko)

97. Who won the first Indianapolis 500? (Ray Harroun)

98. What did Charles Atlas discover that made him "the world's most perfectly developed man"? (Secret of Dynamic Tension)

99. What famous product was advertised by the slogan "good to the last drop"?   (Maxwell House Coffee)

100. What extinct form of man was first discovered in a valley near Dusseldorf, Germany? (Neanderthal)

101. Shakespeare produced most of his plays in what theatre?   (Globe)

102. What is the name of the cards used to predict the future?   (Tarot)

103. Who was the first settler and founder of Oshkosh?   (Webster Stanley)

104. By what name is the Yeti better known? (Abominable snowman)

105. Who succeeded Curly Lambeau as coach of the Green Bay Packers?   (Gene Ronzani)

106. By what name was Captain Edward Teach better known?   (Black Beard)

107. In what year did man first land on the moon?   (1969)

108. The cause of Bonnie Prince Charlie ended in 1746 at what battle?   (Culloden)

109. What major sport is played with an oblate spheroid?   (Football)

110. What Pennsylvania city was almost wiped out by a major flood in 1889?   (Johnstown)

111. If you had only one match and entered a room in which there was a kerosene lamp, an oil burner, and a wood burning stove, which would you light first?   (Match)

112. What nation developed the first jet aircraft?   (Germany)

113. What was the food given to the Israelites by God during their journey out of Egypt? (Manna)

114. What is the minimum speed necessary to place an object in orbit around the earth? (18,000 mph)

115. What was the name of the jeep on the "Roy Rogers Show"?   (Nellybelle)

116. Corner stones is what kind of game of cards?   (Solitaire)

117. The Silver Ghost and the Silver Shadow were produced by what automobile company? (Rolls Royce)

118. What famous ship struck an iceberg and sank in the Atlantic on her maiden voyage? (Titanic)

119. What is the eve of May Day called? (Walpurgis Night or Feast of St. Catherine of Siena)

120. In 1848 the United States flag had how many stars?   (30 or 29)

121. What advertisement asks "Does your shoe have a boy inside"?   (Buster Brown)

122. If a doctor gave you three pills, and told you to take one every half hour, how long would they last?   (1 hour)

123. What was the ransom paid in the Frank Sinatra Junior kidnapping?   ($240,000)

124. What was Johnny Appleseed's real name?   (Jonathan Chapman)

125. What was the first musical created by the team of Richard Rogers and Oscar Hammerstein? (Oklahoma)

126. Who killed Cock Robin?   (Sparrow)

127. What century was the television series "Star Trek" set in?   (23rd)

128. What is the width in yards of a football field?   (53⅓ yards)

129. The Rhine Institute, where many famous ESP experiments were carried out, is located at what university?   (Duke)

130. What are the two bronze sculptures by the old main entrance to the Oshkosh Public Library?   (Lions)

131. Who is famous for, but never said, "Judy, Judy, Judy"?   (Cary Grant)

132. What was the name of Pecos Bill's horse?   (Widow Maker)

133. What famous female singer, now deceased, was a member of the Mugwumps? (Cass Elliot)

134. What famous Grant Wood painting was used in a cornflake commercial?   (American Gothic)

135. What is the name of the Hindu scripture containing 1,200 hymns to the gods of fire, sunlight, wind, etc.?   (Rig Veda or Veda)

136. What American invented the first successful reaper?   (Cyrus McCormick)

137. How many drawers are there in the main adult card catalog, including the separate adult audio visual catalog, in the Oshkosh Public Library?   (576)

138. Divide 30 by halves and add 10. What is the answer?   (70)

139. Who was responsible for the dance craze "The Twist"?   (Chubby Checker)

140. What Chinese game, similar to rummy but played with small tiles, was very popular in the United States in the early 20th century?   (Mah Jongg)

141. What radio character of the 1930s was played by Fanny Brice?   (Baby Snooks)

142. When was the great Oshkosh fire? (April 28, 1875 or May 10, 1859)

143. "Joltin' Joe . . . we want you on our side" was the line of a popular song in the 1940s. Who was "Joltin' Joe"?   (Joe DiMaggio)

144. What is Spiderman's secret identity? (Peter Parker)

145. What are the last two lines of the quotation which begins "Our country, right or wrong"? (When right, to be kept right; When wrong, to be put right.)

146. What artist painted the "Garden of Delights"?   (Hieronymus Bosch)

147. H_2SO_4 is the formula for what chemical compound?   (Sulfuric Acid)

148. Who was the artist, born in 1853, who cut off his own ear in a fit of depression?   (Vincent Van Gogh)

149. Who discovered the Book of Mormon? (Joseph Smith)

150. What states border the gulf of Mexico? (Texas, Louisiana, Mississippi, Alabama, Florida)

151. What Pope commissioned Michelangelo to paint the Sistine Chapel?   (Julius II)

152. What was the fermented mares milk drunk by the ancient Mongols called?   (Kumiss or Koumiss or Coumos)

153. What was the name of Robert Fulton's first steamboat?   (Clermont)

154. Who is the children's show host named after an Australian animal?   (Captain Kangaroo)

155. What circus job was held by Emmet Kelly?   (Clown)

156. Who created the music and lyrics for the play "Kiss Me Kate"?   (Cole Porter)

157. What famous Black singer sang with the Supremes?   (Diana Ross)

158. What is the popular name for the 18th amendment to the United States Constitution? (Prohibition)

159. What is the eve of All Saints Day called? (Halloween)

160. As a circus performer, for what was Clyde Beatty best known?   (Wild animal trainer)

161. What is the head of state in Luxembourg called?   (Grand Duke)

162. In golf, if you are two strokes under par for a hole, what is it called?   (Eagle)

163. What was the real name of the "Red Baron"?   (Manfred von Richthofen)

164. What animal is the symbol for "MGM"? (Lion)

165. Name the seven wonders of the ancient world?   (Statue of Zeus at Olympia, Tomb of King Mausdeus at Halicernassus, Temple of Diana at Ephesus, Colossas of Rhodes, Pyramids, hanging Gardens of Babylon, Pharos or Lighthouse of Alexandria)

166. Name the only marsupial found natively in North America.   (Opossum)

167. What does the Beaufort scale measure? (Strength of the wind)

168. Who said "You can fool all of the people some of the time and some of the people all of the time, but you cannot fool all of the people all of the time"?   (Lincoln or P.T. Barnum)

169. Who was George McGovern's eventual running mate in the 1972 election? (Sargent Shriver)

170. What woman aviator disappeared mysteriously on an around the world flight in 1937? (Amelia Earhart)

171. What article of swimwear was named after a hydrogen bomb explosion? (Bikini)

172. Thor Heyerdal made a famous voyage from Peru to Polynesia on what raft? (Kon Tiki)

173. In what year did the stock market crash which preceded the great depression occur? (1929)

174. What was Red Grange's nickname? (Galloping Ghost or Red)

175. Who has the world's smallest army? (San Marino)

176. Chief Oshkosh was Chief of what tribe of Indians? (Menominee)

177. The lost continent of Lemuria was located in what ocean? (Indian or Pacific)

178. What were the names of all seven of the Ringling Brothers? (Al, Otto, Charles/Carl, Alfred, Gus, Henry, John)

179. Who invented the first safety pin? (Walter or William Hunt)

180. What is an annuity purchased by a group and collected by the last survivor called? (Tontine)

181. How many outs are there in one inning of baseball? (6)

182. What is the largest selling phonograph record to date? (White Christmas)

183. What was the name of Paul Bunyan's Ox? (Babe)

184. When was V-J Day? (September 2, 1945 or August 14, 1945)

185. Name the seven deadly sins. (Pride, Avarice, Sloth, Gluttony, Wrath, Envy, Lust)

186. What town in Wisconsin was destroyed by fire on the same day as the great fire of Chicago? (Peshtigo)

187. What is Sergeant Joe Friday's badge number? (714)

188. What is the longest side of a right triangle called? (Hypotenuse)

189. What famous city, described in Homer's "Iliad," was discovered by Heinrich Schliemann? (Troy)

190. If you divide the Roman numeral D by the Roman numeral XX what is the answer? (XXV)

191. Who was the wife of Osiris, Egyptian God of the Dead? (Isis)

192. What is the technical name for the small four toed "Down Horse"? (Eohippus)

193. What is the common English translation of the name Lucifer? (Light Bearer)

194. What Mexican musical instrument similar to the Xylophone has wooden bars as keys? (Marimba)

195. What ice cream chain serves the world's largest number of flavors? (Baskin Robbins or Howard Johnson or Breslers)

196. How many Justices are there on the Supreme Court? (9)

197. What beer is made "In the land of sky blue waters"? (Hamms)

198. What was the name of the oldest person in the Bible? (Methuselah)

199. If you went to bed at eight o'clock at night and set your alarm to get up at nine o'clock in the morning, how many hours of sleep would this permit you to have? (1 hour)

200. What is the world's largest theatre? (Radio City Music Hall or National Congress Building in Peking)

201. What was the name of Walt Disney's first cartoon character? (Oswald the Rabbit or Alice)

202. What was the first recorded message? (Mary had a little lamb)

203. Who was the author of the play "Our Town"? (Thornton Wilder)

204. In what president's inauguration was an automobile first used? (Warren G. Harding)

205. Clytemnestra's daughter and a play by Sophocles shared what name? (Electra)

206. List two names used by the Beatles before they became "The Beatles." (Moon Dogs, Quarry Men, Moonshiners, Silver Beatles)

207. What sinister Chinese literary character has "eyes of the true cat green, a brow like Shakespeare, and a face like Satan"? (Fu Manchu)

208. What famous pirate became the lieutenant governor of Jamaica? (Henry Morgan)

209. What was the name of Edgar Bergen's radio sidekick? (Charlie McCarthy)

210. How many pounds did the largest birthday cake in the world weigh? (25,000 lbs.)

211. In what part of the body are the metatarsals found? (Bones in the feet)

212. What is a group of ferrets called? (Business)

213. What is the common name for the number 3.14159? (Pi)

214. Tennyson's "Idylls of the King" is based upon ancient stories of what famous king? (King Arthur)

215. What was the name of the computer in "2001: A Space Odyssey"? (Hal)

216. What made Popeye strong? (Spinach)

217. What kind of a car held the world speed record in 1906? (Stanley Steamer)

218. What relationship was Ruth to Naomi in the Bible? (Ruth was a daughter-in-law to Naomi)

219. In the 1954 TV comedy series "Private Secretary," Ann Sothern played under what name? (Susie McNamara)

220. What are the leggins worn by Boy Scouts and Doughboys called? (Puttees)

221. What famous German general commanded the Afrika Korps? (Erwin Rommel)

222. What was Albert Einstein's most famous scientific formula? ($E=MC^2$)

223. What was King Tut's full name? (Tutankhamen)

224. How many bookmobiles does the Oshkosh Public Library have? (2)

225. What two monsters did Bela Lugosi and Christopher Lee both play? (Dracula and Frankenstein's monster)

226. Who played James Stark in "Rebel without a Cause"? (James Dean)

227. Translate the following familiar proverb back into familiar language: members of an avian species of identical plummage congregate. (Birds of a feather flock together)

228. Translate the following familiar proverb back into familiar language: male cadavers are incapable of yielding any testimony. (Dead men tell no tales)

229. Translate the following familiar proverb back into familiar language: the stylus is more potent than the claymore. (The pen is mightier than the sword)

230. How many beans are in the jar near the circulation desk? Check the library outlet at which you looked at the jar of beans.
__ Main Library
__ South Side
__ County Bookmobile
__ City Bookmobile
(Main - 4167; South Side - 4348; City Bookmobile - 4547; County Bookmobile - 1919)

Questions (and answers) used for the youth contest:

1. In which country does the Loch Ness monster live? (Scotland)

2. Who wrote the "Star Spangled Banner," our American National Anthem? (Francis Scott Key)

3. Whose picture is on the $100 bill? (Benjamin Franklin)

4. What is the name of Roy Roger's horse? (Trigger)

5. Name any five of the seven dwarfs. (Doc, Grumpy, Happy, Dopey, Sneezy, Bashful, Sleepy)

6. What is the name of Dennis the Menace's dog? (Ruff)

7. Name the two letters that do not appear on telephone dials.   (Q and Z)

8. What is the name of the Magic Dragon who lived in the land of Honalee?   (Puff)

9. What was the name of Davy Crockett's rifle?   (Old Betsy or Bessy)

10. What is the normal body temperature of a human being?   (98.6)

11. What did Edgar Allen Poe's raven like best to say?   ("Nevermore")

12. What are the names of Mickey Mouse's nephews?   (Morty and Ferdy)

13. What was the name of the ship which brought the Pilgrims to America?   (Mayflower)

14. What is the area of the United States in square miles?   (Approximately 3,615,123—all answers close to that were accepted.)

15. Name two of the states that border Wisconsin?   (Michigan, Minnesota, Illinois, Iowa)

16. What was the 50th state to be admitted to the United States?   (Hawaii)

17. In what American city is the tallest building, the Sears building, located?   (Chicago)

18. In which state is the "painted desert" located?   (Arizona)

19. What are the names of the two moons of Mars?   (Deimos and Phobos)

20. Who is the bad guy in McDonaldland? (Hamburgler, Captain Crook, Grimps, the Evil Grimace)

21. Who plays the piano in the Charlie Brown cartoon series?   (Schroeder)

22. What does Popeye eat to give him super-human strength?   (Spinach)

23. In the movie Bambi, Thumper was what kind of animal?   (Rabbit)

24. What kind of animal could Dracula turn into?   (Bat)

25. What are the statues beside the old front entrance of the main library?   (Lions)

26. What is the ancient Egyptian picture writing called?   (Hieroglyfics, Hierglyphics)

27. What is the colored part of the human eye called?   (Iris)

28. Who is Donald Duck's lucky cousin? (Gladstone Gander)

29. What is the total length of the mission of the Starship Enterprise?   (5 years)

30. What is the name of Mickey Mouse's girl-friend?   (Minnie)

31. What was the name of Abraham Lincoln's assassin?   (John Wilkes Booth)

32. Who flew the first successful airplane at Kitty Hawk, N. Carolina?   (Wright Brothers)

33. Who is Batman's partner?   (Robin)

34. Who is the baseball player who hit the most home runs in a season?   (Roger Maris)

35. What was the nickname of the German general, Erwin Rommel?   (Desert Fox)

36. What president made his home at Mount Vernon?   (George Washington)

37. How many senators are there in the U.S. Senate?   (100)

38. What is the highest land speed ever recorded?   (650 mph)

39. The platypus is found in the wild on only one continent, what is it?   (Australia)

40. What famous race horse won the Triple Crown last?   (Secretariat)

41. What state's license plates have the motto "America's Dairyland"?   (Wisconsin)

42. Who is Winnie the Pooh's donkey friend? (Eeyore)

43. In ancient Greece there were two powerful city states. One was Athens. What was the other? (Sparta)

44. Who was considered one of the greatest football coaches of all time and coached in Green Bay for many years?   (Lombardi)

45. What is the name of the tuna fish in the "Star Kist" ads?   (Charlie)

46. Casper is "the friendly ghost" but who is "the tuff little ghost?"   (Spooky)

47. What is the name of the automobile race held every Memorial Day in Indianapolis, Indiana? (Indianapolis 500)

48. Who was the only non-Indian survivor of Custer's last stand? (Comanche—a horse)

49. Add the final line to this nursery rhyme—
It's raining it's pouring
The old man is snoring
He went to bed
And bumped his head
(And couldn't get up in the morning)

50. William H. Bonney, the famous western gunman, was better known by what name? (Billy the Kid)

51. What is the world's record for non-stop talking? (138 hours or 5 days and 18 hours)

52. What is the name of Paul Bunyon's big blue ox? (Babe)

53. What is Alfred E. Neuman's most famous saying? ("What, me worry?")

54. What two major league baseball teams play for Chicago? (Cubs, White Sox)

55. What is the name of Tarzan's wife? (Jane)

56. What is maize? (Corn or the color yellow)

57. In the poem "The Owl & The Pussycat," what did they go to sea in? (A beautiful pea-green boat)

58. What is the name of the television detective who works from a wheel chair? (Ironsides or Raymond Burr)

59. From what animal does mutton come? (Sheep or Lamb)

60. Who is the present coach of the Packers? (Bart Starr)

61. What is the motto of the United States? (In God We Trust or E Pluribus Unum)

62. When was the first recorded Olympics held? (776 B.C. or 1896)

63. How many legs does an arachnid have? (8)

64. In what state was Laura Ingalls Wilder, the author, born? (Wisconsin)

65. What is the name of the elephant on Sesame Street? (Snuffleupagus)

66. What character in Peanuts is the dustiest little boy in the world? (Pig Pen)

67. What Italian is America named for? (Amerigo Vespucci)

68. What is the name of the cat that is always trying to eat "Tweety Pie"? (Sylvester)

69. What did "Peter Piper" pick? (A peck of pickled peppers)
or (You don't really want to know)

70. What is the name of the giant trees that grow in California? (Redwood or Sequoia)

71. What is the name of the family that Mary Poppins lived with? (Banks family)

72. What reptile is well known for changing its color to match its surroundings? (Chameleon)

73. What is Spiderman's real name? (Peter Parker)

74. What is the name of the aircraft which transports the president of the U.S.? (Air Force I or the Spirit of '76)

75. What is the name of the pirate villain in Peter Pan? (Captain Hook)

76. Where is the baseball hall of fame located? (Cooperstown, New York)

77. What is the smallest planet in our solar system? (Mercury)

78. What country in Europe is shaped like a boot? (Italy)

79. What are the Hardy Boys' names? (Frank and Joe)

80. What is the longest running TV western? (Gunsmoke)

81. What is the national language spoken in Brazil? (Portuguese)

82. What was the name of the Apollo 11 lunar module? (The Eagle)

83. In what year did Wisconsin become a state? (1848)

84. What is a pirate flag of a skull and crossed bones usually called? (Jolly Roger)

85. What is the name of the Indian woman who saved Captain John Smith's life?   (Pocahontas)

86.   Who was the fourth Musketeer? (D'Artagnan)

87. Name two of the six major groups of musical instruments.   (Woodwinds, Strings, Keyboard, Brass, Percussion)

88. In what European country did Joan of Arc live and die?   (France)

89. In what years was the American Civil War fought?   (1861 to 1865)

90.   What is Superman's dog named? (Krypto)

91. What is the chemical name for white granulated sugar?   (Sucrose)

92. Who was the youngest president to be inaugurated?   (Teddy Roosevelt)

93. From what German town did the Pied Piper chase the rats?   (Hamlin)

94.   What kind of animal was King Kong? (Gorilla or ape)

95. Is a horse chestnut an edible nut?   (No)

96. What river is on the western boundary of Wisconsin?   (Mississippi)

97. What was the name of King Arthur's wife? (Guinevere)

98. Which side is considered proper for mounting a horse?   (Left)

99. Who invented the game of football? (Walter Camp)

100. What makes blood red?   (Hemoglobin)

101. How many miles around is the Earth at the equator?   (Approximately 25,000 miles. All answers reasonably close were accepted.)

102. Guess how many beans are in the jar at the circulation desk? Check the library outlet at which you looked at the jar of beans.
__ Youth Services at the Main Library
__ South Side
__ County Bookmobile
__ City Bookmobile
(Main - 4444; South Side Branch - 4340; City Bookmobile - 4547; County Bookmobile - 1919)

Appendix IV: Sample Campaign Timetables

Timetable Used by Withers Public Library, Bloomington, Illinois, in November Campaign for New Library Building

In addition to this general monthly listing, a detailed timetable for each week in October, immediately preceding the election, was also prepared.

I. July
Letter of acknowledgement sent to the approximately 90 people who have indicated help and support.

II. July and August
A. Preparation of calling list by precinct:
    1. Registered voter-by-precinct list checked against library card registration file.
B. Preparation of fact sheet and speech material for coffees.
C. Committees set up and continued recruitment of volunteers.
    1. Committees will consist of volunteers with one board member and one library staff member as liaison.
    2. Committees are:
        a. *Publicity*
        b. *Correspondence* (fact sheet, brochure, etc.)
        c. *Speakers Bureau* (coffees and civic groups) Note: Will only talk to clubs, etc., if an invitation is offered. Will not solicit speeches.
        d. *Coffees*—Set up precinct coffees.
        e. *Telephone and Calling List Committee*—Will prepare briefing sheet for precinct callers to use in contacts with each potential *yes* vote.
        f. *Special Groups*—Make special effort to contact potential yes votes among school personnel, non-property tax paying retirees, the handicapped, minority groups, downtown merchants, etc.

III. September
A. Kickoff meetings—morning and evening meetings with board, library director and architect. Initial organization of committees at this meeting.
B. Committees meet, complete organization and begin work.
    1. Coffee dates/time set to begin in mid-September.
    2. Precinct calling lists completed and initial contacts made to identify favorable voters.

IV. October
A. Coffees continue.
B. Open house at library scheduled for all identified favorable voters.
C. Brochure mailed to all favorable voters by name.
D. Favorable voters called and reminded of upcoming election.
E. Newspaper series identifying Library's problems.
F. Brochures mailed to all registered voters using bulk mailing rates.

V. November—Election Day
A. Poll watching during voting.
B. Three hours before polls close precinct lists checked to determine favorable voters who have not yet cast ballots and these voters called and reminded to vote.
C. Transportation to polls provided for favorable voters in need.
D. Babysitting provided for favorable voters in need.

Forms Used for Telephone Calls in Withers Public Library, Bloomington, Illinois Campaign for New Library Building

The calls were initiated shortly after a mailing of a brochure to all registered voters.

Introductory Call

Good evening. This is _____. I'm calling for the Bloomington Library Board. We're doing an information canvass to determine voter awareness of the new public library building proposal. Were you aware that on _____ the citizens of Bloomington will be voting on whether they want a new public library building?

    Yes   (Continue down this sheet)
    No   (Go to yellow sheet—#1)

You've probably read that the site for the new library will be the southeast corner of Olive and Albert Streets, just across the street east from the City Hall. Do you think that's a good location for the new library building?

    Yes   (Continue down this sheet)
    Undecided   (Continue down this sheet)
    No   (Go to pink sheet—#2)

What about the idea of building a new library . . . are you in favor of the new library?

    Yes   (Continue down this sheet)
    Strong No   (Go to blue sheet—#3)
    Undecided or weak No   (Go to green sheet—#4)

I'm happy to hear that, because we're very enthusiastic about the prospect of a new facility. I appreciate your time in chatting with me. Please be sure to vote on _____. By the way, if you need a free ride to the polls, just call _____. If you want to write that number down . . . I'll repeat it _____. Thanks, again, and have a pleasant evening.

Yellow Sheet—Continuation #1

You should have received a copy of our fact sheet in the mail. Would you like another copy sent to you?

The Library Board, which is composed of _____ citizens who serve without pay, has been studying the library situation for _____ years. The Board determined that the present building, built in _____, just can't handle the volume of current users and certainly not the expected number of users in the near future. There are right now _____ people using the library every week and of course the number is increasing all the time. Also, the present building doesn't offer the book protection, such as from fire, that we feel a library should.

The site selected for the new $2.4 million library is the southeast corner of Olive and Albert Streets, just across the street east from the City Hall. It's anticipated it will cost the average homeowner about _____ a year.

Does that seem like a price you would be willing to pay for a new library?

    Yes   (Continue down this sheet)
    Strong No   (Go to blue sheet—#3)
    Undecided or weak No   (Go to blue sheet—#3)

I'm happy to hear that, because we're very enthusiastic about the prospect of a new facility. I appreciate your time in chatting with me. Please be sure to vote on _____. By the way, if you need a free ride to the polls, just call _____. If you want to write that number down . . . I'll repeat it _____. Thanks, again, and have a pleasant evening.

Pink Sheet—Continuation #2

What site do you prefer?

You should have received a copy of our fact sheet in the mail. Would you like another copy sent to you? Let me quickly give you some additional background information. The Library Board, which is composed of _____ citizens who serve without pay, has been studying the Library situation for _____ years. The Board determined that the present building, built in _____, just can't handle the volume of current users and certainly not the expected number of users in the near future.

Forms Used for Telephone Calls in Withers Public Library, Bloomington, Illinois Campaign for New Library Building (continued)

There are right now __ people using the library every week and of course the number is increasing all the time. Also, the present building doesn't offer the book protection, such as from fire, that we feel a library should. It's anticipated the new $2.4 million library will cost the average houseowner about __ a year. Does that seem like a price you would be willing to pay for a new library?

Yes   (Continue down this sheet)
No   (Go to blue sheet—#3)

I'm happy to hear that, because we're very enthusiastic about the prospect of a new facility. I appreciate your time in chatting with me. Please be sure to vote on __.

By the way, if you need a free ride to the polls, just call __. If you want to write that number down . . . I'll repeat it __. Thanks, again, and have a pleasant evening.

Blue Sheet—Continuation #3

As I mentioned, we're calling merely to learn the public's feelings on this important issue.

I appreciate your time in chatting with me and have a pleasant evening.

Green Sheet—Continuation #4

You should have received our fact sheet in the mail. Would you like another copy sent to you? Let me quickly give you some additional background information.

The Library Board, which is composed of __ citizens who serve without pay, has been studying the library situation for __ years. The Board determined that the present building, built in __, just can't handle the volume of current users and certainly not the expected number of users in the near future. There are right now __ people using the library every week and of course the number is increasing all the time. Also, the present building doesn't offer the book protection, such as from fire, that we feel a library should.

It's anticipated the new $2.4 million library will cost the average houseowner about __ a year. Does that seem like a price you would be willing to pay for a new library?

Yes   (Continue down this sheet)
No   (Go to blue sheet—#3)*

I'm happy to hear that, because we're very enthusiastic about the prospect of a new facility.

I appreciate your time in chatting with me. Please be sure to vote on __. By the way, if you need a free ride to the polls, just call __. If you want to write that number down . . . I'll repeat it __. Thanks, again, and have a pleasant evening.

Timetable of Toledo-Lucas County, Ohio Campaign for Library Levy

January: Need for additional funds shown as Library Trustees propose to close three branches.

February: Plans laid for Friends of the Library membership drive.

March: Membership drive underway with distribution of membership application forms through banks and savings and loans.

March & April: "Grim Facts" brochure distributed to all patrons of the Library.

April: Appointment of Citizen's Task Force.

May 7:   Auction-on-the-Lawn (fund-raising event).

May & June: "Q's and A's" distributed to all Library patrons.

June: Report of Citizen's Task Force recommends that Library seek additional funds by placing a levy on the ballot in November.

July 21:   Library Board of Trustees votes to place an operating levy on the November 8 ballot.

July 29:   Children's Safair Parade (library event).

August: Tent at Lucas County Fair sponsored by the Friends of the Library.

August 11: Library trustees adopt resolution setting millage at 0.7 of a mill for a five-year levy.

August: Public Relations consultant hired.

August: Concerned Citizens for the Library Committee formed.

September 19:   Headquarters for Library levy campaign opening (buttons and posters distributed—$10,000 contributed by Friends of the Library to the campaign fund).

September & October: Staff of Library undertakes intensive speaking campaign.

October 1: Bus signs installed; banners placed on Library buildings.

October: Flyers distributed to all Library patrons and organizations.

October: Request for endorsements of Library levy mailed to organizations and churches.

October 8: "Rally-on-the-Lawn."

October 11: Phone-a-thon extended (10 phones at Main Library used Tuesday through Friday evenings until election).

October 25: Radio and television ads begun; newspaper ads begun.

October 30: Door-to-door distribution of literature.

November 1 - 7:   Phone-a-thon further extended with use of 16 phones in real estate offices.

November 6: Door-to-door distribution of literature in areas not previously covered.

November 7: Distribution of literature on downtown street corners.

November 8: Yard signs erected at all polling places in Toledo; distribution of literature at selected polling places; election night party.

Index

Compiled by Sanford Berman